Raúl Ruiz's
CINEMA OF INQUIRY

Contemporary Approaches to Film and Media Series
A complete listing of the books in this series can be found online at
wsupress.wayne.edu

General Editor
Barry Keith Grant
Brock University

Advisory Editors
Robert J. Burgoyne
University of St. Andrews

Caren J. Deming
University of Arizona

Patricia B. Erens
School of the Art Institute of Chicago

Peter X. Feng
University of Delaware

Lucy Fischer
University of Pittsburgh

Frances Gateward
California State University, Northridge

Tom Gunning
University of Chicago

Thomas Leitch
University of Delaware

Walter Metz
Southern Illinois University

Raúl Ruiz's
CINEMA OF INQUIRY

Edited by
Ignacio López-Vicuña and
Andreea Marinescu

WAYNE STATE UNIVERSITY PRESS
DETROIT

ISBN 978-0-8143-4106-3 (paperback); ISBN 978-0-8143-4107-0 (ebook)
Library of Congress Cataloging Number: 2017953529

Wayne State University Press
Leonard N. Simons Building
4809 Woodward Avenue
Detroit, Michigan 48201-1309

Visit us online at wsupress.wayne.edu

Contents

Interviews

Editors' Note

Unless otherwise indicated, all translations into English are by the editors. Available English translations of Ruiz's works and interviews, as well as secondary bibliography have been supplied whenever possible. Notes added by the editors are indicated.

Acknowledgments

This book arose out of the desire to bring together distinct perspectives on this important and complex filmmaker. The contributors to this volume were instrumental in helping us achieve that goal. We feel very fortunate to have worked with such a dedicated and enthusiastic group of authors, whose passion for Ruiz's work extends well beyond this volume. We thank them wholeheartedly.

For having introduced us to Raúl Ruiz's eccentric yet fascinating universe, we wish to thank our former professors Catherine Benamou and John Beverley, respectively. Gareth Williams introduced us to each other at a LASA conference almost seven years ago and we have been close intellectual interlocutors ever since. Alberto Moreiras graciously hosted Andreea at the University of Aberdeen in 2008, where she met and interviewed Ruiz.

Valeria Sarmiento and Bruno Cuneo provided invaluable resources and advice for the successful completion of this project. Tessa Allen de Oliveira translated parts of the book and provided general support. Kirsten Strayer and Ivan Mayerhofer read drafts and offered critical feedback and suggestions throughout. Paula Dittborn selected and prepared several images in the collection. The anonymous reviewers provided useful insights and recommendations, greatly improving the quality of the collection.

At Wayne State University Press, we are grateful to Annie Martin and Barry Keith Grant, series editor, for their support and encouragement throughout this process. It has been a pleasure to work with the other team members at WSUP, including Kristin Harpster, Rachel Ross, Emily Nowak, and Ceylan Akturk.

This book received generous funding from Colorado College and the University of Vermont, to facilitate exchanges of ideas at critical junctures in the conceptualization of the project.

Our gratitude to those closest to us, fellow travelers on this long journey: Ivan Mayerhofer and Matthew Webb. This book is dedicated to the memory of Maria Marinescu.

Introduction

Ignacio López-Vicuña and Andreea Marinescu

Most widely known for his filmic productions, Raúl Ruiz (1941–2011) was a highly prolific, erudite, and innovative artist, whose work is located at the intersection of diverse locations, languages, and aesthetic traditions. In addition to directing over one hundred films, among them features, shorts, television serials, and videos, Ruiz's eclectic body of work includes two books on the theory of cinema, *Poetics of Cinema 1* (1995) and *Poetics of Cinema 2* (2007), and genre-defying fiction books such as *Le Transpatagonien* (1989), *Le livre des disparitions* (*The Book of Disappearances*, 1990) and *L'esprit de l'escalier* (*The Wit of the Staircase*, 2012). Among other artistic endeavors, he wrote and directed plays, composed and organized a radio show, and exhibited a multimedia installation. His films have been a constant presence in high-profile venues, such as the New York Film Festival, the Cannes Festival, International Film Festival Rotterdam, and the Toronto International Film Festival.

Despite these accomplishments his vast body of work is little known and explored. For years Ruiz was seen as an elite, art house filmmaker, occupying a marginal position in both European and Latin American film industries. While highly regarded by critics and scholars, the experimental nature of his art and the scarce circulation of his films in commercial circuits restricted access and critical engagement. At the same time, Ruiz's uncompromising dedication to artistic experimentation drew the attention of international film stars, such as Marcello Mastroianni, Catherine Deneuve, and John Malkovich. His collaboration with them on big-budget films such as *Le temps retrouvé/Time Regained* (FR/IT/PT, 1999) and *Klimt* (AT/FR/DE/UK, 2006), as well as the critical success of his film *Mistérios de Lisboa/Mysteries of Lisbon* (PT/FR, 2010), brought Ruiz to a wider international audience.

More importantly, however, Ruiz's relevance to cinema and the growing interest in his work are due to his legacy as a global filmmaker.

Viewers, filmmakers, and film scholars keep returning to his works because his films continue to pose the question of what cinema can be, especially at a time when cinema is increasingly seen as displaced by television and new media. In his recent study *The Cinema of Raúl Ruiz*, Michael Goddard argues that "rather than simply being an anachronistic, 'European' auteur, Ruiz used this role as a way of conducting research into cinematic images and their combinations that is highly resonant with the emergence of the new media sphere that we are inhabiting today."[1] Goddard and other contributors to this volume focus on Ruiz's role as an original philosopher and thinker of the cinematic image, an approach that parallels work being done in Chile, for example by filmmaker and critic Cristián Sánchez and philosopher Willy Thayer.[2]

Because Ruiz is strongly geohistorically situated, but able to move comfortably across diverse film traditions and genres, he offers a unique way of engaging with the global that is quite different from the trajectory of a globalized Hispanic and Latin American cinema that has embraced a transnational aesthetic of gritty urban realism and a Hollywood style of narrative. Ruiz's cinema thus also poses the question of what "independent" cinema can mean today. At a time when "independent" cinema has all but been co-opted by mainstream global cinema, Ruiz's artisanal modes of production and distribution invite reflection on what it means to make and enjoy films.

In spite of growing international recognition and an increasing interest in his work, Ruiz's place within the history of cinema has remained eccentric. While he is seen as an inspiration and as an important figure in the history of Latin American film, he does not fit neatly within any category, period, or style. Part of the purpose of this book is to show how Ruiz's creative work draws from and crosses over into film theory, art history, theater, television, and aesthetic traditions such as the baroque, surrealism, and global storytelling traditions. Contributors in this collection approach Ruiz by emphasizing the interstitiality of his films, their exchange with other aesthetic discourses, and their understanding of the making and viewing of films as play and exploration. In this introduction, we will first give an overview of Ruiz's life and career, highlighting important developments that defined his aesthetic theory and influenced his artistic practice, while also registering his unwavering commitment to artistic experimentation. A brief synthesis of salient trends in Ruiz scholarship will be followed by a presentation of our approach through Ruiz's main aesthetic principles. We will conclude by summarizing what the collection as a whole sets out to do and by giving a brief overview of each essay and interview.

Biography and Filmography

Early Years

Ruiz was born on July 25, 1941, in Puerto Montt, a port city in the south of Chile. His father and grandfather were both sailors, and his mother was a schoolteacher.[3] His early life had lasting influence, especially notable in his films: the prevalence of maritime themes, images of the sea and seafaring, and folklore tales from Chiloé, an island adjacent to Puerto Montt. From an early age he was an avid cinemagoer; the majority of films screened in theaters at the time were North American productions, such as those by John Ford, Howard Hawks, and such.[4] As Ruiz has stated in interviews and in *Poetics of Cinema*, Hollywood "B" movies were also part of his formation as a young boy and served as inspiration as their technical imperfection and narrative contradictions served to open up the cinematic medium to fantasy and imagination, a theme that recurs in Ruiz's own films.

With his family's move to Valparaíso and Santiago, Ruiz emerged onto the national artistic scene by famously writing one hundred theater plays in two years at the age of eighteen.[5] This prolific production was motivated by a Rockefeller Foundation grant. Ruiz explains his humorous logic: "I thought I had to produce a lot, lest they think I did not deserve the grant."[6] As a university student, Ruiz began studying law, but abandoned the study after three years.[7] Afterward, he enrolled to study theology as an act of provocation[8] at a time when he and all his friends were overtly left leaning. Throughout his university studies, however, he kept writing plays and, as a natural extension, film scripts. He received support from the Universidad de Chile's Department of Experimental Film to shoot his first film, *La maleta/The Suitcase* (CL, 1962). In addition, the cultural context of the time was such that in cinema political limitations were less strict than in theater.[9]

With his interest in film growing, Ruiz decided to attend Fernando Birri's highly regarded documentary film school in Santa Fe, Argentina.[10] As before with law and theology, Ruiz left the school once he felt he had learned all he needed.[11] His experience in Argentina taught him the importance of positionality—"when one lives in Latin America, it's not possible to make the same kind of images as when one lives in Europe or the United States"[12]— but he also became convinced that the documentary form privileged at Birri's film school was mostly subservient to political ideology. Back in Chile, he continued writing scripts and began working as editor for TV news and sports. For a brief period, he also traveled to the United States, where he attended some classes at Louisiana State University[13] and worked in Mexico as a telenovela scriptwriter.[14] Back again in Chile, he was hired to work in

TV as a scriptwriter, mainly to adapt novels for TV. In characteristic Ruizian fashion, he could not resist playing some creative tricks: "Evidently, I could not help making some false adaptations, of non-existent stories."[15] While working for TV and teaching screenwriting, he also continued producing films, among them *El tango del viudo/ The Widower's Tango* (CL, 1967), an unfinished fiction film in 16 mm.[16]

In 1968, having already acquired a vast experience as screenwriter, editor, and director, he produced his first finished full-length film, *Tres tristes tigres/ Three Sad Tigers* (CL, 1968). A groundbreaking film, *Tres tristes tigres* followed in the footsteps of Chilean antipoet Nicanor Parra (to whom it is dedicated) by paying homage to the contradictions and baroque forms of Chilean popular speech. Just as Parra had smashed and reinvented poetic language with his antipoetry, now Ruiz was setting out to develop a new language for cinema. Ruiz stated that in *Tres tristes tigres*, even the position of the camera was unconventional: "The idea was to put the camera not where it would see best, but where it should be, in the normal position. This means that there is always some obstruction and things are not seen from an ideal standpoint."[17] The film was a commercial flop, but it won the admiration of national and international film critics: it won the Premio de la Crítica in Chile and the top prize at the 1969 Locarno Film Festival. It was also screened at the legendary 1969 Viña del Mar Film Festival, a key event in the emergence of the New Latin American Cinema of the 1970s.

The Allende Years, the Coup, and Exile

During the Popular Unity government of Salvador Allende (1970–73), Ruiz was affiliated with the Socialist Party, one of the many parties that composed Allende's government coalition. However, he insisted on maintaining a critical distance from dogmatic tendencies at state-sponsored institutions such as the national production company, Chile Films. Filmmaker Miguel Littín took over the directorship of Chile Films, although he would resign within a year, frustrated with the bureaucracy and internal squabbles.[18] According to King: "No feature films funded by Chile Films were completed under Allende. Increasingly, therefore, the filmmakers decided to make their own films outside the official sector, though they would still use the facilities of Chile Films."[19] During this period Ruiz was tremendously productive, shooting several films and giving interviews in which he developed and defined his aesthetic principles. The films from this period show a range of styles, from the more personal to the more overtly political.[20] Films such as *La colonia penal/ The Penal Colony* (CL, 1970), *Nadie dijo nada/ No One Said Anything* (CL, 1971), *La expropiación/ The Expropriation* (CL, 1972), and *El realismo socialista/Socialist Realism* (CL, 1973) often used irony and were meant to provoke debates within the Left. In 1969 Ruiz married filmmaker Valeria Sarmiento, who became a lifelong artistic collaborator, editing the vast majority of his films.

In 1973, following the military coup in Chile, Ruiz left for Europe, arriving first in Germany and then in Paris, where he was to remain.[21] Following the forced exile of many intellectuals and artists, a Chilean cinema of resistance emerged, associated in particular with the films of Miguel Littín and Patricio Guzmán. In spite of his left leanings and exilic condition, Ruiz did not fit comfortably within the Chilean cinema of exile. His first film produced in France, *Diálogos de exiliados/Dialogues of Exiles* (FR, 1974), alienated the Chilean community in Europe because of its ironic view of the exiles' inability to adapt to their new surroundings. To add insult to injury, the film also flouted the narrative and political conventions of Latin American cinema of the time: "The film's humorous, flippant and surreal treatment of the adventures and tribulations of a group of exiles, compounded with a sketch-like narrative, diverged from the predictable authenticity of social realism."[22] In an interview from 1975, Ruiz discussed the importance of irony for artistic and political lucidity:

> It is not a question of pessimism, but for me irony is an important tool of political analysis. The present tragic situation is the result of a certain political process: it is important to be lucid rather than bemoan our fate; irony is necessary to refresh and clarify our perception of things.[23]

While Ruiz remained faithful to his principles of incisive political critique even in the face of repression and exile, the Chilean community in France was not ready to welcome this self-critique because they perceived it as taking away from denouncing the abuses of the Chilean dictatorship.

Very soon Ruiz would start exploring new creative avenues, such as highly imaginative, Borgesian fictions, at first inspired by the works of Pierre Klossowski. *La vocation suspendue/The Suspended Vocation* (FR, 1978) was based on Klossowski's novel of the same name, although Ruiz made it his own. *L'hypothèse du tableau volé/The Hypothesis of the Stolen Painting* (FR, 1979) was inspired by Klossowski's philosophical ideas and incorporated elements from his novel *The Baphomet* (1965).

In 1981, Ruiz began collaborating with Portuguese film producer Paulo Branco, which allowed him to shoot most of his feature films of the 1980s in Portugal. *Les trois couronnes du matelot/Three Crowns of the Sailor* (FR, 1983), for example, was filmed on the Portuguese island of Madeira, which stands in for the Chilean port town of Valparaíso. Portugal was a perfect location for Ruiz, since it served as a bridge between Europe and Latin America, overlooking the sea, one of Ruiz's sources of inspiration.

> I felt the need to explain Latin America to my European friends and Europe to my Latin American friends. [Some of my films] are bridges between the cinema I would like to do in Latin America and the cinema I make in Europe. This idea of a bridge came naturally when I got to know Portugal, which for me is a deformed mirror in regard to Spain and also to Latin America and Chile.[24]

There is an analogy between the idea of Portugal as a bridge and Ruiz's exilic status; exile became a central point of his cinema, allowing him to experiment with "intercultural and inter-representational forms of dialogue."[25] Accordingly, Ruiz's films of this period are marked by a strong sense of extra-territoriality and transnational wanderings, which reflected not only his diasporic situation but also his method of cinematic production. Since his arrival in Europe, Ruiz had worked in both film and television, and had made films in France, Germany, the Netherlands, and Portugal. The sense of extraterritoriality was also apparent in Ruiz's self-reflexivity in language, as illustrated by the multilingual film *Het dak van de Walvis/On Top of the Whale* (NL/FR, 1982), shot in the Netherlands, with dialogues in Dutch, German, Spanish, and English, in addition to an invented Patagonian language.[26]

Since early 1970s Ruiz's work had been featured in specialized French film journals such as *Positif* and *Cahiers du cinéma*, which regularly published film reviews and interviews with the filmmaker.[27] In 1983, *Cahiers du cinéma* organized a retrospective of his films in Paris[28] and devoted a special issue to Ruiz—now "re-baptised" as *Raoul* Ruiz (March 1983).[29] The critical acclaim cemented Ruiz's status as auteur in France and abroad. By 1984, Ruiz was fully integrated within the system of French cultural institutions. He was appointed director of the audiovisual section of the Maison de la Culture, first in Grenoble and then in Le Havre,[30] and continued to produce work for the Institut national de l'audiovisuel (INA) and for French public television.

Big Budget Films, The United States, and Reengagement with Chile

In the 1990s and 2000s, Ruiz began making European films with major stars such as Catherine Deneuve, Marcello Mastroianni, John Malkovich, and Mathieu Amalric. Although his film style remained surrealistic and baroque, these films were more polished, had stronger narrative lines, and were less brazenly avant-garde. Films such as *Généalogies d'un crime/Genealogies of a Crime* (FR, 1997), *Le temps retrouvé/Time Regained* (FR/IT/PT, 1999), based on the novel by Proust, and the biopic *Klimt* (AT/FR/DE/UK, 2006), belong to this group. Perhaps *Mistérios de Lisboa/Mysteries of Lisbon* (PT/FR, 2010), one of Ruiz's final films, is the highest expression of this type of cinema.

In the United States Ruiz's growing profile as filmmaker attracted the attention of both experimental theater groups, such as the New York–based Wooster Group, and of Hollywood. In Hollywood he made *Shattered Image* (US/CA/UK, 1998). By his own admission, his Hollywood adventure did not last long, as his filmmaking style received critical acclaim but did not prove to be commercially successful.[31] In New York, Ruiz made *The Golden Boat* (BE/US, 1990) with James Schamus[32] as first-time producer, featuring appearances by Jim Jarmusch and other now-major players on the independent cinema circuit.[33] Ruiz continues to inspire a new generation of North American avant-garde filmmakers.[34] In the United States Ruiz was also visiting professor at Harvard University and Duke University. At Duke he wrote a series of lectures on cinema, which would become his *Poetics of Cinema*.

Ruiz renewed his artistic relationship with Chile very late. Although he had been back as early as 1983, when the Pinochet dictatorship began allowing some exiles to return to the country, in the 2000s he began to cultivate a more consistent presence in his native country.[35] The first volume of *Poetics of Cinema* appeared in Spanish translation in 2000.[36] A retrospective of Ruiz's films was organized in Santiago in 2003, along with a series of conversations with French and Chilean intellectuals later collected in the book *Conversaciones con Raúl Ruiz* (*Conversations with Raúl Ruiz*).[37] This was to reawaken audience interest in the filmmaker as well as consolidate Ruiz's "return to Chile" in his cinema. Films such as *Cofralandes, rapsodia chilena/Cofralandes, Chilean Rhapsody* (CL/FR, 2002), *Días de campo/Days in the Country* (CL/FR, 2004), and the TV series *La recta provincia* (CL, 2007) and *Litoral* (CL, 2008) constituted an exploration of Chilean folk tales and cultural myths. Ruiz's return to Chile would culminate in his final film, *La noche de enfrente/Night across the Street* (CL, 2012).

Salient Trends in Ruiz Scholarship

Scholars have conceptualized Ruiz's work in diverse ways in response to the historical trajectory above, emphasizing themes such as his status as an exilic filmmaker, his relation to surrealism and the baroque, and his subversion and reinvention of the role of the auteur. Critics such as Zuzana Pick and Hamid Naficy, for example, have emphasized the exilic and diasporic aspect of Ruiz's work.[38] Discussing Ruiz's multilingual film *On Top of the Whale*, Naficy writes: "the film points to the constructedness of all languages—a fact that becomes more apparent in exile and displacement, where languages cease to be 'natural.'"[39]

Christine Buci-Glucksmann has analyzed Ruiz's films in terms of their baroque multiplication of angles and perspectives as well as tracing Ruiz's connections with baroque authors of the Spanish Golden Age such as Francisco de Quevedo and Pedro Calderón de la Barca, and with modern philosophers such as Walter Benjamin and Gilles Deleuze.[40] Buci-Glucksmann describes Ruiz's cinema in terms of Pasolini's "cinema of poetry" and Deleuze's "cinema of the seer."[41] The baroque also relates, in her view, to spectral presences that appear in Ruiz's films, ghosts that "haunt, as if repressed, the Latin American imaginary."[42] Laleen Jayamanne has placed Ruiz's cinema at the intersection of Benjamin's understanding of baroque allegory and surrealism. For Jayamanne, Ruiz is more properly a "late-twentieth-century baroque allegorical filmmaker."[43] She notes that "Ruiz perceives cinema as an allegorical system,"[44] while at the same time distancing himself from some of the deeper tenets of surrealism: "I am not a surrealist. What interests me in surrealism is the slapstick aspects, decorative and stereotypical aspects. . . . I am not at all convinced by the surrealist metaphysics."[45] Similarly, Michael Richardson concludes: "Ruiz's cinema is situated in traditions of the baroque rather than surrealism."[46] He sees Ruiz "as a kind of 'heretical' surrealist . . . because he uses surrealist devices for purposes that are not against surrealism but outside of it."[47] Richardson emphasizes the political intent in Ruiz's films, especially his critique of cultural imperialism.[48]

Ruiz's status as an auteur has also been a theme in the critical literature. Jonathan Rosenbaum wrote of how Ruiz's unique situation working on "assignments" for European television enabled him greater creative freedom than North American production methods, thus freeing him from the constraints of genre-driven cinema. Pointing out parallels with Orson Welles (in particular *The Immortal Story* and other European productions), Rosenbaum argues that Ruiz's situation in Europe allowed him to be an original filmmaker with certain obsessions and repetitions, while at the same time remaining an anti-auteur. His works never take themselves too seriously, they are always "closet comedies" that adopt the mannerisms of European auteur cinema, but also undercut them, as in *The Hypothesis of the Stolen Painting*, which also showcases what Rosenbaum calls Ruiz's "playful metaphysical system."[49]

A different approach is what we might term a critical-regional or place-based study, exemplified by Verónica Cortínez and Manfred Engelbert in

La tristeza de los tigres y los misterios de Raúl Ruiz, which analyzes in detail one feature film, namely *Tres tristes tigres*. The authors undertake a granular analysis of this foundational film, considering its specific historical, cultural, and biographical context.[50]

In the past few years, scholarly interest in Ruiz has grown further due to several factors, such as the greater availability of his films, the publication of many of his writings and interviews in Spanish and other languages, the creation of the Ruiz Archive,[51] and the public recognition of his importance by institutions such as the Cinémathèque Française. The critical rediscovery of Ruiz's early Chilean films from before 1974 has allowed for a reevaluation of his legacy in relation to Chilean and Latin American cinema. In France there has been continued interest in and appreciation of Ruiz's work, most emblematically expressed in a recent two-month retrospective at the Cinémathèque Française, which included showings of seventy-five of his films, accompanied by a wide range of conferences by his collaborators and discussions of Ruiz's impact on the history of cinema.[52] In the United States Ruiz is well known and respected by experimental filmmakers, and his films are routinely rescreened at the Film Society of Lincoln Center, New York, in addition to several retrospectives, such as the Pacific Film Archive at the University of California at Berkeley in 2012.[53]

We seek to expand this reception in light of growing availability of resources and through an analysis of his aesthetic principles, which remain surprisingly consistent throughout his films, writings, and interviews. We feel that the various angles and themes of Ruiz's earlier scholarly reception represent discrete aspects of his work but do not convey a unified image, which can only be achieved by approaching Ruiz's oeuvre as an organic whole. It is through an analysis of his aesthetic principles, followed by rigorous close readings of his films, that we may better capture the uniqueness and significance for modern cinema of Ruiz's oeuvre.

Aesthetic Principles

Ruiz's cinematic practice is inseparable from his poetics and thinking on cinema, disseminated through books, interviews, conversations, and lectures. Central to Ruiz's aesthetic is the idea of a "cinema of inquiry," a way of looking that seeks to reveal underlying cultural habits and ways of communicating and being. Ruiz's filmic practice seeks to activate peripheral and overlooked elements in the cinematic image, thus allowing latent stories to emerge and opening up cinema's expressive capabilities while resisting the centralized narrative mode of mainstream cinema. Ruiz also conceives of film as a quasi-living structure and presupposes an active spectator whose viewing experience is one of invention and imagination, not purely passive enjoyment. Finally, Ruiz's approach to film also privileges a critical interest in folklore as a transnational phenomenon and the activation of postcolonial perspectives latent in particular locations and forms of storytelling. This section will examine and synthesize Ruiz's aesthetic principles.

Cinema as Intervention into Reality

In a series of interviews that Ruiz gave during the early 1970s in Chile, he defined an aesthetic that would form the basis for his film practice at the time and later. For example, he cautioned against the uncritical imitation of Soviet and Cuban film styles that were not appropriate to the Chilean situation: "We are not in the position of takeover yet, as we all know, but in an earlier stage. But the *compañeros* presuppose a certain euphoria that does not exist and a number of positions gained that are not gained."[54] In an interview with the journal *Primer Plano* (1972), Ruiz declared that he "would prefer to register the political process rather than mystify it."[55] Perhaps most importantly, in an interview with Enrique Lihn and Federico Schopf for the journal *Atenea* (1970)—translated in this volume—Ruiz formulated his notion of a "cinema of inquiry" (*cine de indagación*): "there is the type of cinema we try to create: a cinema of inquiry, in the sense of searching for national issues. By filming a situation, you complete it; you resolve it. This is the idea of the cinema of inquiry."[56] Cinema becomes a privileged avenue to modify one's relationship to the world. It is in this sense that, for Ruiz, film can do political work: "It is all about these gestures becoming a language, reflecting themselves in film, which can come to define them. I suspect that the culture of resistance conceals a great capacity for subversion, and that this resistance can only become subversion by completing itself through the medium of film."[57] Film can register new "gestures" and transform them into a language, which can in turn change one's ways of being in the world. This means that film, even what we would call fiction film, does not exist in a realm separate from reality, but that filmic images do have direct impact on reality. This is in stark contrast to the pretense of Hollywood-style films, which allege the existence of a clear barrier between film and real life. Thus, all films and filmic images inevitably restructure our reality. But how do they do this? To address this point, Ruiz gives an example of a group of filmmakers who went to a fishing village, recorded one of the fishermen talking for days, and then projected the film for the whole village to see. He states that the fishermen saw the film and *changed*, although one could not tell with certainty *how*.[58] It was "the intent of film to influence reality ('influir sobre la realidad'), establishing a connection between cinematic activity and real events that would not have happened without cinema."[59]

Surface Effects and the "Photographic Unconscious"

Ruiz's concept of a "cinema of inquiry" also suggests that seemingly unimportant gestures, ways of talking and relating to each other, when captured on film, visually express the repressed ways of being of a people in alienation, whether in a neocolonial situation such as Latin America in the 1960s and 1970s, when Ruiz first formulated these ideas, or in a context in which the dominant paradigms of mainstream commercial cinema, following the model of Hollywood, capture and organize images and experience around the globe, a theme Ruiz continued to develop in his writings on cinema and which speaks to the struggle for original modes of cinematographic insight and expression today.

The unconscious is not hidden, but visible on the surface of discourse, gesture, and performance, the same way the unconscious manifests in the peripheral detail of the photograph or film shot. Ruiz thus argues that cinema registers gestures and speech patterns that configure an underlying language of resistance. Cinema captures *styles* of being, what Ruiz calls "stylemas." Pier Paolo Pasolini had used the term *stylema*, understood as "a unit of style," in the essay titled "The Cinema of Poetry" (1965).[60] Ruiz references Pasolini's concept in his conversation with Lihn: "My idea is that cultural methods of resistance make up a nonverbal language whose only way to become formalized and ascend to an ideological level—I employ this phrase with some reservations—is through film. These self-referential, decanted techniques form a group—not so much of syntagmas, but of *stylemas*."[61]

In *Poetics of Cinema 1* (1995), Ruiz would present a series of reflections and thought experiments in cinema and on the film image. In the section titled "The Photographic Unconscious," Ruiz elaborates on his notion of the unconscious as expressed on the surface of the image, further developing Benjamin's discussion of the "optical unconscious" in "Little History of Photography."[62] Ruiz's interest in the term "unconscious" has to do with the antirepresentative potential of "unnecessary" elements. For example, in order to say what a photograph is about, we must construct a narrative that takes into account some elements and that marginalizes others that are present in the photograph but do not fit the narrative created around the image. That narrative, Ruiz argues, is presented as representative of the photograph, a complete story, but it is not the whole story. Peripheral elements have been discarded, and thus a single narrative has effectively suppressed other possibly contradictory accounts of the photographic image.

> All these unnecessary elements have a tendency, curiously, to reorganize themselves forming an enigmatic corpus, a set of signs that conspires against the ordinary reading of the picture, adding to it an element of uncanniness, of suspicion. We will call that conspiracy . . . the photographic unconscious.[63]

So, Ruiz is interested in using and activating these elements that do not fit an "ordinary reading" in order to destabilize the pretense of totality that narrative cinema often has. Ruiz continues:

> I gradually came to understand that every spectator of the movies today is really a "connoisseur" in Benjamin's sense: in cinema as in sports, the spectators understand what's going on, to the point where they can anticipate what happens next, because they know the rules, by learning or by intuition (the rules of a cinematic narration are verisimilar, that is, made to be believed, easily legible, because they must be identical to those of the dominant social structure). That is why commercial cinema presupposes an international community of connoisseurs and a shared set of rules for the game of social life. In that sense, commercial cinema is the totalitarian social space par excellence.[64]

Ruiz locates repression in the forms of organizing and limiting the stories that images tell, in attaching a particular narrative to the image. His concept of photographic unconscious attempts to break open and liberate cinema's expressive—and political—possibilities. As Ruiz once stated: "What I am trying to do is extend the expressive capabilities of cinema."[65]

Film as Open System

In his *Conversaciones* in Chile, Ruiz mentions Giordano Bruno's treatise on magic, *A General Account of Bonding* (1591), describing it as "an excellent treatise on cinema" because it explains how to bind or subjugate humans by means of the combination and manipulation of images. "Now," says Ruiz mischievously, "are we or are we not talking about American cinema?"[66] Mainstream narrative cinema employs a sort of magical bonding, a manipulation that creates the "totalitarian social space" mentioned above. Ruiz's approach is to try to liberate the stories or narrative potential contained in every image, as if a film were composed of hundreds of possible films latent in each shot.

During the same visit to Chile in 2003, Ruiz gave a lecture in Valparaíso where he discussed his theory of the six functions of the shot.[67] In the Valparaíso lecture he gives some key insights and formulations, in particular Ruiz's description of the film as an intersubjective space. Ruiz suggests that the unconscious is intersubjective, existing between images (between shots) and also between the spectator and the film, which functions as an open, quasi-living structure:

> And my purpose when it comes to cinema is to allow all those functions to be activated with the same intensity. So that when we see a movie we are seeing 350, at least. That is to say, we are being seen from 350 points of view, by 350 eyes.[68]

Thus, not only is a film made up of 350 virtual or possible films, and each of those films constitutes a possible way of looking at the film, but furthermore, each shot represents a way in which the *spectator is being viewed by the film.* This connects with Ruiz's assertion later in the lecture that film is similar to a living organism, an intelligence:

> Now let us imagine a film that has all these functions activated . . . [this] is the point of departure, this is my ambition. . . . I mean the possibility of creating a film of such complexity that it resembles the structure of a library, so that when we go in to see a movie we have the impression of entering into the head of a living being of a more than average intelligence.[69]

Ruiz's view of cinema thus exceeds the mere sense of baroque complexity (the idea that the film has many levels of meaning and interpretation) and opens up a more radical view in which the individual and the film interact in a creative, dynamic way. The film is a living organism, an intelligence that itself looks at (questions, challenges) the spectator, thus breaking down the wall between subject and artwork.

Ruiz's view of film as an open system extends to his approach to the creation and distribution of films. For example, at the production level one can observe a concerted effort to relinquish creative control: he does not use a film script when shooting, the actors are free to improvise their parts, and most of the films are true collaborations with cinematographers, editors, and music composers.[70] Also, at the level of reception, if we consider authorship as the product of the negotiation between directors and audiences, his artistic career can be seen more as a continuous renegotiation. While it was fairly clear that his films up to 1973 had a national audience in mind, Ruiz "killed" his potential audience of Chilean exiles by making *Dialogues of Exiles* (1974), a biting critique of the exiles' refusal to accept the realities of Pinochet's coup and an acid condemnation of French paternalistic voluntarism. While art-house audiences in France and abroad embraced him as an auteur, Ruiz's own declarations complicate the issue; there is a certain tension between Ruiz's idea of spectators as "friends" and his insistence on not having a spectator in mind when filming. For example, in a 1990 interview, Ruiz stated: "I have a lot of friends, and these friends are from different countries and from different cultural and economic levels. My idea is to put all my friends together . . . so maybe the model of my audience is those friends."[71] On the other hand, Ruiz has been adamant about not having a "spectator" in mind. In fact, he has actively refused to imagine an "ideal spectator" (see the 2008 interview in this volume, for example). The unstable relationship between the director and his real or imagined audience can be interpreted as a continuing attempt to thwart cinema's populist potential and its rigidifying tendencies.

In this respect, Ruiz's absolute lack of interest in the distribution of his films is notable. Beyond screenings at art film festivals and a few DVD releases, his films are very difficult to access through official means. This situation speaks to the director's refusal to participate in the commercialization of his films, which signals a politically motivated rejection of the profit-driven aspect of the film industry. However, precisely these difficulties have led to the creation of informal networks for exchange and discussion among filmmakers, film students, and scholars in Latin America, North America, Europe, and Australia. YouTube and Vimeo have become dynamic yet unofficial spaces of exchange for Ruiz fans and scholars alike.

Paradoxically, for Ruiz the function of the filmmaker is to fade into the background in order to give way to film as an "open system," as a living organism. Without the expectations of a specific audience, the spectator is allowed to become an active producer of meaning, transforming and being transformed by film. The aim of this approach—with its political implications—is not to illustrate a preexisting thesis through film; it is to reorganize experience.

Transgenre Crossings and Geohistorical Situatedness

Ruiz's cinema is characterized by an aesthetic of impurity and a strong interest in transgenre crossings. Curiosity and a ceaseless search for new combinations mark Ruiz's idea of filmmaking as a pleasurable and joyful activity. During his formative years in Chile, Ruiz came to reject what he saw as the dogmatism of Latin American documentary realism of the late 1960s and early 1970s. Once filmmaking became "working with statistical data, investigating the social situation in the field," then it "was ultimately very boring."[72] Ruiz thus distanced himself from the Latin American Left's view of film as a "moral instance," which implied that "everything that prompted pleasure was a sin."[73]

While rejecting the dogmatism and moralism of a certain Latin American cinema, Ruiz's films retain a strong interest in decentering colonialism and Eurocentric perspectives. Nowhere is an anticolonial perspective more evident than in the film *On Top of the Whale*, which parodies the attempts of two European anthropologists to understand the mysterious language of the only two remaining members of a Patagonian tribe. As Ruiz explains, however, what might appear as a fanciful allegory in fact has a basis in reality. Wealthy landowners in the south of Chile and Argentina exterminated the Patagonian Indians, and in some cases only a few members of some tribes remained alive in the twentieth century.[74]

Ruiz's awareness of coloniality also informs his suspicion of any form of nationalism. Even the cultural nationalism of the 1960s and 1970s, conceived as a form of emancipation and anti-imperialism, could give rise to a form of xenophobia that recalled, for Ruiz, the search for ethnic purity in the Spanish Peninsula: "I was shocked upon first reading Américo Castro. I suddenly realized that our fight for Latin American identity and the expulsion of the foreigner (whoever they were) for the best reasons, could be read as a parallel to Spain's actions of expelling the Moors and the Jews."[75] Although Ruiz constantly engages in ethnographic explorations of Chilean identity, myths, and folklore, these forms of cinematic inquiry should be taken for what they are: a playful deconstruction of national mythology that often exposes the transnational roots of all folklore.

Ruiz's critique of authenticity extends to how he views his artistic role. Leaving behind Romantic and Modernist notions of authorship, Ruiz conceives of filmmaking as a combinatory art, a collective exploration of the possibilities latent in images, stories, words, and their combinations. Ruiz's interest in pastiche and in constantly crossing and mixing art film, melodrama, thriller, Hollywood "B" serials, documentary, and many others, speaks to a rejection of the role of the filmmaker as a virtuoso within a given film genre or form. Likewise, Ruiz's explorations of the cinema's intersection with literature, painting, installations, theater, poetry, philosophy, television, radioteatro, fotonovela, and such, all work to destabilize the cinematic apparatus itself. His combinatory art cultivates an open system of permutations that ushers in an endless multiplication of expressive possibilities.

Essays and Interviews

Due to his transnationalism and prolific output, Ruiz's work has created multiple contexts of reception in different places and at different stages of his career. Ruiz was not only a Chilean expatriate working in Europe but also a transnational filmmaker who worked in several languages and in different countries—Chile, France, the United States, and Portugal, among others—and scholarship on Ruiz has developed independently in English, Spanish, French, and Italian. Due to this, Ruiz's work is difficult to classify. He has been seen as an exilic filmmaker, as a European "auteur," as a surrealist, as a baroque (or neobaroque) artist, and as a philosopher of cinema whose writings and films constitute thought experiments. This may give the impression that there are many different "Ruizes" but no single "Ruiz."

In contrast, our collection posits the unity of Ruiz's oeuvre and investigates the conceptual similarities between his very diverse artistic productions. The notion of "cinema of inquiry" frames our reading of Ruiz's films and poetics as a system. Ruiz is a thinker of the image who expands the domain of cinema, incessantly probing the interstices between cinema and other arts and forms of knowing. Because it originates in the context of 1970s Chile, Ruiz's notion of "cinema of inquiry" also captures an undertheorized political dimension in his artistic productions.[76]

The first three chapters offer a broad focus on Ruiz's aesthetics by highlighting themes such as joy and play in his films; his commitment to transgenre explorations; and the way his teaching practice, literary writings, and television work inform his philosophy and poetics of cinema.

In "Childhood and Play in the Films of Raúl Ruiz," Valeria de los Ríos examines the figure of the child in Ruiz's work to argue that childhood and play become foundational tropes and strategies for the filmmaker's aesthetic project. Ruiz bases his aesthetic project on childhood, thus achieving his ludic and playful cinematic style. The figure of the child serves as a device that challenges the normativity of classical narration by introducing formal and diegetic categories, such as anomie or resistance to regulation, visual and linguistic experimentation, and the existence of possible worlds. De los Ríos seeks to demonstrate that the figure of the child points not toward an idealized state but rather toward a space of potentiality that eludes the regulated and normative world of adulthood, a space tied to formal and narrative experimentation. Looking at instances of childhood and play in several films spanning over thirty years—from *Het dak van de Walvis/On Top of the Whale* (NL/FR, 1982) to his last film, *La noche de enfrente/Night across the Street* (CL/FR, 2012)—de los Ríos shows how the image of the child allows the filmmaker to resist normativity and to break through spatiotemporal limitations so that viewers can experience new worlds and new ways of seeing. Using Giorgio Agamben's notion of infancy as a stage prior to entering into discourse, de los Ríos views Ruiz's films as intentionally "infantile" in the sense of privileging playful formal games, such as breaking the 180-degree rule, the use of false match-cut (*faux raccord*), multiple exposures, playing with the depth of field, and the use of mirrors and filters. In addition, Ruiz employs childhood as an affective trigger that retrieves both individual and collective memory, thus uniting the pursuit of memory with play and experimentation. The ubiquitous presence of child characters, games, and toys opens new fields of visibility normally inaccessible to the human eye. Thus, childhood and play in Ruiz's cinema have a narrative, visual, and political yield.

In "Television, Tractations, and Folklore: Raúl Ruiz as Transmedia Filmmaker," Michael Goddard expounds on Ruiz's work beyond cinema, especially his work in television and his literary and theoretical writings, in order to establish Ruiz as a transmedia artist. Goddard reminds us that Ruiz had worked in television throughout his career in Chile and in Europe. While he had an idiosyncratic approach to audiovisual production, he also had a pragmatic attitude toward the support and exposure that television offers. His partnership with France's Institut national de l'audivisuel (INA), a state-funded experimental TV producer, allowed him to experiment with available resources and to use structural constraints to harness his creativity, as demonstrated in *Petit manuel d'histoire de France/A Small Guide to French History* (FR, 1979), where a delirious collage of archival footage presents the country's history as a pervasive collection of stereotypes. In this and other TV documentaries Ruiz "enacts an implosion of the documentary form itself" by exposing the deceptive rhetorical fictions of standard television documentary. In addition to sustained work in television, Ruiz's transmedia explorations extend to literature, theory, performance art, and installations, demonstrating a willingness to experiment with (and within) any available context or medium while at the same time rendering unstable any rigid medium distinctions. The discussion of Ruiz's work as teacher and as theorist in *Poetics of Cinema* allows Goddard to demonstrate how theory and practice inform each other. The transmedia perspective opens up the cinematic field to a broad range of techniques and aesthetic choices, which allowed Ruiz to escape the confines of central conflict narrative and to create a "shamanic cinema"—the crafting of singular films, irreducible to genre, story line, or particular aesthetic formulas. Finally, Goddard argues, Ruiz's penchant for "complex, ludic constructions of multiple fictions" would lead him to a more explicit engagement with folklore in the last decade of his life. With films produced for Chilean TV, such as *Cofralandes* (CL, 2002), *La recta provincia* (CL, 2007), and *Litoral: Cuentos del mar/Litoral: Tales of the Sea* (CL, 2008), Ruiz explores the idea of folklore as ruins, offering a multifaceted vision of Chile's past and its bearing on the present.

In her essay titled "Raúl Ruiz, Speculative Bricoleur: Pedagogical and Televisual Ruptures," Alejandra Rodríguez-Remedi analyzes Ruiz's work as teacher and his television productions to illustrate the many ways in which the artist has sought to stimulate creativity. Rodríguez-Remedi looks beyond Ruiz's filmic productions to explore two long-standing activities: his work as teacher of film studies at institutions of higher education in Chile, the United States, and Europe as well as his work in television, in particular two recent TV miniseries inspired by Chilean folklore. Ruiz contests the commercial film industry's narrative uniformity and sterilization of cinema's poetic potential, which is the source of aesthetic emotion. The poetic resources that exist beyond the prescribed visual and narrative recipe enable the spectator to see his or her own film, to interact with it in an active and sustained dialogue. To illustrate, Rodríguez-Remedi provides a number of concrete examples from Ruiz's filmmaking classes at the University of Aberdeen in 2008–9. Exercises enhance the nonplot ways of making film, such as generating narratives by reordering diverse photographs and combining seemingly disparate everyday objects or improvising scenarios that intentionally deviate from a preexisting screenplay. By pointing to and attempting to break established patterns, Ruiz sought to empower students with creative awareness and to help them develop their own expressive capacity and personal poetics. Ruiz talked about filmmaking as a "collective joy," where aesthetic challenges for the crew members infuse joy into the creative process so as to combat a mechanistic attitude to filmmaking. He located free play at the epicenter of his teaching methodology to stimulate creative thinking and speculation, but backed by a solid background in readings, personal obsessions, and recurring themes. In his work made for Chilean television, Ruiz employed his childhood memories as a creative source of inquiry. Based on Chilean folklore, *La recta provincia* (CL, 2007) and *Litoral* (CL, 2008) combine echoes from national history and references to contemporary Chile. Ruiz explores folklore's capacity to stimulate audiences' viewing experience as a process of discovery.

The next five chapters offer close film analyses, focusing on different aspects such as aesthetic affinities with Orson Welles, dialogues with the European avant-garde (in particular Walter Benjamin and visual art theory of early twentieth-century Vienna), and Ruiz's complex relationship with memory and postdictatorship in Chile.

In "Inter-*auteurial* Itineraries and the Rekindling of Transnational Art Cinema: Raúl Ruiz and Orson Welles," Catherine L. Benamou brings attention to the filmmaker's global reach and appeal, accomplished through hybrid, multilingual constructions, one of them being Ruiz's multifaceted relationship with Orson Welles. Film critics and Ruiz himself have made explicit references to Welles's work, so this extended study seeks to provide a deeper analysis of biographical and artistic points of connection and resonance. Both directors were public intellectuals, engaging with their cultural and political circumstances in a variety of ways; both were influenced by their exilic experience in Europe to produce self-reflexive works that privilege open narrative discourse and uneasy plot endings, and examine sociocultural displacements. Their life experiences inspired a neobaroque take on modernity, in which they are both concerned with transforming viewers' perceptions of historical events and inspiring new interpretations of canonical works. Conceptually, Benamou identifies three broad categories of resonance, divergence, and tension in Ruiz's and Welles's work: architecture, the baroque, and adaptation. Shared reflexive attention to architectural form and detail underscores their metaphorical and para-narrational dimensions. The built environment (streets, buildings) resonates visually and aurally with the characters' existential states, while spatial distortions (such as objects placed in extreme foreground or exaggerated proportions) intentionally prevent the spectator from becoming fully immersed in the diegesis. Mirrors, especially for Ruiz, become portals for narrative insight, replacing the conventional reverse shot and thus refracting the spectator's attention away from the character's viewpoint. Their interest in (neo)baroque constructions reveal not just a passageway into memory, but also offer a means of de-suturing narrative and revealing the cyclical nature of time. For example, shifts in filmic style are linked to shifts in cultural sensibility or temporal register, creating relationships between different historical periods. Baroque melancholia, a fusion of distinct temporalities where the realms of the dead and the living coexist and intersect, signals the lingering presence of the past. In her discussion of adaptations, Benamou underlines the importance of storytelling for both directors. Inspired by other storytellers, they allegorize historical events and personal experiences, thus allowing the spectators to participate in the production of meaning. Nevertheless, of course, there are significant differences between the two filmmakers, such as in generation and personality, but most importantly in their approach to their modes of production: Welles's formative yet conflicted relationship to Hollywood stands in contrast to Ruiz's willingness to test the limits of iconoclasm, perhaps best captured by his self-description as "bricoleur."

Janet Stewart's chapter, "Filming Vienna 1900: The Poetics of Cinema and the Politics of Ornament in Raúl Ruiz's *Klimt*," seeks to show how Ruiz's nontraditional biopic makes a contribution to wider debates on the politics of film aesthetics. In particular, Stewart argues that Ruiz sets out to put into cinematic form aspects of the visual art theory of early twentieth-century Vienna as a way to address the relationship between theory and history in film and art. Vienna's iconic Café Central, as a site of urban modernity, offers the ideal location to explore ways in which art historians rethought space and spatial relations at the turn of the twentieth century, and which cinema reimagines at the turn of the twenty-first century. Using the location as a starting point, the film begins by exploring the tension between architecture's experiential dimension and its cognitive dimension and goes on to visually highlight the dissonance between lived experience and the distant gaze in one's perception of space. In this struggle between exterior and interior, the film visually engages with and explores the contested concept of the ornament in art theory. In particular, the film sets out to rethink the function of Klimtian ornament; Ruiz reactivates earlier textual debates on the role of ornamentation in art, translates them into filmic images, and thus retheorizes ornament not as something that is placed *on* a surface, but as something indistinguishable from the surface.

By accentuating the primacy of surface over depth in cinema, Stewart argues, Ruiz rejects the "penetrative" logic of traditional cinematic ways of displaying knowledge. Ruiz thus comments on cinema's historical complicity in displaying otherness to the Western (male) gaze in ways that produce and reproduce colonial and patriarchal structures. Stewart contends that Ruiz explores ways to construct a new cinematic language that emphasizes a more involved tactile and sensorial perception of the image, reactivating the potential of a haptic visuality that complements the more detached optic visuality associated with the traditional Western gaze.

In "Ghosts with Open Wounds: Benjamin's Photographic Unconscious and Raúl Ruiz's Spectral Turn," Sabine Doran traces Ruiz's dialogue with Walter Benjamin through a close reading of the film *Three Crowns of the Sailor*. She argues that Ruiz reworks Benjamin's reflections on technology and media after the supposed death of cinema in the wake of the digital revolution. Ruiz awakens the spectator to "the photographic unconscious," an alternate technique of vision Doran characterizes as "a form of carnal vision." Doran sees this film about a ghost ship that travels the seas populated by corporeal living-dead as materializing the ghosts of collective histories, which reemerge to haunt the present, breaking through the barrier of repression and amnesia in our mass-mediated society. The open wounds the ghosts display transform the film itself into a porous membrane, a site of passage between worlds.

Paying close attention to Ruiz's cinematography and editing technique, Doran demonstrates how the film leads the spectator through a state of intoxication into a dream world that challenges conventional perceptions of reality and opens up new fields of visuality. Ruiz's use of extreme close-ups and jolting montage as well as his wandering narrative and camerawork reawaken the revolutionary potential of cinema, exposing the fictive structure of film itself by drawing attention to the space felt between shots. It is in these spaces between shots that Doran discerns the film's ability to gaze back at and haunt the spectator. Just as the visual style of the film draws attention to its own constructedness, it also underscores the constructedness of family and community bonds, revealing how they are held together by various forms of inscription that serve to incarnate a sense of belonging. Throughout the film, forms of inscription such as stitching, tattoos and marks upon the body, wounds and sores on the skin expose the wounds and vulnerabilities upon which family and community are based. The family bonds the sailor has created on his meandering journey across the world is the construct of a scattered global family, which Doran reads as an invocation of Giorgio Agamben's "community to come," a community without unity or identity, made up of "universal exiles" who co-belong in their diversity.

In "Raúl Ruiz's 'Lost' Chilean Film: Memory and Multiplicity in *Palomita blanca* (1973)," Ignacio López-Vicuña explores how the film, which was believed lost but was rediscovered and screened in 1992, constitutes an untimely irruption of the Popular Unity period into the postdictatorship cultural landscape of Chile, and thus provides a unique intervention into the ongoing debate on memory. The film is an ironic adaptation of a popular love story across social classes by conservative writer Enrique Lafourcade, again demonstrating Ruiz's penchant for "creative imitation," that is, imitating something so closely that it becomes distorted and ultimately turns into something else entirely. The film's uncanniness resides not only in its documentation of everyday life under Allende but also in the way Ruiz's aesthetics of dissonance and fragmentation challenge the idea of memory as linear narrative, multiplying perspectives in a baroque manner. Formally, the film rejects the dominant aesthetics of documentary realism and opts for aural and visual experimentation. The film embraces a nonlinear narrative style and refuses to offer a clear-cut political message. Instead, the film focuses on dissonances and fragmentation and thus offers a visual representation of a past that was heterogeneous, full of dark humor, and absurd. Using irony as a political and aesthetic strategy, Ruiz seeks to create new forms of consciousness while remaining grounded in regional history and narrative. The film challenges the idea that the nation's past or future can be ordered into a coherent narrative. Its fragmented and nonlinear presentation of discourse and subjectivity emphasizes the dissonances created by everyday discourse to reflect the constitutive heterogeneity of the nation and of political subjects. The film reflects the director's ongoing commitment to exploring the complexity of reality through a cinema of subconflicts and story lines that proliferate, as well as through characters with multiple conflicting internal motivations. López-Vicuña contends that the film embraces the revolutionary through a cinematic rendering of the heterogeneous nature of temporality and subjectivity.

In "Raúl Ruiz's Surrealist Documentary of Return: *Le retour d'un amateur de bibliothèques* (1983) and *Cofralandes* (2002)," Andreea Marinescu seeks to demonstrate how in Ruiz's hands, documentary film functions as an inquiry into the fleeting and fragile nature of documentary realism, memory, and narratives of the nation. Ruiz does not set out to provide a unified narrative of the nation or a better grasp of truth, but rather to explore the limits of knowledge and the impossibility of a unified narrative. Central to this endeavor is Ruiz's understanding of documentary not as a record of truth but as an interpretation of it. Inspired by Brazilian Cinema Nôvo and French New Wave, Ruiz problematized the documentary realism of Latin American Cinema. He uses film techniques to expose the mechanisms documentary deploys for creating coherence and truth, for example by using asynchronous sound and voice-over narration that contradicts the images being shown. Using surrealist techniques, Ruiz creates a distanciation to expose the artificiality of documentary. In *Return*, the narrator, a returning exile like Ruiz himself, seeks to remember the day before the military coup, but keeps getting derailed by memories of childhood and by the search for a book he lost. The irony is that the one thing he can only partially remember is a poem he failed to memorize in childhood. Thus the film stages memory as necessarily incomplete and fragmented, and documentary as an exploration of this fragmentation, rather than as a recovery of a unified narrative. In his later documentary film *Cofralandes*, Ruiz uses childhood memories and associations of images to reconstruct a surrealist view of national history, layering sounds and images from history in incongruous or comical juxtapositions, exposing the impossibility of any synthesis of national history, identity, or culture. Surrealism emerges from the material's discontinuities, non sequiturs, and absurdities. Thus documentary becomes a tool for probing reality's absurdist dimensions rather than a vehicle for truth.

The three interviews in this volume have been selected in order to give a sense both of the consistency of Ruiz's obsessions and of the evolution of his ideas over time. Roughly twenty years apart from each other, they capture important moments of self-reflection in the filmmaker's trajectory. The 1970 interview is previously unpublished in English. What we offer here is a selection that contains some of Ruiz's early ideas on cinema and the political, including his original formulation of the notion of a "cinema of inquiry." The 1989 and 2008 interviews are published here for the first time. Together, these interviews give the reader a sense of the variety, erudition, and creativity of Ruiz's thinking. Although the interviews come at the end of the book, they should not be seen as a mere appendix, but rather as engaging in a conversation with the preceding essays. These interviews have been critical in shaping our sense that Ruiz's ideas on cinema maintain a strong unity over time.

In his 1970 interview Ruiz conveys an understanding of the politics of cinema that diverges from the documentary realism prevalent at the time in Latin America. Already at this early stage of his career, Ruiz conceives of the process of filmmaking as involving elements of storytelling and play, which allow meaning to emerge from the images themselves. It is this whole process of discovery that Ruiz calls "cinema of inquiry." Speaking during the highly politicized period of Allende's socialist Popular Unity government in Chile, Ruiz describes cinema's ability to capture the nonverbal language that expresses a culture's resistance to cultural imperialism. In the context of the colonized Third World, cinema explores how people in subjugated cultures subvert modernizing discourses and developmentalist projects.

In the 1989 interview with Catherine Benamou, Ruiz articulates some of the ideas that will become central to his *Poetics of Cinema* books, such as the importance of the overlooked detail at the margins of the film image. He discusses how unexpected visual effects result from the play of light and shadow and from "accidents" in the filmmaking process. Rather than smoothing out or erasing these phantom effects, Ruiz argues that they should be embraced—in this regard, he says, film can learn from other visual arts. Looking back at his trajectory, he also recalls how he resisted the didacticism and the moralism of Latin American left-wing filmmaking, citing Brazilian cinema and Akira Kurosawa as decisive influences on his early work, because they showed him how cinema could be politically aware, yet also artistically playful, and how it could investigate national identity through a collage of cinematic styles and cultural influences. In this interview, Ruiz also provides key information about layers of meaning in his films, such as political resonances in *The Suspended Vocation* and references to the history of colonialism in *On Top of the Whale*. Far from providing a definitive reading of the films, however, such information creates allegorical levels that enrich the films' combinatory potential, ultimately understood as an open system.

Finally, in his 2008 interview Ruiz, toward the end of his career, reflects upon his films and describes them as encouraging a "contemplative playfulness" and as resisting any form of moralism, whether from the right or the left. Ruiz describes his use of voice-over narration and other devices to create a space for the viewer to become both involved and detached from the film, to develop an active experience of spectatorship in which viewing becomes a form of daydreaming, remembering, and inventing. He discusses how his films attempt to reawaken forgotten connections with myth, drama, and folklore that are most evident in his reworking of elements of Hispanic popular culture that intersect with the Spanish baroque and with global storytelling traditions. Ruiz also discusses how cinema does not function as a representation of reality but rather serves to "awaken the capacity for invention" both with regard to everyday life and in relation to the political, insofar as cinema undermines any conception of politics as a unitary narration and opens up our awareness to the complex and ambivalent nature of political emotions and desires. His reflections come full circle, back to the notion of a cinema of inquiry that engages with history, politics, and the (trans)national through a questioning of unitary narratives and identities.

Notes

1. Michael Goddard, *The Cinema of Raúl Ruiz: Impossible Cartographies* (London: Wallflower; New York: Columbia University Press, 2013), 1.

2. Filmmaker Cristián Sánchez is the author of *Aventura del cuerpo: El pensamiento cinematográfico de Raúl Ruiz* (Adventure of the Body: The Cinematographic Thinking of Raúl Ruiz) (Santiago: Ocho Libros, 2011). Philosopher Willy Thayer has taught courses on philosophical approaches to Ruiz's poetics of the image at the University of Chile and at Universidad Metropolitana de Ciencias de la Educación (UMCE) in Chile. He is the author of ongoing research on the cinema of Raúl Ruiz.

3. This biographical sketch relies upon Ruiz's interview with Benoît Peeters (1986–1987), reprinted in Bruno Cuñeo, ed., *Ruiz: Entrevistas escogidas—filmografía comentada* (Santiago: Ediciones Universidad Diego Portales, 2013), 47–90.

4. Cuneo, *Ruiz*, 50–51.

5. Ibid., 51–53.

6. "Pensé que debía producir mucho, porque si no iban a pensar que no me merecía la beca." Ibid., 52.

7. Ibid., 55.

8. Ibid., 60.

9. Ibid., 62.

10. Ibid., 63.

11. Ibid., 64.

12. Ibid.

13. Ibid., 67.

14. Ibid., 68.

15. Ibid., 69.

16. Ibid., 308.

17. Ruiz quoted in John King, *Magical Reels: A History of Cinema in Latin America* (London: Verso, 2000), 172. Scholars such as John King have commented on the relationship between Parra's antipoetry and Ruiz's cinema. See *Magical Reels*, 172. For a fuller discussion, see Verónica Cortínez and Manfred Engelbert, *La tristeza de los tigres y los misterios de Raúl Ruiz* (Santiago de Chile: Cuarto Propio, 2011), 111–19.

18. King, *Magical Reels*, 175.

19. Ibid.

20. Ibid., 176.

21. Cuneo, *Ruiz*, 88–89.

22. Zuzana M. Pick, "The Dialectical Wanderings of Exile," *Screen* 30, no. 4 (1989): 52.

23. Ruiz quoted in King, *Magical Reels*, 177.

24. In Zuzana M. Pick, *The New Latin American Cinema: A Continental Project* (Austin: University of Texas Press, 1993), 30.

25. Ibid., 161.

26. Ruiz also collaborated with cinematographers Sacha Vierny (*Hypothesis of the Stolen Painting*, 1978, and *Three Crowns of the Sailor*, 1983) and Henri Alekan (*The Territory*, 1981, and *On Top of the Whale*, 1983).

27. *Positif* and *Cinéma* began covering Ruiz's work in 1970, after he had won the Golden Leopard at Locarno Film Festival with *Tres tristes tigres* (1969), while *Cahiers du cinéma* published their first film review in 1978. See Pamela Biénzobas, "Amor a primera vista: Cuando la crítica francesa conoció a Raoul," *Mabuse: Revista de cine*, June 11, 2005. Website. For a complete list of titles, see the "Articles de presse" section in *Le Cinéma de Raúl Ruiz*. Website.

28. Pick, "Dialectical Wanderings of Exile," 52.

29. See "Raoul Ruiz," *Cahiers du cinéma*, special issue, 345 (1983): 1–82.

30. Pick, "Dialectical Wanderings of Exile," 52.

31. See the 2008 interview in this volume.

32. James Schamus is an Academy Award–nominated screenwriter, producer, and film executive. As CEO of Focus Features, he oversaw the finance, production, and distribution of numerous films, including a number of Oscar winners. He has also produced or executive-produced many of the most important American independent films of the past decade, including four Grand Prize winners at the

Sundance Film Festival. Faculty profile website at Columbia University School of the Arts. Website. Accessed September 1, 2016.

33. See here James Schamus's touching piece written on the day of Ruiz's passing, "Raúl Ruiz: First Thoughts," *Filmmaker Magazine*, August 19, 2011. Website.

34. For example, the 2012 Migrating Forms Festival (formerly the New York Underground Film Festival) dedicated a section to Ruiz's films and writings.

35. Ruiz had returned to Chile in 1983 and documented his experiences in a short film, *Lettre d'un cinéaste ou Le retour d'un amateur de bibliothèques/Letter from a Library Lover* (FR, 1983).

36. Raúl Ruiz, *Poética del cine*, trans. Waldo Rojas (Santiago: Editorial Sudamericana Chilena, 2000).

37. Eduardo Sabrovsky, ed., *Conversaciones con Raúl Ruiz* (Santiago: Ediciones Universidad Diego Portales, 2003).

38. Pick, "Dialectical Wanderings of Exile" and *New Latin American Cinema*; Hamid Naficy, *An Accented Cinema* (Princeton, NJ: Princeton University Press, 2001).

39. Naficy, *Accented Cinema*, 50.

40. Christine Buci-Glucksmann, "The Baroque Eye of the Camera," in *Raúl Ruiz: Images of Passage*, ed. Helen Bandis, Adrian Martin, and Grant McDonald (Melbourne, Australia: Rouge Press, 2004), 31–44.

41. Ibid., 32–33.

42. Ibid., 34.

43. Laleen Jayamanne, "*Life Is a Dream*: Raúl Ruiz Was a Surrealist in Sydney—A Capillary Memory of a Cultural Event," in *Toward Cinema and Its Double* (Bloomington: Indiana University Press, 2001), 161.

44. Ibid., 166.

45. Ruiz quoted in ibid., 163.

46. Michael Richardson, *Surrealism and Cinema* (New York: Berg, 2006), 160.

47. Ibid., 163.

48. Ibid., 157.

49. Jonathan Rosenbaum, "Mapping the Territory of Raúl Ruiz," in *Placing Movies: The Practice of Film Criticism* (Berkeley: University of California Press, 1995), 224.

50. An important Spanish-language study on Ruiz, which together with *El cine de Raúl Ruiz: Fantasmas, simulacros y artificios*, eds. Valeria de los Ríos and Iván Pinto (Santiago: Uqbar Editores, 2010), Sánchez's *Aventura del cuerpo*, and Cuneo's *Ruiz*, contributed to sparking the renaissance of academic interest on Ruiz in Chile, it features a meticulous and extensive close film analysis. Cortínez and Engelbert examine Ruiz's early practice and thinking on cinema, as well as concepts such as *cine de indagación* and *seis funciones del plano*, which the filmmaker will develop throughout his career. See especially the second chapter, "La estética de Ruiz," in Cortínez and Engelbert, *La tristeza de los tigres*, 63–81.

51. The Ruiz Archive, available at the Institute for Contemporary Publishing Archives (IMEC), France, and the Art Institute of the Pontifical Catholic University of Valparaíso, Chile, contains the vast majority of Ruiz's films and film scenarios, as well as a vast collection of interviews (1960–2013), articles, and press

conference excerpts, a collection of books that directly influenced Ruiz's filmmaking, and most importantly, a number of manuscripts by Ruiz that include short stories, theater plays, film scripts, notes on film theory, and Ruiz's diary from the last twenty years, which is currently being transcribed and edited for publication. See IMEC (France): www.imec-archives.com/fonds/ruiz-raul/ and Archivo Ruiz-Sarmiento at Pontificia Universidad Católica de Valparaíso: www.arte.ucv.cl/index .php/archivo-ruiz-sarmiento/.

52. The retrospective dates were March 30 to May 30, 2016. www.cinematheque. fr/cycle/raoul-ruiz-315.html.

53. In December 2016, The Film Society of Lincoln Center organized a three-week-long retrospective featuring sixteen of Ruiz's films: www.filmlinc.org/series/ life-is-a-dream-the-films-of-raul-ruiz-part-1/#about.

54. Raúl Ruiz, interview by Federico de Cárdenas, Paris, *Hablemos de Cine*, July 1971, 10. The original quote is: "No estamos aún en el momento de la toma del poder, como todos sabemos, sino en el previo. Pero los compañeros se dedican a presuponer una cierta euforia que no existe, una serie de posiciones ganadas que generalmente no lo están."

55. The original quote is: "Prefiero registrar antes que mistificar el proceso chileno." See Raúl Ruiz, interview in *Primer Plano* 1, no. 4 (1972): 3.

56. The original quote is: "el tipo de cine que intentamos hacer nosotros: de indagación, en el sentido de buscar las claves nacionales. Al filmar una situación, tú la completas, la resuelves. Esta es la idea del cine de indagación." See Raúl Ruiz, "Diálogo con Raúl Ruiz por Enrique Lihn," *Atenea: Revista de ciencia, arte y literatura de la Universidad de Concepción* 500 (2009): 276. For the English version, see the 1970 interview in this volume.

57. "De lo que se trata es de que estos gestos se conviertan en un lenguaje, reflexionando, por sí mismos, a través del cine, el cual puede llegar a definirlos." Ibid., 277. See also the 1970 interview in this volume.

58. Ibid., 276–77. See also the 1970 interview in this volume.

59. Ibid., 277. See also the 1970 interview in this volume.

60. Pier Paolo Pasolini, "The Cinema of Poetry," in *Heretical Empiricism* (Bloomington: Indiana University Press, 1988), 167–86.

61. The original quote is: "Mi idea es que las técnicas de resistencia cultural conforman un lenguaje no verbal, cuya única manera de formalizarse y de elevarse a un nivel ideológico—empleo esta palabra con mucha reserva—es a través del cine. Estas técnicas decantadas, comentándose a sí mismas, conforman un conjunto, más que de sintagmas, de estilemas." Ruiz, interview by Lihn, 274. See also the 1970 interview in this volume.

62. Walter Benjamin, "Little History of Photography," in *Selected Writings, Volume 2 (1927–1934)*, ed. Michael W. Jennings, Howard Eiland, and Gary Smith (Cambridge, MA: Harvard University Press, 1999), 507–30.

63. Ruiz, *Poetics of Cinema 1*, 2nd ed., trans. Brian Holmes (Paris: Dis Voir, 2005), 57.

64. Ibid., 58.

65. The original quote is: "Lo que yo trato de hacer es extender las capacidades expresivas del cine." Ruiz quoted in Sabrovsky, *Conversaciones con Raúl Ruiz*, 78.

66. Ibid., 32–33.

67. Raúl Ruiz, "Conferencia en el Instituto de Arte: Pontificia Universidad Católica de Valparaíso, 23 de septiembre de 2003," *Pensar y poetizar* 10 (2012): 93–101. For Ruiz, each shot can potentially activate up to six functions: centrifugal, centripetal, critical, holistic, allegorical, and combinatory. The notion of six functions of the shot is one that Ruiz returned to and reformulated in several texts and interviews, most notably "The Six Functions of the Shot," in Bandis, Martin, and McDonald, *Raúl Ruiz: Images of Passage*, 57–68; "The Making of Films" in Ruiz, *Poéticas del cine* (Santiago: Ediciones Universidad Diego Portales, 2013), 295–331; and the Valparaíso lecture. Although they all discuss six functions of the shot, these versions differ somewhat. For further discussion of Ruiz's notion of "six functions of the shot," see Cortínez and Engelbert, *La tristeza de los tigres*, 73–74, and Adrian Martin, "Hanging Here and Groping There: On Raúl Ruiz's 'The Six Functions of the Shot,'" *Screening the Past* 35 (December 2012).

68. "Y mi propósito cuando hago cine es decir que todas esas funciones pueden ser activadas con la misma intensidad. De manera que cuando vemos una película estamos viendo 350, por lo menos. Es decir, estamos siendo vistos desde 350 puntos, desde 350 ojos." Ibid., 94.

69. "Ahora imaginemos una película que tenga activadas todas esas funciones . . . es el punto de partida, es mi ambición. . . . Me refiero a la posibilidad de crear un film de una complejidad tal que semeje la estructura de una biblioteca, para que cuando entremos a verlo tengamos la impresión de entrar en la cabeza de un ser vivo de una inteligencia más que mediana." Ibid., 96–97.

70. See, for example, "El guión lo hago al final: Declaraciones de Raúl Ruiz a José Román," *Enfoque* 7 (1986): 37–41.

71. See Jonathan Rosenbaum, "Ruiz Hopping and Buried Treasures: Twelve Selected Global Sites," in *Essential Cinema: On the Necessity of Film Cannons* (Baltimore: Johns Hopkins University Press, 2004), 238–39.

72. See Ruiz 1989 interview included in this volume.

73. Ibid.

74. Ibid.

75. Ibid.

76. See Ruiz 1970 interview included in this volume.

Childhood and Play in the Films of Raúl Ruiz

Valeria de los Ríos

According to *Cahiers du cinéma* critic Alain Bergala, it is in their childhood when cinephiles encounter the essential films in their relationship with cinema—they carry those films for all their lives, as a sort of "inexhaustible traveling allowance."[1] Raúl Ruiz's *Poetics of Cinema*[2] begins precisely with a glance at childhood. In the first chapter, titled "Central Conflict Theory," Ruiz considers the context of the 1950s and '60s, when that theory began to circulate in an optional manner, not with the compulsory nature that characterizes it today. Ruiz recalls that in those times, many American "B" movies were screened in cinemas in the Chilean provinces, which later became part of his childhood memories:

> Around 1948 or 1950, a gang of us kids were just about to leave elementary school. We liked to use our .22 long rifles to shoot the bulbs out of streetlights, or we'd fight with the great-grandchildren of German immigrants, who had arrived in Chile at the end of the previous century and who the wave of anti-Nazi films portrayed as abhorrent. From time to time we would call a truce and go to the movies together. There were two theaters in our town. One showed Mexican adult movies, Italian neorealist dramas, and French "thesis" films. The other one specialized in American kids' movies. That was the one we went to, and even if some of us occasionally found our way to the other in the hope of seeing a naked woman, still we much preferred the films for kids. Long after we'd stopped being kids, we maintained that same preference. I think that's where I got something that could be called my first "value system."[3]

The value system Ruiz refers to was born closely tied to those films, and it materialized in linguistic expressions imbued with the language and iconography of cinema. Children at the time used expressions such as "slower than the villain's horse"; when someone cheated in a game, it was said that the dice were as fixed "as the last fight in a Western"; rainy Sundays were said to be "longer than a movie's last kiss," and a bad guy was always "meaner than Fu Manchu."[4]

Rather than focusing on the autobiographical turn of Ruiz's cinematographic poetics, I am interested in the productivity that the Chilean-born filmmaker assigns to play and childhood. Far from looking at that period as a bygone or primitive stage of the future filmmaker, Ruiz bases his aesthetic project on childhood and play. In fact, his poetics of cinema is based on the rejection of central conflict theory—the idea that every narrative plot must have a conflict structuring it as its backbone—in favor of those "bad movies" that contributed to his primal canon. Here I understand "bad movies" as those that do not comply with the basic requirements of a traditional narrative according to Aristotelian poetics: a central conflict motivating the actions of the characters, where the narrative threads are perfectly structured and nothing is in excess. Ruiz's poetics, by contrast, proposes a concern with secondary objects and events,[5] a praise of boredom[6] and distraction,[7] and an openness to the complexity involved in the process of montage of different shots where several threads coexist, not merely the narrative one. This approach to cinema—focused on the objects, involving circumstance and incorporating the spectator, even in states of boredom or distraction—can be characterized as ludic or playful.

Ruiz's image corresponds mostly to the Deleuzian time-image—since movement is subordinated to the temporal axis—but it could also be metaphorically seen as *imago ludens* or "playful image," that is, as an image constantly playing with its technical possibilities while refusing to conform to the normative aesthetics of classical narration. In Ruiz's films, the presence of the child is associated with formal experimentation, while at the same time, the child's presence narratively justifies visual anomalies without fully explaining them—doubt always remains about their causes, or uncertainty concerning whether what is being shown is real or a dream. Thus childhood, rather than an ideal or pure state, represents a space of pure potentiality.

In this chapter, I reflect on the figures of childhood and play in Raúl Ruiz's cinema, considering several of his films: *Het dak van de Walvis/On Top of the Whale* (NL, 1982); *La ville des pirates/City of Pirates* (FR/PT, 1983); *Manoel dans l'île des merveilles/Manoel on the Island of Wonders* (FR/PT, 1984); *L'île au trésor/Treasure Island* (UK/FR/US, 1985); *Le temps retrouvé/Time*

Regained (FR/IT/PT, 1999); *Comédie de l'innocence/ Comedy of Innocence* (FR, 2000); *Le domaine perdu/ The Lost Domain* (FR/RO/ES/IT, 2005); *Mistérios de Lisboa/Mysteries of Lisbon* (PT/FR, 2010); and *La noche de enfrente/Night across the Street* (CL/FR, 2012).

I will analyze how the image of the child serves as a device that allows the filmmaker to resist the normativity of classical narration, introducing categories linked to infancy and childhood at the formal and diegetic levels—such as anomie or resistance to regulation, visual and linguistic experimentation, and the existence of possible worlds. By linking Ruiz's work with that of authors such as Giorgio Agamben and Walter Benjamin, I will examine how childhood in Ruiz's cinema is both aesthetically and politically productive. Additionally, I will study the presence in Ruiz's films of toys—as technical gadgets signaling the presence of cinema within cinema—and ghosts—like children, beings capable of breaking through spatiotemporal limitations and passing from one world to the other.

Infancy and Childhood[8]

According to Giorgio Agamben, etymologically, the word *infant* alludes to one who cannot speak, but not because of a certain dumbness, but because of a privation of language—a privation that also grants access to language. For Agamben, infancy presents itself as a machine, transforming pure, pre-Babel language into human discourse, and nature into history.[9] To situate oneself in infancy implies then to suspend the passage from nature to history and to linger in play as a practice prior to the entrance into discourse—here understood in a Foucauldian way as a system of representation, both individual and collective.

Richard Bégin states that Ruiz practices cinema as a child practices adult language.[10] With that, he directly references Agamben's notion of infancy—as a stage prior to entering into discourse—explaining Ruiz's formal experimentation as a freedom that relieves him from classical cinematic conventions (here understood as "adult language" or "hegemonic cinematographic discourse"). In this way, for Bégin—who marginally alludes to infancy—the "infantile" character of Ruiz's cinema emerges in the multiple games Ruiz plays with the cinematographic language. Some examples of these procedures are sudden spatiotemporal changes, breaking the 180-degree rule, the persistent use of the *faux raccord*,[11] multiple exposures, playing with the depth of field, and the use of mirrors and color filters. The persistent use of these procedures results in a confusion of the spatiotemporal planes, the presence of phantasmatic elements, and an emphasis on the perceptive and corporeal character of cinema—while leaving the strictly narrative intentions in the background.

Not only does infancy appear in Ruiz's cinema at the diegetic and formal levels—recall that in addition to experimenting with an "infantile" cinematographic language, children have taken part and starred in many of his films[12]—it is also linked to affection. In an interview with Bruno Cuneo, Ruiz declared:

> Childhood memories are important not just for me, but for everyone. You are the first generation to have actually broken up with Chile's past. I mean an emotional breakup. For you, the younger ones, *El Peneca* doesn't mean a thing; neither does the magic of radio dramas. But when we were children, there was nothing besides than radio. At night you would turn off the lights, listen to radio dramas in silence and imagine things. And when I was even younger, I thought very small people who lived inside the radio were talking to me. Those kinds of images cannot be lost.[13]

In this quote, Ruiz includes several elements: his own childhood memories, a technical device (the radio) around which the child's imagination generates fantasies, and the need to record the images of that lost childhood. The imperative idea that these images "cannot be lost" appeals not only to individual memory but also to a collective memory, and up to a certain point, to a common history.

All these elements appear somehow re-created in *The Lost Domain* (2005), an audiovisual narrative mixing several temporalities: the childhood past, the 1973 Chilean coup d'état, and the beginning of the twenty-first century, all stemming from an intertextual reference to Alain Fournier's *Le Grand Meaulnes* (1913)—the only novel by the French author, who died in World War I. It tells the story of two young friends in search of a magic domain that signals the passage from childhood to adulthood. In one sequence in the film, Ruiz recreates his childhood vision of radio drama: Max, the child character, listens to the radio and recounts his first experience attending a radio show, with the actors in costume reading in front of several microphones. In this film, the radio operates as a toy and as a device suturing the different spaces and times that coexist in the film. The "lost domain" that the film's title alludes to is precisely infancy, since just as in Chilean poet Jorge Teillier's verse—from the poem (inspired by Fournier's novel) that lends the film its title—life is conceived as a playground: "There is no house, nor parents, nor love; there are only the companions of our play."[14] For Ruiz, the recourse to childhood is an affective procedure of retrieving a memory that is both individual and collective. At the same time, it is an artifice to escape rational laws while signaling the presence of possible worlds. In this way, the retrieval of memory and experimentation appear in Ruiz as two nonexclusive, simultaneous activities. Childhood is precisely the device that allows this conjunction.

Another example comes from *Manoel on the Island of Wonders*, a three-chapter French-Portuguese miniseries made for television. The main character is Manoel, a child living multiple adventures, who travels in time and changes his destiny. In a sequence in the third chapter, titled "The Little Chess Champion," Manoel is overcome by an insatiable curiosity to look through a keyhole. In an extreme close-up, we see Manoel's eye peeping through the keyhole; then, in the reverse shot, we see the focused vision of the spectacle he witnesses. Here the gaze of the child identifies with the mechanical eye of the subjective camera, so we could say that the camera literally takes a child's perspective at times.

What the camera shows is the black contour of the keyhole and, through the opening, smoke and two fast-moving hands making figures. The frame's dark background suddenly lights up, and we see Manoel's cousin Pedro appear—a young man always dressed in pajamas and behaving like a child, in the manner of the Lost Boys from James M. Barrie's *Peter Pan*. Pedro is in profile, watching with delight through his clenched hand as if it were a monocular. After a cut, we leave the point-of-view shot and see Manoel in profile. In the background, we see the keyhole he was watching through, thanks to the shot's depth of field. Through the opening, we see the man who was moving his hands peeking out: a man with a sailor hat who appears in another part of the telefilm as the pirate Pombo de Albuquerque. With Pedro's help, the pirate makes the child pass through the keyhole, covering him with crochet cloths. Then, Manoel is freed from the cloth and the now acousmatic pirate voice says to him, "you are very curious." Thus, they begin a dialogue about curiosity and the act of seeing:

—Can you see?

—Yes.

—Look closely . . . Can you really see?

—Yes.

—Is that what you wanted to see?

—Yes.

—Look!

The images accompanying the dialogue are a close-up of Manoel observing through the frame of his hands, as if he were a filmmaker trying out the framing of a shot. The reverse shot is the image of a light source. Over the image, we hear Manoel's voice off screen; he is now looking toward the screen through Pedro's hand-as-monocular. The child-narrator says, similarly to the narrator of Borges's "El Aleph," "I don't have the words to tell you what I saw." The montage shows us a shot with the shadows of three hands projected over a white wall, in the manner of Chinese shadows. The hands move until they form Pedro's profile. Manoel tells us off screen that Pedro's shadow asked for help and after that, Pedro's body disappeared.

In the film, Manoel eludes all kinds of limits, even spatiotemporal restrictions. He is able to communicate with fantastic beings, change his fate and visit parallel worlds. The presence of children as a device justifies the formal experimentation and the use of visual tricks inherited from cinema's "infancy," many of them invented by Georges Méliès.

Play

Despite his wariness of scholarly quotes, Ruiz had read Walter Benjamin early on[15] (his theory on boredom,[16] in fact, is partly based on Benjamin and Kracauer), and consequently he is likely to have known about Benjamin's reflections on childhood. Benjamin believed that until the nineteenth century, children were not regarded as creatures furnished with a spirit of their own, and so the adult—the ideal "educator"—would try to mold the children into their own image and likeness—as a "little adult"—from a perspective both rationalist and Rousseauian.[17] For Benjamin, however, children are not just men and women on a reduced scale. In his opinion, the twentieth century revealed the "cruel, grotesque, and grim side of childhood."[18] Removed from public life, children have a certain callousness that Benjamin describes with a 1916 quote by philosopher Salomo Friedlaender, alias Mynona:

> The fact that little children laugh at everything, even the negative sides of life, is a glorious extension of radiant cheerfulness into all the spheres of life it had so shamefully neglected and that are so utterly dreary as a result. . . . Wonderfully successful little bomb plots, with princes who fall apart but are easily put back together again. Department stores with automatic outbreaks of arson, break-ins, thefts. Victims who can be murdered in a multitude of ways and with every appropriate weapon. . . . My children would not like to be without their guillotines and gallows, at the very least.[19] (Original ellipses.)

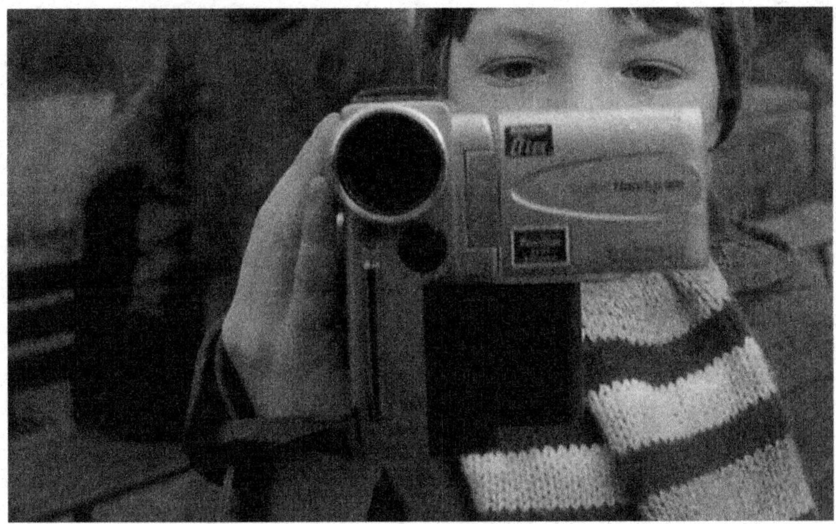

Camille's favorite toy, a video camera. *Comedy of Innocence.*

Like Benjamin, Ruiz does not mythicize childhood. Brats populate his cinema: in *City of Pirates*, Malo[20] is an unscrupulous child who kills his entire family and then proceeds to murder his adoptive father and the lover of his adult mistress, Isidore. After escaping with her to an island, he abandons her at the mercy of the island's only inhabitant, a young man with multiple personalities. In *Comedy of Innocence*, the boy Camille declares that his mother is not his mother, and another woman turns up, whom he starts calling "mom." This instance of childish rebellion is what triggers the plot. As in the Mynona quote, what these badly behaved children embody is the notion of play, proceeding under their own internal laws and constantly challenging the established norms—hence their being considered "bad."

But what is the specificity of play? And how can we characterize its mode of operation? Benjamin says that the child proceeds according to this verse by Goethe: "All things would be resolved in a trice / if we could only do them twice." But the child "is not satisfied with twice, but wants the same thing again and again, a hundred or even a thousand times."[21] "This is not," he continues, "only the way to master frightening fundamental experiences," but it also "means enjoying one's victories and triumphs over and over again, with total intensity."[22] The essence of playing—says Benjamin—is not so much "doing as if" but "doing the same thing over and over again."[23] If the adult is overcome by an urge to play, this is not simply a regression to childhood—although play is always liberating. For Benjamin, children, surrounded by a world of giants, play in order to create a smaller world of their own. In the same way, the adult, cornered by reality, minimizes the impact of an unbearable existence by creating a reduced image whose terrifying elements are erased.[24] In other words, play provides the joy of repetition, liberating the world and making it smaller and, consequently, safer.

Benjamin celebrates the idea that in children's play even the most princely doll, after being mislaid, broken, repaired, and readopted, may become a "capable proletarian comrade in the children's play commune."[25] For Agamben, as much as for Benjamin, childhood and play—as areas that escape adult normativity—represent a potential space that may even become revolutionary.

According to Susan Buck-Morss, Benjamin was interested in what is lost in the path to adulthood: the creative fantasy, the restriction of the child's flow of consciousness through bourgeois education, the seamless connection between perception and action, and the ability for mimetic improvisation.[26] Children's cognition has revolutionary potential because it is tactile and linked to action; instead of simply accepting the given meaning of things, children learn to know by experience, holding and using objects in ways that transform their meaning.[27] Analogously, the new technologies (camera and cinema) are potentialities for developing a mimetic language.[28] Thus, their ability to access the optical unconscious ensured an unanticipated field of action by incorporating previously imperceptible elements. Cinema corresponds to the perceptive form of an audience that is dispersed as a result of the industrialization process. Perception as shock gains relevance in cinema as a formal principle: the montage rearranges fragments of reality as semantic units.[29] Unlike the Frankfurt School, Benjamin is optimistic about cinema; industrial technology fragments experience, but at the same time, it provides the means by which to reunify it.

Children instinctively imitate objects in order to dominate their world, argues Benjamin. Thus, at a collective and social level, it is possible to use this mimetic ability as a defense against the trauma of industrialization and as a way to reappropriate the subjectivity previously alienated in the process.[30] For Ruiz, then, cinema as play is interesting not just at the diegetic level, but for the possibilities it presents as a technique. Play as a form of experimentation is analogous to a cinematographic technique that allows us to approach images in a creative way. Ruiz understands cinema and play as potentially counterhegemonic forms, hence their revolutionary potential. Ultimately, play as an aesthetic category is revolutionary in Ruiz's cinema as it underlines the tactile and not merely visual aspect of the image, and because it is able to transform an object's preestablished meaning.

In *Aventura del cuerpo*, Cristián Sánchez claims that Ruiz discovered the artistic dimension of play thanks to Johan Huizinga.[31] According to Huizinga, play is

> a free activity standing quite consciously outside "ordinary" life as being "not serious," but at the same time absorbing the player intensely and utterly. It is an activity connected with no material interest, and no profit can be gained by it. It proceeds within its own proper boundaries of time and space according to fixed rules and in an orderly manner. It promotes the formation of social groupings that tend to surround themselves with secrecy and to stress their difference from the common world by disguise or other means.[32]

Starting from Huizinga's definition, Roger Caillois in *Les jeux et les hommes* (*Man, Play, and Games*, 1958) develops his own, an emended version in which play appears as a free activity separated in a specific time and space; uncertain—as its value is not determined in advance; unproductive—as it doesn't create either goods or wealth; regulated—as it is subject to conventions suspending ordinary laws and installing a new legislation; and fictitious—as it is accompanied by a consciousness of either a secondary reality or blatant unreality compared to ordinary life.[33]

Caillois classifies play under four fundamental categories, namely: *Agon*—games of competition and fight; *Alea*—games of dice and chance; *Mimicry*—games assuming the acceptance of illusion or disguise; and *Ilinx*—games based on vertigo, attempting to destroy the stability of perception for a moment. All of these categories are present without exception in Ruiz's cinema. *Treasure Island* (1986), for example, more than an adaptation of Robert Louis Stevenson's novel, is the staging of a permanent game.[34] In the film, the boy narrator and protagonist, Jim Hawkins, reads from Stevenson's novel in order to find out the location of a treasure. At the beginning of the film, he confesses that he had been watching a violent film on TV, and after falling asleep, reality and fiction started to blend together in his mind— to the point that he mistakes the guests at the little hotel where he lives for the characters in the film. The game of the island is clearly one of physical confrontation (*Agon*, in Caillois's terms), but it is also a game of imitating Stevenson's characters (Caillois's *Mimicry*).

In the third part of *Manoel on the Island of Wonders*, we see several forms of play between Manoel and the other children: fighting (*Agon*), games of dice (*Alea*), costumes (*Mimicry*), and vertigo (*Ilinx*). In one sequence, a couple of children invite Manoel to come up to a high archway, and he repeatedly replies, "No, I can't." When he closes his eyes, however, he rises up in thin air, and while he does, he keeps repeating, "No, I can't"; "I can't"; "I can't." The next sequence is a point-of-view shot of Manoel's flight through a fantastic garden; a pair of twins with whom he had been fighting before are pushing him around from side to side as if he were a balloon or a ball. The camera rises up, crosses the water, and reaches one of the playmates' hands. For a moment, we see a close-up of Manoel, and a bird's-eye view of a glass of water. While a spoon stirs up the contents of the glass, the silhouette of a person in a boat waving a hand appears inside by double exposure. Here it is clearly the children's play that allows for formal experimentation, but at the same time, these experimentations constitute a plot built from the outrageous possibilities of the child character, the agent of the wonders announced by the title: Manoel meets himself in the future and is able to change his destiny at least three times; he exchanges bodies with an adult and retrieves his child-body after swallowing a magic coin (a kind of Borgesian *Zahir*); he passes from the real world to a fantasy world with the help of a pirate illusionist.

In a 1987 interview by Christine Buci-Glucksmann and Fabrice Revault d'Allonnes, Ruiz stated that, after his exile, he began to relate "logical games with popular games (since for me, they're just games and not beliefs or myths)."[35] Popular games are linked to jokes and wordplay. In an interview with Bruno Cuneo, he says that joking "is the Chilean way to philosophize."[36] That is why in Ruiz's cinema, games are not just physical, but they involve language as well. In *On Top of the Whale* (1982), for example, one can see several elements related to language games that defy the established norms both in the visual and narrative planes. These games are expressed in particular through the character of Anita. An androgynous looking girl, she becomes pregnant after looking at herself in a mirror. This event constitutes the mise-en-scène of wordplay: it is the confusing embodiment of Borges's quote in "Tlön, Uqbar, Orbis Tertius": "mirrors and copulation are abominable, because they increase the number of men."[37] Her mother, Eve, declares that poetry is dangerous because "metaphors become religion, and religion is the opiate of the masses." Despite the fact that Anita is not the film's protagonist (the protagonist is the narrator, an anthropologist attempting to study a couple of Patagonian Indians), her presence is associated with formal experimentations. For example, in a sequence representing the Deleuzian time-image, she appears phantasmatically as she is playing, due to the use of multiple exposures and color filters.[38] Anita empathizes with the aboriginal couple Adán and Edén (Adam and Eden), whom the anthropologist-narrator is studying. She observes them from a distance but with intense

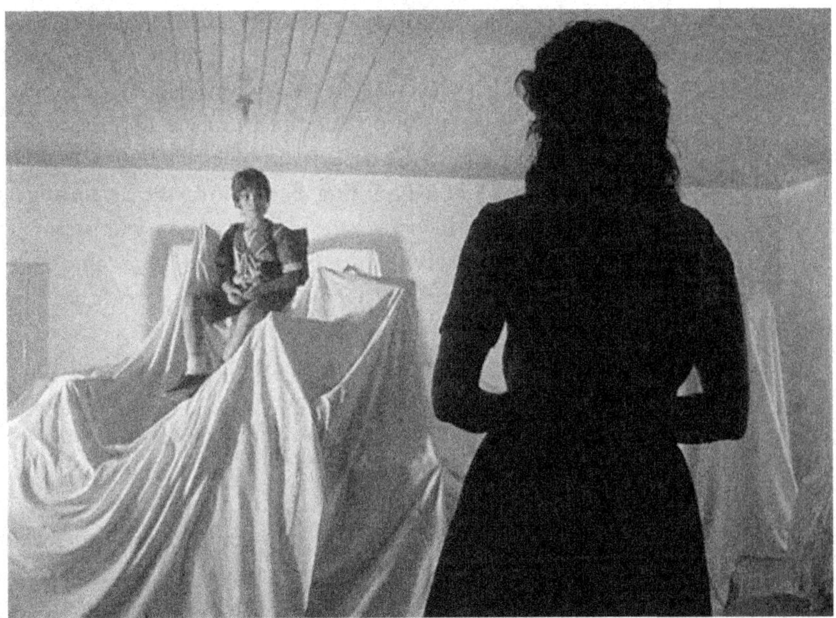

Bad children: Malo in *City of Pirates*.

dedication, attempting to communicate with them and to imitate the facial gestures they practice in front of the photographic camera—a parody of Guillaume Duchenne's photographs for Charles Darwin's 1872 book, *The Expression of the Emotions in Man and Animals.*

In her conversations with her mother, Anita refers to the natives as "proletarians" or "victims of exploitation" in a way that reveals a relation between her as a child—a being who has not yet become a proper subject—and these individuals who are considered a minority in terms of ethnicity or social class. As unstable subjects, both Anita and the indigenous peoples represent a challenge to the established norms. Anita defies nature's laws by becoming pregnant, and the indigenous people quickly acculturate: with each of the anthropologist's visits, they learn Italian, German, and French, discuss classical music, and fluently quote seventeenth-century philosopher Baruch Spinoza.[39]

As in the previous example, play presupposes a suspension, or rather a transformation, of spatiotemporal categories. Agamben argues that there is a correspondence and opposition between play and ritual. Both engage in a relationship with the calendar and with time, but this relationship is an inverse one: while the ritual fixes and structures the calendar, play changes and destroys it.[40] This ability of play is precisely its capacity to destabilize the established social norms. Following Claude Lévi-Strauss in *The Savage Mind*, Agamben maintains that ritual transforms events into structures, while play transforms structures into events. The purpose of ritual is to resolve the contradiction between mythical past and present, reabsorbing events into the synchronic structure. Play, by contrast, breaks the connection between past and present, making the structure crumble into events. Thus, play becomes a machine that transforms synchrony into diachrony.[41] In temporal terms, games serve to break the linearity of the story and put any and all certainties into question.[42]

In his anthropological investigations, Lévi-Strauss had discovered that games are closely related to the funeral rites of primitive peoples. In Agamben's reading, the land of toys corresponds to Lévi-Strauss's land of *larvae*. Therein lies the difference between the world of the living and the world the dead, between nature and culture—through rituals, the *larva* must become a dead person. If the *larva* is a living-dead, or a half-dead person, the baby is a dead-living, or a half-alive person—as the child also represents a threat to be neutralized.[43] Adults submit to becoming *larvae* so that the *larvae* can become dead, and the dead become children so that the children can become men.[44] The unstable signifiers exist to ensure that the phantoms can become dead and the babies living men.[45]

What interests me here are not the anthropological implications of Lévi-Strauss's proposal as Agamben understands it in *Infancy and History*, but rather how it can illuminate a particular interpretation of Raúl Ruiz's notions of infancy and play. In this regard, what Agamben retrieves from Lévi-Strauss is enlightening, as infancy is characterized there as a space preceding the entrance into discourse, and consequently, preceding the passage into adulthood and history (according to Agamben's view, in the strict sense, the child is still not a proper subject). This condition is not seen as an inevitable teleological step, but acquires instead—just as in Benjamin—creative and revolutionary potentiality, which is central to Ruiz's conception of cinema. The game of oppositions between play and ritual that Agamben establishes through Lévi-Strauss is of particular interest in the case of Ruiz because the opposite of infancy is phantoms, which are so prominent in Ruiz's films.

Play and ritual are the devices that allow the passage between these domains. As in the previous examples, Max moves between different temporalities, and Manoel crosses from one world to the other with ease—he literally passes through a keyhole. His cousin Pedro's disappearance could be read as the definitive passage into adulthood, since crossing permanently from one world to the other is to lose the child's condition and become either an adult or a phantom. Both children and phantoms are "unstable signifiers" populating Ruiz's cinema, and both are capable of passing from one world to the other, connecting present with past and future, here and there.

Toys and Ghosts

Benjamin noted that before the nineteenth century, toys were a part of the "production process that bound parents and children together"[46] and demanded the parental[47] presence much more dearly. In the nineteenth century, with industrialization begins the emancipation of the toy; it eludes parental control and becomes increasingly alien, more attractive, but at the same time, less apt for playing.[48] In Ruiz's cinema, toys occupy a preeminent place. Many of them have an archaeological character—they are old toys. The most memorable case is the prostitute's dolls with luminous eyes in *Les trois couronnes du matelot/ Three Crowns of the Sailor* (FR, 1983).

For Agamben, the essence of the toy is something eminently historical, or history in a pure state—in no other place may we catch history's temporality like in a toy, in its pure differential and qualitative value. Toys in Ruiz's films tend to have a technical stamp. In *Comedy of Innocence*, the video camera that Camille receives as a birthday gift is the favorite toy that comes to disrupt family ties. In *Time Regained*, the images in young Marcel's magic lantern serve as a model to blend past and present in a permanent flow of projected images. In *Mysteries of Lisbon*, the small theater given to Pedro by his mother serves as an ellipsis, as a seam between shots, and as a framing to narrate the staging of multiple stories. What joins these visual devices together is the idea of play, embodied in an object for a child's amusement. These visual devices signal toward cinema as a medium, just as the young Manoel points out at the end of "The Picnic of Dreams," the second chapter of *Manoel on the Island of Wonders*: "Adults also played, conjuring the ghosts' shadow. They called it cinema."

According to Agamben, when the game is over, the toys become an embarrassing residue to be hidden and taken away, as they are unstable signifiers belonging neither to diachrony nor synchrony, neither to ritual nor to play.[49] In many of Ruiz's films, however, they remain in sight, signaling their uncomfortable place in adult life—like the doll that Helene, the au pair, secretly plays with in *Comedy of Innocence*, or the maid's dolls in Juan Carlos's house in *Palomita blanca/ Little White Dove* (CL, 1973).[50]

The third part of *Manoel on the Island of Wonders* is paradigmatic in signaling the toy's role in crossing from one world to another. Marylina, the girl genius and chess champion (*Alea* in Caillois's terms) lives with a group of children and is surrounded by toys, giant dolls or mannequins. When Pedro disappears, they ask Marylina (who is celebrating her birthday that day) for help. The pirate Pombo de Albuquerque turns up and gives Marylina the gift of dancing music. While he plays the music with the movement of his hands, we see his shadow projected on the wall as if in a small theater. Another shadow comes up by his side, puts on a pirate hat, and murders Pombo by stabbing him in the back. As he dies, he says his mission was to cross boundaries and borders, taking the characters from one world to the other, smuggling them from here to there. Marylina approaches Pombo and discovers that he was a doll, not a human being. Thus, the pirate/toy is marked as the one who takes children from one world to the other and as a sinister, spectral object: he appears to be alive, but is dead.

The toy is a central element of play, as it participates in that which play makes possible: the passage from one world to another. In the case of Ruiz, the toy is a symbol of the cinematographic apparatus—that is why it is linked on the one hand to infancy and play and on the other to ghosts—as a residual instance of the game and as a technical element of cinema, as Ruiz himself points out in several interviews. In the 1983 *Cahiers du cinéma* special issue, when referring to the ghosts in *Three Crowns of the Sailor*, Ruiz notes: "They live like everyone else. In the film they are alive, but they are being projected by a machine. That allows the film to work as a game of mirrors."[51] And then he reaffirms this: "When we see a film, it may be that what we're seeing is just dead people's shadows. The only thing is that here it is a matter of dead people who don't know they're dead: they eat, etc. They are shadows that appear to eat, to live."[52] Thus, at the same time, cinema is used to conjure up ghosts and to make them visible. For Ruiz, ghosts "represent the questioning of the border between the living and the dead. Dead people going among living men; living people entering the world of the dead. . . . And that is exactly what happens in cinema in some way."[53]

Night across the Street—the last film Ruiz made in Chile—follows a character from infancy to adulthood. Celso, the protagonist, converses with ghosts and becomes one himself. The world of the living and the world of the dead coexist, but they are divided by an insurmountable temporality. The cyclist Ugalde, for example—who had died years before in an accident—asks don Celso whether he can see the new buildings in Antofagasta, which are conspicuously shown in the background of the frame. He replies, "no, not yet," delaying this visibility for a future time. The spectators, who clearly see the buildings in the background, realize that they are placed in another temporality, different from the diegetic one. On the other hand, the conversation between Ugalde and don Celso could be seen as a dialogue about technique,

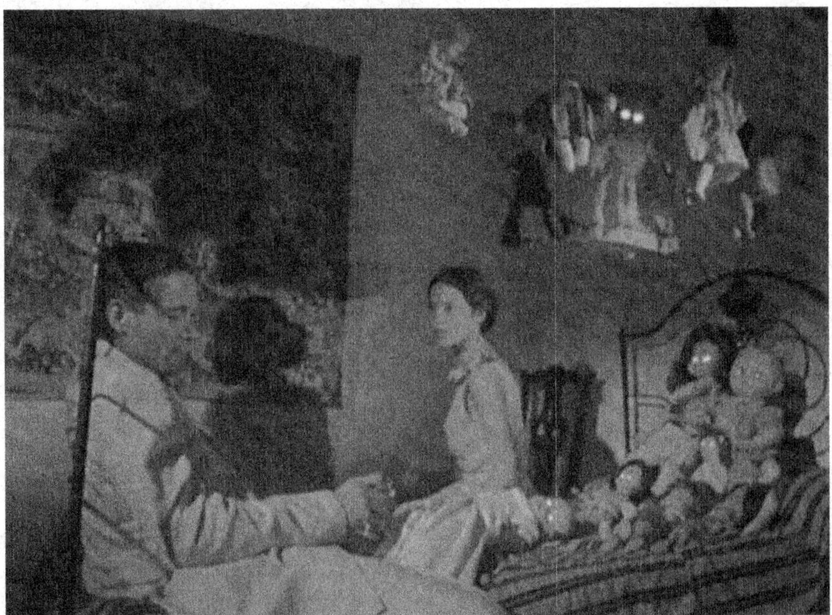

Ghostly dolls in *Three Crowns of the Sailor*.

as the sequence—like many others in the film—uses the chroma key (color keying) procedure for the background—a technique created in 1950 and used when it was too expensive or impossible to shoot a character in a specific scenery. The technique consisted of filming a character against a colored backdrop, and then removing the color from the image and replacing the colored area with another image. Thus, when the cyclist asks the question, don Celso truly is not seeing the buildings, as they would be included later on.

In conclusion, childhood and play in Ruiz's cinema have a narrative, visual, and political yield. To a great extent, the presence of child character allows Ruiz to engage in radical experimentation. Children are commonly associated with visual experiences and tricks linked to the Benjaminian notion of "optical unconscious"—cinema's mechanical eye opens a new field of visibility previously inaccessible to the human eye.

Play as a characteristic element of childhood manifests itself in Ruiz's cinema through the use of multiple technical procedures that allow, among other things, the crossing from one world to another, the challenge of spatiotemporal limits, and the confusion of reality and fiction. The toy as a child's device is associated with cinema as an apparatus, and thus audiovisual experimentations are linked to childhood as aesthetic form.[54]

Child characters are also associated with ghosts. For Ruiz, children and ghosts are not properly subjects, but this nonbelonging, far from making them uniform, gives them a certain freedom: they are a revolutionary power in a Benjaminian sense because they are able to resist all normativity and are linked to a mode of doing—play—that defies hegemonic practices. Children and ghosts are the ones who embody Ruiz's idea of cinema most precisely: if cinema works as a mirror,[55] then it is ghosts and children who are called to cross from one side to the other, destabilizing and challenging the present and its normativity.

Translated by Felipe Fernández Lavanderos and Tessa Allen de Oliveira

Notes

1. Alain Bergala, *L'hypothèse cinéma* (Paris: Cahiers du cinéma, 2006), 61.

2. Raúl Ruiz, *Poetics of Cinema 1*, 2nd ed., trans. Brian Holmes (Paris: Dis Voir, 2005).

3. Ibid., 9–10. The editors took the liberty of using various translations of *Poetics of Cinema* in order to communicate Ruiz's original words as faithfully as possible. See the select bibliography for citation information.

4. Ibid., 10. See editorial note above.

5. Ibid., 15.

6. Ibid., 13.

7. Ibid., 12.

8. In Spanish, the word *infancia* can be used indistinctly to mean infancy or childhood (*niñez*). There is thus a certain amount of overlap between "childhood" and "infancy" in the text. Editors' note.

9. Giorgio Agamben, *Infancy and History: Essays on the Destruction of Experience* (New York: Verso, 1993), 60.

10. Richard Bégin, "Raúl Ruiz o el Barroco en acción," in *El cine de Raúl Ruiz: Fantasmas, simulacros y artificios*, ed. Valeria de los Ríos and Iván Pinto (Santiago: Uqbar Editores, 2010), 200.

11. Youssef Ishaghpour, "Entre espejos y cuadros: *La hipótesis del cuadro robado*," in Ríos and Pinto, *El cine de Raúl Ruiz: Fantasmas, simulacros y artificios*, 178–79. According to Youssef Ishaghpour, Ruiz insistently resorts to the *faux raccord* ("false match cut"). To invalidate the *raccord*—guaranteeing identity and reality—Ruiz does not hesitate to tamper with the image, crushing it with the use of lenses and colored filters. Ruiz also commonly uses *faux raccord* in sound.

12. Including *On Top of the Whale, City of Pirates, Manoel on the Island of Wonders, Treasure Island, Time Regained, Comedy of Innocence, The Lost Domain, Mysteries of Lisbon,* and *Night across the Street.*

13. See Bruno Cuneo, ed., *Ruiz: Entrevistas escogidas—filmografía comentada* (Santiago: Ediciones Universidad Diego Portales, 2013), 207.

14. Jorge Teillier, "Los dominios perdidos"/"The Lost Domain," in *In Order to Talk with the Dead: Selected Poems of Jorge Teillier*, trans. Carolyne Wright (Austin: University of Texas Press, 1993), 102–5. The original quote is: "No hay casa, ni padres, ni amor; sólo hay compañeros de juego."

15. Ruiz notes: "Regarding the previously discussed issue of the redemption of reality, Walter Benjamin claims that photography is to reality what the unconscious is to conscious life. In this way, cinema makes evident a series of behavioral mechanisms, which are generally nullified or forgotten in habitual activity. I'm excited about the possibility of cinema becoming an art of compiling arts; that is, that cinema nullifies itself as autonomous art and becomes a compiler of the art of climbing stairs, of sitting down, of watching through windows, of registering a series of gestures, which by adjusting to a series of rules, are art in themselves." Raúl Ruiz, "Interview with Raúl Ruiz," *Primer Plano* 1, no. 4 (1972): 7. In the same way, Ruiz cites Benjamin's "photographic unconscious" and postulates that this notion could be extended to "phenomena which he probably never imagined," in *Poetics of Cinema 1*, 57.

16. Ruiz comments on boredom through the story of a monk. According to Ruiz, early Christian Fathers understood boredom in the Middle Ages as the eighth capital sin, called *tristitia* or sadness. It had three stages: a feeling of imprisonment, evasion by sleep, and finally, anxiety. The remedy against the affliction was entertainment; that is, "distract distraction by means of distraction, use poison to heal," in Ruiz, *Poetics of Cinema 1*, 12. Entertainment on the other hand empties the world (of boredom). Against this idea, Ruiz is interested in films that produce a "high quality boredom," exemplified in the works of Snow, Ozu, Tarkovsky, Warhol, and Straub-Huillet (ibid., 13). The central conflict theory is secured against boredom. The films that produce boredom, on the other hand, have an effect on the viewer: "we spectators begin to fall asleep, really or metaphorically" and "we begin to lose the thread of the story" (ibid., 119). "It is at this point," says Ruiz, "that we can finally say that we are in the film" (ibid., 119). According to Ruiz, identification should not be established with the film's main character, but with the manipulated objects, landscapes, multiple characters—dissociation that is only possible beyond the hypnotic threshold. Before that point, we are merely watching a spectacle (ibid., 119). Editors' note: The sentence, "Let's say they possess a high quality boredom" ("Digamos que poseen una elevada calidad de aburrimiento") occurs in the Spanish edition of the *Poetics of Cinema* but is omitted in the English translation. See *Poética del cine*, 22; *Poetics of Cinema 1*, 13.

17. Walter Benjamin, *Selected Writings, Volume 2 (1927–1934)*, ed. Michael W. Jennings (Cambridge, MA: Harvard University Press, 1999), 118.

18. Ibid., 101.

19. Ibid.

20. *Malo*, a common name in French, means "bad" or "wicked" in Spanish, making the child's name an instance of wordplay in Ruiz's film.

21. Walter Benjamin, *Selected Writings, Volume 2*, 120.

22. Ibid., 120.

23. Ibid.

24. Ibid., 100.

25. Ibid., 101.

26. In "One Way Street," Benjamin affirms: "In waste products, they [the children] recognize the face that the world of things turns directly and solely to them. In using these things, they do not so much imitate the works of adults as bring together, in the artefact produced in play, materials of widely differing kinds in a new, intuitive relationship." Walter Benjamin, "One Way Street," in *Selected Writings, Volume 1 (1913–1926)*, ed. Marcus Bullock and Michael W. Jennings (Cambridge, MA: Harvard University Press, 2004), 449–50.

27. Susan Buck-Morss, *Walter Benjamin, escritor revolucionario* (Buenos Aires: Interzona, 2005), 63.

28. Ibid., 67.

29. Ibid., 70.

30. Ibid., 76.

31. Cristián Sánchez, *Aventura del cuerpo: El pensamiento cinematográfico de Raúl Ruiz* (Santiago: Ediciones Universidad Diego Portales, 2013), 130.

32. Johan Huizinga, *Homo ludens: A Study of the Play-Element in Culture* (Boston: Routledge and Kegan Paul, 1980), 13.

33. Roger Caillois, *Man, Play, and Games*, trans. Meyer Barash (Urbana: University of Illinois Press, 2001), 9–10.

34. In a 1987 interview, Ruiz notes that *L'île au trésor* "is still a film about the simulacrum, a role game; in it, we see people playing 'treasure island.' This film is a digest, a trivialization, a vulgarization of games of simulacra. In some sense it is a synopsis, a trailer, or an instructions manual of all my cinema." See Christine Buci-Glucksmann and Fabrice Revault d'Allonnes, *Raoul Ruiz* (Paris: Dis Voir, 1987), 104.

35. Buci-Glucksmann and Revault d'Allonnes, *Raoul Ruiz*, 98.

36. Cuneo, *Ruiz*, 203.

37. Jorge Luis Borges, *Labyrinths*, ed. Donald A. Yates and James E. Irby (New York: New Directions, 1964), 3.

38. It can be said that the visuality of the child's presence spreads throughout the whole film. In another sequence, through a series of multiple exposures, we see the anthropologist's hand starting to dissociate, to unrealize itself while taking notes in his field journal. With the phantasmatic multiplication of the anthropologist's hand, the linearity of the writing begins to wander. Illegible scribbles appear on the paper, and the ethnographer ends up abandoning his research. This signals to Ruiz's relation with writing—and therefore with the narrative—on a scale: for Ruiz, cinema is a procedure that exceeds writing and challenges it by generating multiplicity. We observe this both in narrative—in the generation of new stories—and visual terms—from the value he grants to the centripetal forces in the construction of the shot. See Adrian Martin, "Hanging Here and Groping There: On Raúl Ruiz's 'The Six Functions of the Shot,'" *Screening the Past* 35 (December 2012).

39. In an interview, Ruiz described three characteristic Chilean attitudes based on the three figures of American aborigines dialoguing and reflecting on the indigenous figures in *On Top of the Whale*: "That of Lautaro, an Indian who was taken by the Spanish as a friend, and who meticulously studied their methods with no other motive than to use them against his masters. That of Jimmy Button [*sic*], an illiterate Indian adopted by the *Beagle's* captain in Darwin's first voyage; although he learned English in three weeks, went to Oxford, and was even called to the bar, he forgot everything upon his return to South America. And that of Valderomat [*sic*], the Chilean Oscar Wilde, who was the darling of the salons before drowning in the sewer." See Zuzana M. Pick, *The New Latin American Cinema: A Continental Project* (Austin: University of Texas Press, 1993), 184.

40. Agamben, *Infancy and History*, 69.

41. Ibid., 74.

42. The TV series *Petit manuel d'historie de France/A Short Guide to French History* (FR, 1979) exemplifies the distinction between the structured time of ritual and the time of play. The history of France, understood as a linear narrative of a series of structured facts—in this sense, a modern ritual—is questioned by its child narrators who end up destructuring it. Ruiz has the children read fragments from French history books while he creates a montage of different films representing the same episodes (play). Thus, the official history, taught in schools as part of a national discipline, is read by those who are just learning to do so—linear history begins to waver, dropping its reputed solemnity—while the images taken from historical films show that the staging varies, thus conveying that there is more than one way of recounting history.

43. Agamben, *Infancy and History*, 83.

44. Ibid., 85.

45. Ibid.

46. Benjamin, *Selected Writings, Volume 2*, 115.

47. Ibid., 114. Benjamin says "the mother's."

48. Ibid.

49. Agamben, *Infancy and History*, 80.

50. The maid character receives batteries for her dolls from Juan Carlos in exchange for sexual favors.

51. Pascal Bonitzer and Serge Toubiana, "Entretien avec Raoul Ruiz," *Cahiers du cinema*, spécial Raoul Ruiz, 345 (1983): 11.

52. Ibid., 11.

53. Buci-Glucksmann and Revault d'Allonnes, *Raoul Ruiz*, 99.

54. As mentioned at the beginning of this chapter, Ruiz's poetics of cinema presents itself as a counterhegemonic practice defying the normativity of central conflict theory.

55. In the 1972 interview published in *Primer Plano*, Ruiz comments: "I use cinema as a mirror, with which I obtain an inverted face of reality, and I use cinema as a distorting mirror. I start from the idea that I see reality with the eyes, and cinema, through distortion, can help me capture certain elements of reality that escape us." See Ruiz, "Interview with Raúl Ruiz," *Primer Plano* 1, no. 4 (1972): 9.

In "The Baroque Eye of the Camera," Christine Buci-Glucksmann, using Deleuze's nomenclature from *The Time-Image*, notices that in Ruiz's cinema there is a confusion between the spectacle and the real, the actual and the virtual. See Helen Bandis, Adrian Martin, and Grant McDonald, eds., *Raúl Ruiz: Images of Passage* (Melbourne, Australia: Rouge Press, 2004), 31. This is what defines, according to Deleuze, the "crystal-image," whose paradigm is the mirror.

Television, Tractations, and Folklore

Raúl Ruiz as Transmedia Filmmaker

Michael Goddard

Introduction

This chapter will examine the transmedia dimensions of the work of Ruiz, arguing that while Ruiz remained throughout his career a filmmaker, his practice was in proximity to a range of other media practices including literature, theory, television, and video installation, tending to make the distinctions between these fields unstable. This can be seen not only in Ruiz's engagements with a range of creative practices including painting, telenovelas, modern dance, and tableaux vivants, in addition to his frequent and inventive adaptation of literature, but also in his own practices in other media such as the writing of theory and short novels as well as in video installation. This chapter will present Ruiz's transmedia engagements with television in the 1970s and writing, especially in his *Poetics of Cinema* project, of the 1990s, culminating with his engagement with folklore in the 2000s, especially associated with his work in Chile. As a paradigmatic example, this chapter will especially examine his *Book of Disappearances/Book of Tractations* (2005), itself based on his multimedia installation *The Expulsion of the Moors* (1990). Reading this strange doubled book featuring mirrored and encrypted writing that can only be deciphered through processes of decoding, in relation to several of Ruiz's other transmedia projects, this chapter will present Ruiz as a transmedia filmmaker, who nevertheless remained fully committed to working in cinema. Ruiz's explicit turn to folklore in the work he made especially in Chile in the 2000s (*Cofralandes, rapsodia chilena/Cofralandes, Chilean Rhapsody* [CL/FR, 2002], *La recta provincia* [CL, 2007]) also attests to this paradox as well as clarifying the reasons for it. As Ruiz stated in an interview in 2009 in relation to the subject of folklore, "I stay in narrative and popular narrative as the basis of all my work of experimentation."[1] This chapter will therefore present both Ruiz's loyalty to cinema and excursions into other practices as emblematic of situating cinema as a contemporary mode of folklore, and hence inseparable from the transnational and post-colonial as well as transmedia dimensions of his work.

Ruiz as a Television Producer in the 1970s

The strictly auteurist approach to art film directors risks leaving unexplored the potential transmedia dimensions of their work. While few contemporary filmmakers work exclusively in cinema, their work in television and other media tends to be either neglected as minor, or considered as if it were cinema even if made explicitly for television, and conforming to television formats in terms of both the use of video or digital technologies and duration. If one also considers the extensive role of television in financing cinematic production, distinguishing the two media in any decisive way becomes impossible.[2] Such questions have more recently been complicated by the adoption of convergent digital media so that film as a materially specific medium has literally ceased to exist even if cinematic formats and, to some extent, relative prestige, continue to exist. But even in the 1970s, there was a good deal of disavowal of the increasing lack of distinction between film and television, despite the involvement of many art cinema filmmakers in various forms of television production. Jean-Luc Godard, for example, was extremely productive in television in series such as *Six fois deux: Sur et sous la communication* (1976) and continued to use video as a more flexible medium in tandem with his film production, culminating in *Histoire(s) du cinéma* (1989, 1987, 1988), which while "on" cinema, can be argued to be not only a video work but one designed more for televisual than cinematic consumption.

Other filmmakers who worked extensively in television, such as Rainer Werner Fassbinder, were much more pragmatic, and relatively free of such medium anxieties. This was no doubt a response to the reactionary nature of the project of keeping cinema free of television or lamenting its inevitable corruption, as can be seen in the discourse of the "death of cinema," not only in the work of Godard but also Fassbinder's New German Cinema peer, Wim Wenders. Ruiz shared this pragmatic attitude to audiovisual production and, especially in the 1970s and early 1980s, was happy to work in a variety of formats, much of which was funded and commissioned by French television institutions. This did not mean he had no preference for making cinema, and indeed in the 1980s and 1990s, he would return to a focus on cinema, once the budgets and institutional support, especially for international coproductions, was available. Nevertheless, connections with television and video never entirely disappeared from his work, and there were several returns to these media ranging from video installations, to the use of video in films like *La maison Nucingen/Nucingen House* (RO/FR/CL, 2008), to the production of television series based around folklore for Chilean television in the 2000s.

Raúl Ruiz as Television Producer

The beginnings of Ruiz's career as a television producer were intimately connected to a rather unique television institution in France, the Institut national de l'audiovisuel (INA). Once Ruiz's films had been embraced by *Cahiers du cinéma* and other critics, and therefore given some exposure in France, Ruiz showed some of his work to the INA, which was interested in producing work that was neither purely experimental, nor straightforwardly narrative but fell somewhere in between these two poles. As this corresponded closely to the type of films Ruiz was interested in making, it became the beginning of a fruitful partnership, beginning with Ruiz making feature films as part of the INA's *Cinema Je* (Cinema I) series, followed by several television commissions. This arrangement enabled Ruiz to work quickly, making the next project as soon as the previous one was complete or even working on more than one project simultaneously. This manner of working did not always mean his work could be easily seen, since often it was shown neither in cinemas, since it was commissioned for television, nor on television, since the end results frequently departed radically from what those who had commissioned the programs had been expecting. Instead, Ruiz's work from this early period of exile was largely shown in retrospectives, reinscribing them as art cinema even if lacking in normal forms of cinematic distribution.

The INA was a state-funded experimental TV producer, and the state-run channels were obliged to show sixty hours of its content per year as a way of ensuring audiovisual diversity in French television. Filmmakers who benefited from this setup form an impressive list and included Jacques Rivette, Chris Marker, Marguerite Duras, Joris Ivens, Maurice Pialat, René Allio, Jean-Marie Straub, and Danièle Huillet among others. According to Susan Boyd-Bowman, the mandate of the INA was not only to commission feature films but also to "invent new modes of television expression and to apply new techniques,"[3] a mandate that was clearly compatible with Ruiz's idiosyncratic approach to audiovisual production. In essence, the INA applied the same "auteurism" that had become influential in French cinema to television production, bringing in cinematic auteurs and more or less giving them free rein to be as creative as possible. Nevertheless, this was not necessarily embraced by the state television channels, leading to significant tensions between the INA and its distribution, with the effect that many programs were either screened at inconvenient times, several years later, or not at all. This led to a shift in emphasis in the INA, which, after succeeding in screening Godard's *Six fois deux* series in 1976 on FR3, had encountered a lot of resistance on the part of television channels and reframed their activities as a cross between creativity and commerce, experimentation and the maintenance of a popular audience.[4]

One way the INA attempted to do this was through a kind of magazine format, at the same time making use of the audiovisual archives, thereby combining both of its main functions. The first of these series was the 1975–76 series *Hieroglyphs*, followed by *Rue des archives* (to which Ruiz made a key contribution), and by *Juste une image*, based on the famous Godard quotation from *Vent d'Est/Wind from the East* (1969), "This is not a just image, it's just an image."[5]

However, the series that Ruiz contributed to, *Rue des archives*, was very different from this series. As the title suggests, it was exclusively based on French televisual archives, and it was entirely shot on video and so, unlike the other two series, there was no material from the history of cinema or commissioned work. Nevertheless, as Ruiz's contribution, *Petit manuel d'histoire de France/A Small Guide to French History* (FR, 1979) demonstrates, this did not render the series any less experimental. The idea behind the series was to give the spectator the impression of strolling around this "vast collective memory"[6] without being organized by conventional categories like genres, themes, and historical periods, and so a project especially suited to Ruiz.

Ruiz fulfilled this commission in his own way, jumping between different historical epochs or showing the same historical personage such as Joan of Arc via five different performers. Ruiz also went beyond the discrete sequences favored by other directors and montaged several images within the same frame as an audiovisual approximation of the multiple interpretations of history. This gave the sense of the event being portrayed as being haunted by other events, not just different versions of the same events but parallel events suggesting other possible or virtual histories haunting the actual one being presented. For Ruiz, French history, not only in its televisual but also in its academic form, was composed less of hieroglyphs than of stereotypes that pervaded radically different works regardless of their author's intentions or political orientation. Ruiz therefore used as the soundtrack school history textbooks as read out for the first time by a variety of children (in an homage or parody of Godard's INA television work), accompanied by associated and equally stereotyped televisual images, to fully bring out the sense of French history as the stereotyped mise-en-scène of the history of the French state. However, a type of audiovisual delirium in fact overwhelmed this political thesis so that by the time it came to the presentation of Napoleon, Ruiz's guide had rendered the history it was presenting almost incoherent. Rather than delivering a preconstituted "real" content, Ruiz was rather investigating the form of the televisual, its stereotypes, rules, and limitations but also its dynamisms, rhythms, and its specific "photographic unconscious." This concept, discussed prominently in Ruiz's *Poetics of Cinema*, will be discussed shortly in more detail.[7]

Another of Ruiz's projects for the INA, *Des grands événements et des gens ordinaires: Les élections/Great Events and Ordinary People* (FR, 1979), went further still in its complete deconstruction of the televisual codes of documentary, which inadvertently became the real subject of the film. The "great events" referred to in the title was a reference to the lack of interest being taken in the local elections by the inhabitants of Ruiz's 11th arrondissement; according to Ruiz 80 percent of the people approached to take part in the documentary declined, mirroring the lack of interest in the elections themselves. In fact, even the electoral results were a disappointment, since the anticipated dramatic turn toward the left failed to materialize. Ruiz's response to these difficulties was to shift the focus of the film from the elections themselves to the problem of their televisual representation, thereby undoing almost every cliché of the televisual documentary, as well as posing some acute questions about the failures of representation more generally in both the political and aesthetic senses of the term. In Adrian Martin's words, this work "is the best, and certainly the funniest, of self-reflexive deconstructions of the documentary form."[8]

The documentary program takes apart the documentary form by presenting itself as a series of versions consisting for most of its duration as the rushes taken on each day of filming the project, to a series of increasingly shorter edits, dramatizing in the process the falsification inherent in all documentary filmmaking. During the "rushes" section, the objectives of each day's filming are announced, but it is soon revealed that there is often a large gap between these objectives and what actually takes place during the shooting. For example, when they plan to shoot customers in a café to provide "local character," we are informed in voice-over that none of the cafés in the district would let them film there, so they had to go to one in a completely different district. This satirically demonstrates the sort of falsified trick of realism that would usually be disguised rather than highlighted. This is only the most obvious example of a constant gap between visible objects and their description as provided by the voice-over; this is a documentary/

film in which, in Foucauldian terms, speaking never entirely corresponds to seeing. When it comes to interviews it is clear that the neighborhood's inhabitants have little understanding of the mechanism of the election, don't know who the candidates are, or have any clear idea what effects the electoral results will have on their lives. More than this, the presentation in the film of these opinions shows that the order they are presented in is enough to completely manipulate their sense, again drawing attention to the falsification inherent in the documentary form. In another example, after a series of banal shots of the neighborhood, the voice-over intones: "the everyday to the point of absurdity."

What this project indicates is not merely the obvious point that finished documentaries falsify their contents by organizing them according to absurd conventions, but that they are structurally false because they pretend to show reality in process whereas in fact they are a type of preprocessed reality, the (film) "reel" rather than the "real." As such it enacts an implosion of the televisual documentary form itself, which is seen in the program to consist of so many rhetorical fictions used by the filmmaker to construct a reality whose model is merely the conventions of documentary form. It is hardly coincidental that this anti-Bazinian denunciation of realism should take place in the inauthentic medium of television, since, by demonstrating the deceptive rhetoric of the standard television documentary, the truth claims of film in turn become implicated. Even if Ruiz would subsequently shift the focus of his activities to more strictly cinematic productions in the 1980s, this televisual episode in his career was a highly significant one and one that would strongly inform his more properly cinematic work.

Ruiz's Transmedia Explorations of the 1980s

The cluster of tropes of the sea, piracy, childhood, and adventure in Ruiz's "return to cinema" of the 1980s was also not without its transmedia supplements, for example by Ruiz's novella, *In Search of Treasure Island* (1989). The film *L'île au trésor/Treasure Island* (UK/FR/US, 1987/1991) itself was already transmedia in many respects, focusing as it does on a well-known work of literature. More than this, it not only begins with images from the central character's favorite television series but also increasingly takes the ludic form of a Treasure Island game, played out in real time and space but resembling the then-emergent form of the video game, another clear transmedia reference. If this internationally coproduced film was a disappointment to its funders, leading to a four-year delay in its release, the book based on this film, which is even more disorienting and dispersive than the film, perhaps constitutes the ultimate statement of this complex in Ruiz's work. It also demonstrates that cinema is far from the only domain in which Ruiz had been working in the 1980s. One of the key characteristics on Ruiz's work in this decade was a tendency toward a transmedia practice that while remaining focused on cinema also traversed a number of other aesthetic domains. We have already seen crossings with literature and television in *Treasure Island*, not to mention Ruiz's television work of the 1970s; in other projects of the 1980s we also find direct engagements with theater, with films of Racine's *Bérénice* (FR, 1983) and Shakespeare's *Richard III* (FR/CH, 1984), as well as *La présence réelle/ The Real Presence* (FR, 1983), at once the portrait of a precariously employed actor and a documentary about the Avignon festival and the film *Mémoire des apparences/ Memory of Appearances: Life Is a Dream* (FR, 1986), which incorporated scenes from Ruiz's own theatrical production; *Mammame* (FR, 1985), which presents a dance performance choreographed by Jean-Claude Gallotta; *A TV Dante* (UK, 1989), which was commissioned by the British TV Channel 4 in its more experimental phase and followed on from a previous episode done by Peter Greenaway; *The Golden Boat* (BE/US, 1990), which was a film made in cooperation with the New York performance art group The Kitchen, and was also a transposition of American and Mexican television melodrama; and finally the beginning of the 1990s saw Ruiz's first forays into installation art with *The Expulsion of the Moors* (1990), which was exhibited in Boston, Santa Barbara, Valencia, and Paris. *A TV Dante* is of particular interest in this respect as it marked a return to television commissions and televisual form, however experimental, notwithstanding reference to cinematic genres ranging from horror to militant documentary. Again, it is the adoption of televisual form that enables a critical reflection on cinematic genres and the medium itself, ironically via a pioneering use of television. It should also be mentioned that Ruiz was at this time further diversifying his activity as a cultural producer by taking on the role of codirector at the Maison de la Culture at Le Havre from 1985, during which time he produced several of his own films alongside live theatrical productions as well as producing some works of his contemporaries, pioneering a mode of artisanal transmedia production.

There is much that could be said about these transmedia explorations, occurring as they did in the decade in which many of Ruiz's contemporaries such as Godard and Wenders were lamenting the state of cinema in its submission to market forces and domination by television. On one level Ruiz's multidisciplinary work can be seen as a pragmatic affirmation that it

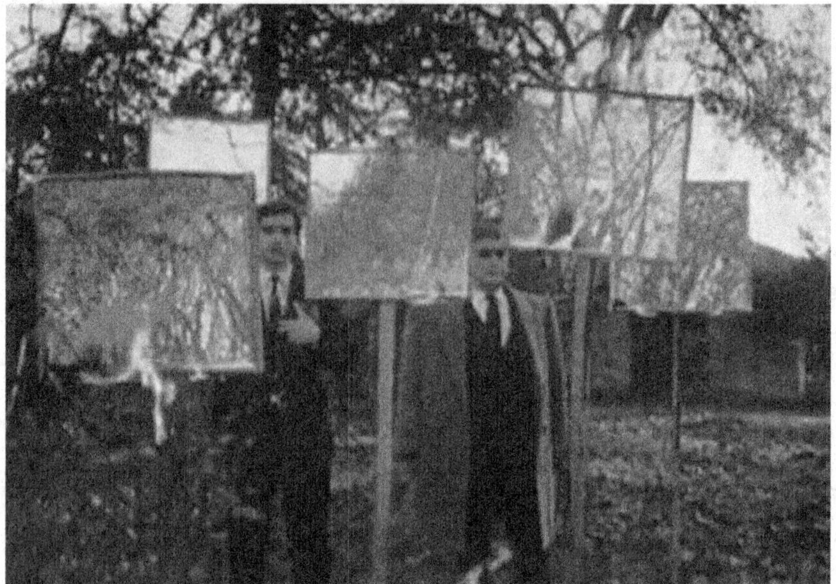

From *A TV Dante*. (Ruiz, 1991), series commissioned for Channel 4.

is always possible to create in whatever medium or context is available, if not a film then a play, an installation, a performance, a work for television, or some crossing between these domains without the slightest trace of ontological anxiety about the medium specificity of cinema. In this respect, Ruiz's aesthetic wanderings mirror the contemporaneous development of Raymond Bellour's concept of "entre-images."[9] According to Bellour, under the pressure of both television and video art, it sought to reposition cinematic images as one form of technical and aesthetic image among a diverse field of media practices, including not only photography and video but also painting, poetry, and philosophy, and in which we are no longer certain exactly what constitutes an image.[10] Ruiz's transmedia voyages, however, have less to do with stories of what is or was cinema, as Godard would subsequently investigate in *Histoire(s) du cinéma* (1989/1998), but rather about the powers of creativity across media in which cinema is caught up. In this respect, from being a threatening enemy, television, for example, was often a way of continuing Ruiz's prolific output, with its own fascinating logics to explore, as was already evident in Ruiz's INA projects of the 1970s. This exploration would also continue through Ruiz's practice of writing and pedagogy that would become an increasingly important part of his work.

Ruiz as a Pedagogue and Writer of Theoretical Fictions

If the early 1990s seem to indicate a slowing down of strictly cinematic activity on Ruiz's part (although he was still producing around three short films per year), this can be accounted for by the fact that he was at this time engaging in a new pedagogical and critical activity as a visiting professor first at Harvard and then Duke University that would continue intermittently up until his appointment at the University of Aberdeen (2007–9), the last two engagements facilitated by Alberto Moreiras. In between, Ruiz also engaged with educational institutions in France and Belgium for varying lengths of time. One aspect of this pedagogical activity was the running of practical filmmaking workshops with students, in some cases leading to collaborative films, as in the production with students of *Vertige de la page blanche/Vertigo of the Blank Page* (BE, 2003) in collaboration with Marie-Luce Bonfanti and students of CIFAS in Belgium, or *Agathopedia* (IT, 2008) produced with students at the University of Calabria. This reflected Ruiz's increasing engagement with pedagogical institutions, culminating in his position as visiting professor at the University of Aberdeen. At the same time, these pedagogical situations enabled Ruiz to concentrate more intensively on writing, most notably resulting in the publication of his key work of film theory, *Poetics of Cinema* (1995), which was based on the lectures he delivered at Duke University. However, it would give a false impression if this suggests that Ruiz's pedagogical activities were strictly divided between theory and practice. In fact his practical classes involved exposing students to a dizzying array not only of cinema but also of theory and philosophy, while his written work, although the product of time devoted to research, tended to continue his practical engagement as a filmmaker, for example, by laying out potential thought experiments, often supposing the production of possible or impossible imaginary films. Furthermore, Ruiz's writing on cinema considerably predates the *Poetics of Cinema* project, even if it was only with this project that Ruiz had the time to elaborate his thoughts in such a full way. Key examples of his theoretical production being "Object Relations in the Cinema,"[11] as well as the "Imaginary Dialogues" he conducted with Jean-Louis Schefer shortly afterward.[12]

The first volume of Ruiz's *Poetics of Cinema* is a rich and complex work that, while absolutely refusing disciplinary boundaries, has had a considerable impact in the field of film theory and reflection on film more generally, as evidenced by its citation as one of the key works on film in a 2010 survey of critics conducted by *Sight and Sound*. While *Poetics of Cinema 1* can be, and usually is, read as a stand-alone volume, it was in fact the first of a series of three works, of which the first has the subtitle "Miscellanies," the second would be called "*Serio Ludens*" (serious play) and be composed of "parodies and conceptual simulations,"[13] while the third would be devoted to methods and consist of exercises and formulae intended as "a method of filming."[14] The second volume only appeared eleven years later, and while it does indeed contain a number of examples of "serious play" in the form of elaborate thought experiments, it no longer carries that subtitle and seems to have departed from Ruiz's original intentions. At the same time, the first volume also contains its share of thought experiments accompanying the more theoretical discourse, demonstrating that for Ruiz theory is never entirely distinct from practice, even if that practice might not necessarily be the practice of cinema but of thinking itself. Arguably, all of this was already embodied in the earlier Ruizian texts on cinema, but it is in the first volume of *Poetics of Cinema* that Ruiz's idiosyncratic practice of theory was given its richest and most powerful expression, exceeding anything he wrote before or after. As for the planned third volume, Ruiz was working on this during his period in Aberdeen, beginning from annotations on Eisenstein's *The Sense of Cinema*, but at the time of his death this had not been definitively completed.[15] In what follows it is principally some key concepts from *Poetics of Cinema 1* that will be addressed.

In the foreword to *Poetics of Cinema 2*, Ruiz describes the earlier volume as a "call to arms,"[16] and this is certainly true of the first chapter, "Central Conflict Theory."[17] In this chapter Ruiz contrasts the fairly anarchic impression that American films made on him as a young Chilean spectator with the surprising discovery later on that they were the product of a method of dramatic construction he refers to as "central conflict theory." This theory is not a global account of classical Hollywood cinema as can be found in the work of Thomas Schatz[18] or Bordwell, Staiger, and Thompson,[19] but rather a pragmatic tendency evident primarily in scriptwriting manuals that dictates how good movies should be formed; exactly the same model advocated by Robert McKee and others that was parodied in Spike Jonze's film, *Adaptation* (2002). By choosing to target the dominant pragmatic way in which stories are produced, rather than Hollywood as an economic or cultural system, Ruiz moves away from the third cinema ideological critique of American cultural imperialism in the direction of an imminent critique of Hollywood and by extension, capitalist pragmatism. As such this is a Foucauldian move, inasmuch as it focuses not on an abstract and imagined center of power but rather on how power is diffused throughout global cinematic production, not ideologically but practically, by the dissemination of certain norms of cinematic construction that are implemented in film schools, funding decisions, and dominant industry practices. As such it is not only more incisive than the critique of cultural imperialism but also more productive in that it immediately raises the practical question of how films might have been made otherwise.

Ruiz proposes as an antidote to this banal narrative realism what amounts to a "politics of boredom" that would seek to affirm precisely those moments such as "a landscape, a distant storm, or dinner with friends" that are "boring" due to the fact that they contribute nothing toward the central conflict. Instead they only provoke detached curiosity and tend to become autonomous from the rest of the film, and in doing so open up other powers of the cinematic image.[20] Elsewhere, I have argued that this constitutes an open or "general economy," after Bataille's term in *The Accursed Share*, as opposed to a restricted one in which there is a direct economic exchange between cinematic images and money.[21] This is both in the sense of the funds required to produce cinematic images and the commodified payoff for the spectator of narratives produced according to the restricted economy of central conflict. To use the dynamic model that Ruiz would adopt later, central conflict operates on a tight centripetal circuit, whereas Ruiz is interested in films that fly off their hinges and open themselves to other films, memories, and experiences through these centrifugal dynamics.

In *Poetics of Cinema*, one of the ways Ruiz approaches this type of strategy is through the idea of the photographic unconscious, the transformation of Walter Benjamin's concept of the optical unconscious that was elaborated in his famous essay, "The Work of Art in the Age of Its Technological Reproducibility." In this essay, Benjamin analyzed the power of cinema and other modern techniques of image reproduction to disturb the conventions of Western art and its modes of reception, famously through the destruction of the aura.[22] While Benjamin had in mind emergent modes of mass perception made possible via newly invented photographic, cinematic, and other technologically mediated imaging techniques, Ruiz's photographic unconscious is somewhat different from this. In the place of Benjamin's focus on optical techniques such as the close-up to "surgically" render visible to the masses the previously invisible structures of reality, Ruiz instead uses the photographic unconscious to refer to a "corpus of signs capable of conspiring against visual conventions."[23] This is Ruiz's particular interpretation of Benjamin's essay. The subversive corpus of signs that Ruiz refers to, however, only has a latent existence in Benjamin's essay and is really an invention of the former, even if it draws on the powers of cinema and technical reproduction identified by the latter. This corpus can take many forms, and rather than being a strictly contemporary phenomenon for Ruiz, is no less evident in treatises on Chinese painting, for example, or the nineteenth-century practice of *tableaux vivants*.

What is central to the concept for Ruiz is the multiplicity of relations between images or between images and other signs that is always in excess of any simple notion of representation. For Ruiz, simple misrecognition opens up onto a whole field of interference between signs and images that refuses any enclosure in stable economies of signification. Therefore, if Benjamin's concept of the optical unconscious can be said to express modernist ideas about technological invention and its impact on mass perception, Ruiz's photographic unconscious is precisely postmodern and transmedia in the sense of connecting any individual image to a field of multiplicity in excess of its place within the narrative economy of a particular film, and instead opening it up to multiple relations with *all* the media images any given image is capable of evoking.

The key idea developed in *Poetics of Cinema* is that in order to escape the confines of central conflict narratives and by implication the film theory that contents itself with these kinds of stories, a type of imaginative engagement with images is necessary in order to grasp them in their full creative multiplicity. This is necessarily a transmedia perspective, opening up cinematic images to the entire field of technical, aesthetic, and imaginary images also explored in Bellour's *Entre-Images* project. In *Poetics of Cinema*, Ruiz proposes a number of ways in which to do this, including the idea of a "shamanic cinema," which—far from being either the transcendental style of Ozu or Tarkovsky, or the mythopoetics of the American underground filmmakers like Stan Brakhage or Kenneth Anger—would rather consist in the crafting of singular films, irreducible to genre, story lines, or particular schools, films that are, in other words, "monsters."[24] While Ruiz refers to this kind of film as the crafting of a poetic object, this has nothing to do with film craft as it is usually understood, even if there is something of the artisanal in Ruiz's description. If the reference here is still to film, it is also clear that these monsters could just as easily take the form of experimental television or video installation:

> It has some elements of the old-fashioned crafts, for instance, a hands-on approach to celluloid or video, a spirit of inventiveness . . . the purpose is to make poetic objects. The rules you need to understand these poetic objects are unique to each film and must be rediscovered by every viewer; . . . in short these are films that cannot respond to the question, "What is this movie about?"[25]

While this quotation might be taken to be the defense of elitist forms of avant-garde or art cinema, it is telling that nowhere in this chapter does Ruiz propose any kind of canon, and indeed the one film singled out as an example of this shamanic cinema is a Hollywood film, Edgar Ulmer's *The Black Cat* (1934), whose poetic qualities derive more from a combination of involuntary narrative, photographic, and performative inconsistencies and Ruiz's "delinquent spectatorship" than they do from any poetic purpose on the part of the filmmakers. Nevertheless, it is a fitting example since Ruiz is proposing a practice of singularity in filmmaking that could never be specified as an aesthetic formula, resulting in films whose multiplicity could never be reduced to being simply "about" something other than the multiple relations constructed with other images.

Ruiz's *Book of Disappearances/Book of Tractations* as Transmedia Artifact

Given Ruiz's tendencies toward considering cinematic images as part of a much broader "photographic unconscious," and his extensive work for television, it is somewhat surprising that he did not work more in video installation, a clear way of exploring the operations of cinematic and other images, as was done extensively by his contemporary Harun Farocki, for example. For theorists like Raymond Bellour, video art became in the 1970s and 1980s not only a key way for artists to reflect on cinematic and other images but also the substitute for the theoretical practice of film analysis that he had pioneered in previous decades—the video facilitated stopping, slowing down, speeding up, and reprocessing of cinematic and other images, combining them with texts and other semiotic material, rendering the laborious theoretical practice of film analysis obsolete. However, Ruiz produced very few installations, mostly in the early 1990s, of which the most well-known was *The Expulsion of the Moors* that was exhibited in Boston and Santa Barbara in the United States as well as in Valencia and Paris, all in 1990. Documentation is difficult to come by concerning this exhibition, even on sites like *lecinemaderaoulruiz* that annotate and document all his films, as well as his writing and theater very minutely. Ironically, the project was very much concerned with logics of forgetting and memory, since its title refers to the Velázquez painting of the same name that was commissioned as a competition by the Royal Court of Spain, which it won, only to be later destroyed in a fire.[26] However, this project also exists in the form of a strange book, *The Book of Disappearances/ The Book of Tractations*,[27] which departs in several respects from being a conventional written text in the direction of becoming a multimedia object. In a sense, it follows *In Search of Treasure Island* as being a parallel or simulacrum of an audiovisual project rather than its script or representation, a transmedia migration that is necessarily falsifying. The focus of this book on official versus secret communications, as well as memory and forgetting, make it fitting that it in a sense translates and keeps alive the memory of the now largely forgotten installation.

The book is a doubled book consisting of a series of tales set in seventeenth century Spain, reminiscent at once of Wojciech Has's *The Saragossa Manuscript* (1965) and of some of Ruiz's own works, especially *Combat d'amour en songe/Love Torn in Dream* (FR/PT/CL, 2000), which shares its puzzle-like structure. These tales, presented as a message to an unknown future reader, cover topics ranging from royal courts, the army, the Inquisition, fear of stars, vowels versus consonants, Velázquez's painting, and the discovery of America. One part is called *The Book of Disappearances* and is written relatively conventionally in prose, albeit consisting of a series of fragments of different origins, and in at least one instance departing dramatically from standard written English in a simulation of archaic English. It is perhaps this page that gives the fullest indication of the book as a whole, since it seems a kind of metacommentary: "this booke, made of chappitres and in quych nohht cleyms to be fynysshed or atchieved."[28] It also contains a seemingly random series of enlarged letters that will be returned to shortly. The other text, *The Book of Tractations*, is a series of dialogues that are written in reversed mirror writing, requiring an optical device in order to decipher it. This device is helpfully included within the book. A tractation is usually understood as the "treatment" of a subject, as in a philosophical "tract" like Wittgenstein's *Tractatus* or a cinematic treatment, but it contains another meaning: that of a discussion intended to resolve a matter or dispute. In this case, there is indeed a series of dialogues between characters of different cultural origins—Spanish, Jewish, and Arabic—but this material is even more heterogeneous than the other part of the book, consisting of a series of letters, and also what appears to be an excerpt of a play "A Morisco Comedy in Three Acts" also described as "a poem for several voices."[29] However, the idiosyncrasies of this textual object do not end here. Within each of these texts are marked letters, which also spell out other sentences, secret messages within the text, even within the mirrored "tractations." This secret writing presents yet another voice addressing issues of prostitution and slavery: in the *Book of Disappearances* it begins: "The price of the captive, agree to twelve thousand, no answer before winter."[30] This encoded message spells out the plight of a captive girl form Marrakech whose fate echoes that of one of the models who posed for Velázquez's painting who is also discussed in the text.

Added to this are visual components such as the chessboard that appear both as the cover and also as two double inlays within the book, around which are a diagram with cryptic writing arranged in a coil within a circle and another diagram of a geometric shape surrounded by lines of *x*'s. As Paul Buck puts it, "Each fiction is like a piece on a chess board, creating a game that works on the surface as well as beneath in the labyrinthine world of illusions and mirrors that shapes the space Ruiz creates for his enjoyment and ours."[31] In fact this labyrinthine construction forms the pretext for expressing a number of Ruiz's key obsessions, including experiences of exile and colonialism, the relations between different media of expression, and fictional multiplicities and complexities. Rather than any narrative whole that could be achieved by synthesizing all the different levels of the book's fictions, each story is like a move in a game, as suggested by the chessboard design, the rules of which are yet to be determined. As such it is strongly related to Ruiz's more game-like puzzle films from *Memory of Appearances: Life Is a Dream* (1986) and *Treasure Island*, via *Love Torn in Dream* to his last widely seen film *Mistérios de Lisboa/Mysteries of Lisbon* (PT/FR, 2010), whose multiple stories within stories reprise this ludic, transmedia aspect of Ruiz's work, despite being the well-made literary adaptation of the work of the nineteenth-century Portuguese writer, Castelo Branco. In all of these cases, Ruiz eschews any linear, conflict-driven narrative in favor of a complex, ludic construction of multiple fictions that is more akin to a type of folklore. It is this folkloric dimension of Ruiz's work that will be explored in the last section.

Ruiz's Cinema and Folklore

One of the reasons that some of Ruiz's later work was less visible internationally is that a good deal of it took place in Chile, some of it for Chilean TV, very little of which has been accessible outside of this context. These projects began with the folkloric "documentary" *Cofralandes* (2002), qualified by the alternative subtitles *Chilean Rhapsody* and *Impressions of Chile*, and the two fictional miniseries, *La recta provincia* (2007) and *Litoral: Cuentos del mar/ Litoral: Tales of the Sea* (CL, 2008). According to Ruiz, "*La recta provincia* is folklore, so folklore is universal. The first thing that you discover when dealing with folklore is that it's not local culture because the stories I found in *La recta provincia*, even the ones I invented, or the stories my grandmother told me, you can find them in Scotland, or in the Germanic tradition . . . everywhere we re-invent the same stories."[32] The key to all these projects was this new engagement with folklore, which Ruiz described in the following terms, in a statement accompanying the release of *La recta provincia*: "I wanted to approach folklore theoretically. . . . I believe folklores are ruins, something that existed before in a more complete manner of which elements persist, like a town that has been destroyed and which several aspects remain: a wall, a mural, and that beginning from these fragments, one can construct other things."[33] It is not that Ruiz has not engaged previously with folklore, in fact most of his cinema has this folkloric dimension of fabulation. However, even in his most delirious tales there was also a certain caution with regard to the subject, whether out of the desire not to be assimilated into Latin American magical realism or simply as an effect of the experience of exile. However, the experience of returning to Chile for these projects enabled Ruiz to approach folklore much more directly and engage with the tales he had both heard in his childhood and through reading, where he "noticed that these stories could be found in many places, in Europe, Arab countries and Spain. And curiously in Germany and Nordic countries."[34] This is not so much a belief in the universality of folk tales, although Ruiz is interested in this idea, so much as an idea that different cultures, for different reasons, come up with related narratives, as if the human brain keeps generating similar stories, even if people are situated in very different contexts.

This folkloric dimension is especially apparent in *Cofralandes*, whose title refers to a popular Chilean utopia of a land of plenty in which even the houses can be eaten. *Cofralandes* is loosely based on the impressions three foreigners—a French writer, a German artist, and an English journalist—have of Chile, to which is added Ruiz's own impressions as an exile returning after many years. The documentary therefore presents a dizzying stream of heterogeneous images and sounds that problematize any clear-cut distinction between documentary and fiction, as Alejandra Rodríguez-Remedi has argued.[35] Instead, what emerges is a multifaceted vision of Chile in which first impressions are conjugated with stories, legends, and historical events to present a type of unfamiliar dream Chile or perhaps in Ruizian terms, its optical unconscious. In Rodríguez-Remedi's words, "the heterogeneous images interlaced with this nominal narrative are charged with multitudinous contents and referents from memory and dream, and therefore rarely correspond to linear reason. Examples include militaristic Father Christmases and blind men evoking the 1973 military coup in the height of summer (in the first part), a sleeping dog's political dream (second part), the Museum of the Sandwich (third part) and a diabolical hen (fourth part)."[36] The film's opening sequence gives some idea of how this complexity functions. After a credit sequence over an image of the sun setting over the ocean, there is a voice-over by Ruiz, describing not being able to sleep due to an earthquake and thinking of a country house he remembered from childhood. As the

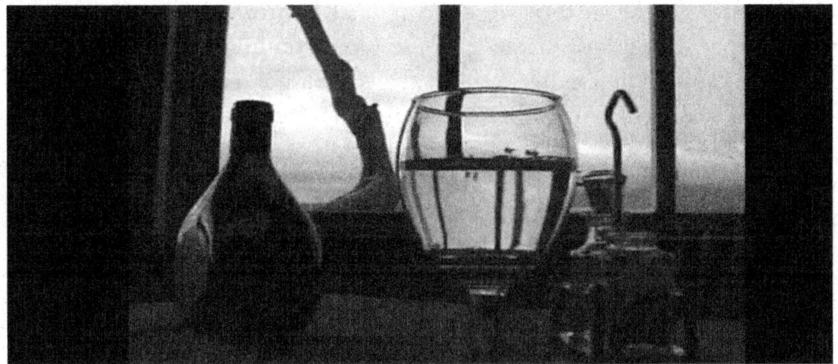

From *Cofralandes, rapsodia chilena* (*Cofralandes, Chilean Rhapsody*, 2002), commissioned for Chilean TV.

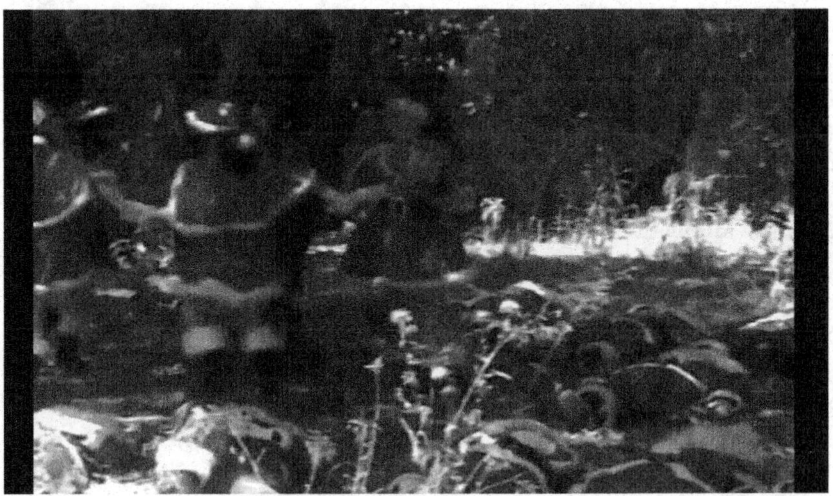

From *Cofralandes, rapsodia chilena* (*Cofralandes, Chilean Rhapsody*, 2002), commissioned for Chilean TV.

camera tracks around this house, a voice recites a Chilean poem typically memorized in school. As the camera tracks back to a previously deserted courtyard, it is now seen populated with Father Christmases.[37] The poem and melancholic music on the soundtrack now give way to a clandestine recording from the day of the Allende coup describing the unfolding military operations surrounding the attack on the presidential palace. This in turn is replaced by the military-style training of the Father Christmases who repeat, "I swear to defend my beard" and other absurdities. Despite the heterogeneity and apparent absurdity of these images, their relations with recent Chilean history are clear; it is as if Ruiz were attempting to devise a type of folklore adequate to the recent traumatic past of Chile, a cinematic fabulation able to perform for contemporary Chile what traditional storytelling did in earlier times. As Rodríguez-Remedi has pointed out, *Cofralandes* is an "anthology or compilation of miscellanea, poetic texts and lessons (*aprendizajes*) about Chilean history, stories, culture, language, landscapes and national identity."[38] At the same time its functioning is not so different from the combinatory methods used in several of Ruiz's later feature films, and it shares the Proustian aims of recapturing lost time, only now in a specific national context.

This brings us to the intimate connection Ruiz saw, toward the end of his career, between cinema and folklore. For Ruiz, both of these forms of fiction at once resist linear, official narratives, and at the same time remain popular culture, appreciated and understood by mass audiences. This might seem an odd claim for a filmmaker generally perceived as difficult and esoteric, and anything but popular. It is certainly hard to imagine a mass audience for projects as labyrinthine as *The Book of Disappearances/The Book of Tractations*, or even *Love Torn in Dream* or *L'hypothèse du tableau volé/ Hypothesis of the Stolen Painting* (FR, 1978). Nevertheless, Ruiz very much explained his choice of remaining in narrative cinema rather than moving to video installation, for example, as being connected to this importance of popular narrative: "We were talking about emotion in cinema. That can explain why I do not want to forget about narrative cinema. Because narrative, much more than narrative cinema is at least human. Games are before humanity: the termite plays, the animal plays, the particles play funny games, but narrative is human."[39] The fact that this explanation was followed by the recounting of an African version of the Scheherazade story, in other words an act of folklore, underlines this link and how it explains why Ruiz stayed within "narrative, and in popular narrative, as the basis of all my work of experimentation."[40] Cinema, especially today when its distinctive analog technologies are rapidly becoming obsolete is, like folklore, a kind of ruin, requiring the archaeological approach evident in media archaeology, for example.[41] But it is a ruin that remains rooted in everyday human life. Ruiz was therefore able to work in relation with a wide variety of media—writing, painting, photography, theory, video, theater, novellas—yet remain throughout all these transmedia explorations a filmmaker, precisely because of film's proximity to the folklore of contemporary popular culture: "what happens in the stars is important, but what is more important is what happens between [people] in everyday life."[42]

Notes

1. Raúl Ruiz cited in Michael Goddard, *The Cinema of Raúl Ruiz: Impossible Cartographies* (London: Wallflower; New York: Columbia University Press, 2013), 184.

2. The recent rise of media archaeological perspective is one of the areas that has profoundly challenged this single medium approach. See for example Siegfried Zielinski, *Audiovisions: Cinema and Television as Entr'Actes in History*, trans. Gloria Custance (Amsterdam: Amsterdam University Press, 1999).

3. Susan Boyd-Bowman, "Imaginary Cinematheques: The Postmodern Programmes of INA," *Screen* 28 (1987): 105.

4. See ibid., 103–17.

5. The third series dispensed with commentary in favor of a stream of audio-visual images that commented on the various regimes of audio-visual production and aspired to the condition of being an "imaginary cinémathèque," expressed in purely visual terms (ibid., 112–14). The content could consist of video art, filmmakers' works in progress, archival photographs, animation, and dynamic moments from the televisual or cinematic past. In this way each episode was itself a work of transmedia heterogeneity, corresponding quite closely to Ruiz's own practice as a filmmaker.

6. INA cited in ibid., 109.

7. Raúl Ruiz, *Poetics of Cinema 1*, trans. Brian Holmes (Paris: Dis Voir, 1995).

8. Adrian Martin, *Rouge 2* (Web journal). *Raúl Ruiz: An Annotated Filmography*. Accessed January 4, 2014.

9. See Raymond Bellour, *L'entre-images 2: Mots, images* (Paris: P.O.L., 1999).

10. Ibid., 9.

11. Raúl Ruiz, "Object Relations in the Cinema," trans. Jill Forbes, *Afterimage* 10 (Fall 1981): 87–94. Translation of "Les relations d'objets au cinema," *Cahiers du cinéma* 287 (April 1978): 26–32.

12. It is also significant that one of the last projects Ruiz worked on was another text, published posthumously, a novella told from the perspective of a spirit of a Belgian "agathopède" who is constantly called up for séances and sessions of spirit photography. Raúl Ruiz, *The Wit of the Staircase*, trans. Paul Buck and Catherine Petit (Paris: Dis Voir, 2012).

13. Ruiz, *Poetics of Cinema 1*, 8.

14. Ibid.

15. A part of this was translated in a three-volume version of *Poetics of Cinema*, published in Chile in Spanish (*Poéticas del cine*, trans. Alan Pauls [Santiago: Ediciones Universidad Diego Portales, 2013]).

16. Ruiz, *Poetics of Cinema 2*, trans. Carlos Morreo (Paris: Dis Voir, 2007), 10.

17. Ruiz, *Poetics of Cinema 1*, 9–23.

18. Thomas Schatz, *The Genius of the System: Hollywood Filmmaking in the Studio Era* (New York: Pantheon, 1988).

19. David Bordwell, Janet Staiger, and Kristin Thompson, *The Classic Hollywood Cinema: From Style and Mode of Production to 1960* (London: Routledge, 1988).

20. Ruiz, *Poetics of Cinema 1*, 11.

21. See Michael Goddard, "Towards a Perverse, Neo-Baroque, Cinematic Aesthetic," *Senses of Cinema* 30 (February 2004).

22. See Walter Benjamin, "The Work of Art in the Age of Its Technological Reproducibility," in *Selected Writings, Volume 3 (1935–1938)*, ed. Howard Eiland and Michael W. Jennings (Cambridge, MA: Harvard University Press, 2002), 101–33.

23. Ruiz, *Poetics of Cinema 1*, 32.

24. Ibid., 78.

25. Ibid., 77.

26. For a brief discussion of these aspects of the installation and the book, see Paul Buck, "Raúl Ruiz and *The Book of Disappearances/The Book of Tractations*," *Vertigo* 2, no. 9 (2005). Website. Accessed September 16, 2014.

27. Raúl Ruiz, *The Book of Disappearances/The Book of Tractations*, trans. Warren Niesluchowski (1990; Paris: Dis Voir, 2005).

28. Ibid., 8.

29. Ibid., 33.

30. Ruiz, *Poetics of Cinema 2*, 4–7.

31. Buck, "Raúl Ruiz and *The Book of Disappearances/The Book of Tractations*," n.p.

32. Ruiz in Goddard, *Cinema of Raúl Ruiz: Impossible Cartographies*, 174.

33. Ruiz cited in *lecinemaderaoulruiz*. From an interview with Pablo Rumel Espinoza, marking the appearance of the program in Chile in 2007.

34. "Raúl Ruiz cautiva en presentación oficial de *Recta Provincia*," *El Mercurio*, August 8, 2007. Website. Accessed September 24, 2016.

35. Alejandra Rodríguez-Remedi, "*Cofralandes*: A Formative Space for Chilean Identity," in *Visual Synergies in Fiction and Documentary Film from Latin America*, ed. Miriam Haddu and Joanna Page (New York: Palgrave Macmillan, 2009), 87–104.

36. Ibid., 91.

37. Apparently based on the multiple Father Christmases that can be seen on Santiago street corners, a sight Ruiz found especially disturbing and that reminded him of the dictatorship.

38. Rodríguez-Remedi, "*Cofralandes*: A Formative Space for Chilean Identity," 93.

39. Ruiz in Goddard, *Cinema of Raúl Ruiz: Impossible Cartographies*, 183.

40. Ibid., 184.

41. See Zielinski, *Audiovisions*, for an example of this.

42. Ruiz in Goddard, *Cinema of Raúl Ruiz: Impossible Cartographies*, 184.

Raúl Ruiz, Speculative Bricoleur

Pedagogical and Televisual Ruptures

Alejandra Rodríguez-Remedi

The prolific Chilean filmmaker Raúl Ruiz was given to speculate about the possibilities emanating from the poetic merging of theory and practice in cinema. This was part of a lifelong commitment to the exploration of new ways to stimulate the "introspection"[1] that he believed crews, audiences, and students require to foster the creativity annulled by the "uniformity of narrative"[2] prevalent in the mainstream film industry. His *Poetics of Cinema* amounted to an ongoing synthesis of such speculations, an intuitive endeavor that informed his creative practice. Ruiz's predilection for *bricolage*, a conscious method for improvisation he used not only as a speculative theorist and maker but also as a teacher of film to create poetic effects, materialized in a permanent combinatory, creative, joyful *play*, offering insights into the knowledge and experience underpinning his praxis.

In this chapter, I shed critical light on two of Ruiz's final parallel bifurcations: firstly, his work as a teacher of film studies in UK Higher Education, specifically at the University of Aberdeen (2007–9) and, secondly, the production and prime-time broadcast in Chile of two folklore-inspired TV miniseries, *La recta provincia* (CL, 2007) and *Litoral* (CL, 2008). Ruiz's usual subversion of the conventional ways of doing signified granting these parallel projects an oblique poetic dimension that made them deviate from the norm, themselves becoming ruptures to the established orders of the education and television systems respectively. I argue that these televisual and pedagogical

---

The translations from Spanish in this chapter are my own. I presented a first draft of this chapter at the Film and Philosophy conference in Dundee in 2009, kindly invited by Michael Goddard to participate in his Ruiz panel there. I am also indebted to Alan Marcus for generously permitting me to attend Professor Ruiz's courses at Aberdeen.

bifurcations are in fact unified by the connective speculative order sustaining this bricoleur's vast oeuvre, through which he promoted a type of learning that transcends the time and space of the institutionalized classroom. Moreover, this chapter is intended to contribute to the understanding of the complexity and role of these late Ruizian ventures, which have not received enough attention in light of the fact that Ruiz acknowledged the challenge he posed himself through these apparently minor side projects.

I begin with a brief overview that traces the recurrent pedagogical and televisual forays Ruiz embarked on throughout his career in order to support the case for their significance to any understanding of his cinema. To contextualize them, I first discuss some *speculations* or *theoretical speculations* (both variations of the filmmaker's evasion of the word "theories" to refer to his reflections on cinema) that Ruiz developed over the years to foster a creative cinema, namely, his proposal of a combinatory system for making a poetic cinema that considers films as *living organisms* and strives for the evocation of uniquely aesthetic, or cinematic, emotions in audiences. A synthesis of these and other speculations are compiled in his *Poetics*, which he regarded as recipes: "Being inside the manufacture of the cookery of cinema, and its projection, is poetic and not to be confused with a general theory of cinema."[3] Second, I offer some reflections about the interdisciplinary nature of these speculations, and the implications of this, and also look into these speculations' underlying concern with human beings, expressed, for example, in the framework for the understanding of human emotions Ruiz takes from Spinoza's philosophy of affects, speculating about cinema's potential to broaden our experience of emotions in view of sustained creativity. Still within this overall contextualization, and in order to make profounder sense of Ruiz's creative way of engaging with theory and practice, I examine his cognitive style, which is infused by a free autodidacticism and his natural predisposition for bricolage, a playful method of improvisation and experimentation he used for combining the most diverse resources available. This last point is a reminder of Ruiz's distinctive way of reasoning: that without his thinking mind, there would be no Ruizian speculations or poetics. This reflection acquires additional significance if we consider that Ruiz's poetic project, through the facilitation of creative perceptions of the world, involves, as all great art does, a transformation of the way we see and thus of our thinking minds, as will be illustrated in greater detail below.

British film studies and Chilean television, two seemingly disparate fields of endeavor, coincided with Ruiz's long-held interests in teaching film and Chilean culture. His early professional development was rooted in teaching and television. In addition to his work at the University of Aberdeen

(2007–9), which will be discussed later, he taught at the Pontifical Catholic University of Valparaíso's Art Institute (1969–72); the Catholic University's Film Institute in Santiago de Chile (1972–73); the Centre d'Aide Technique et de Formations Théâtrales (CATFT) in Brussels (1987); Harvard University (1989–90); the École cantonale d'art de Lausanne (ECAL); the Superior Academy of Arts of Bogotá (ASAB) (1993); Duke University (1994 and 1996); and the University of Calabria (2008). Ruiz participated in various conferences in Chile after 2000, in particular in August 2002 and October 2005 and, though he received a Doctorate Honoris Causa from the University of Valparaíso in March 2011, he did not resume teaching there in his later years. Teaching offered Ruiz a source of creative reflection and experimentation, which imbued his oeuvre, reflected also in his films' many representations of classrooms and teachers. His work in television production began as a writer and editor in Chile and Mexico in the mid-1960s but became more prominent as a writer-director in France in the late 1970s and Portugal in the mid-1980s. It was not until his final years that Ruiz, in the context of Chile's Bicentenary celebrations, made two large-scale works for Chilean television: *La recta provincia* and *Litoral*. These televisual projects are both explorations of the evolving sense of "Chileanness" at the center of his imaginary, a theme that finds its most radical cinematic treatment in *Cofralandes, rapsodia chilena/Cofralandes, Chilean Rhapsody* (CL/FR, 2002), a documentary series Ruiz in fact made for the country's Ministry of Education.

Ruiz's Speculations for a Poetic Cinema: Sovereign Films and Spectators

One of the least known of the major filmmakers of his generation, Ruiz's provisional approximation of cinema as the "totality of all the arts connected by poetry,"[4] a totality located in the "haphazard intersecting of sequences" and "instances of narrative incoherence,"[5] goes some way to forewarning the unwary of what can seem "sometimes embarrassing" filmmaking.[6] In his own terms, Ruiz is speculating about inventing "new ways of telling stories with images using the ambiguity and richness and polysemia of the image,"[7] a mode of invention for which he proposes "an open structure based on *ars combinatoria*" (combinatory art): "A system of multiple stories, overlapping according to certain established rules. This process is capable of generating new stories. . . . This is not just a way of writing, but a way of filming."[8]

Through variations of this poetic system for combining and generating stories, Ruiz sought to contest the conformity of repetition, sterilization of expressive potential, narrative uniformity, and automatism propagated by the commercial film industry. He denounced the "central conflict"-based narrative in mainstream Western filmmaking, the oft-cited starting point of his *Poetics of Cinema*, arguing that its hegemony kills cinema's poetic potential, the source of aesthetic cinematic emotion: those unique, "non-repertory" emotions that emerge when narrative conflict is in stasis[9] and which he provisionally called "humanity."[10] When filmmakers remove "arbitrary, involuntary, unnecessary elements"[11] from their films for fear that they may disrupt the central narrative and the audience's fascination, they are excising precisely the poetic resources the audience needs to imagine and see *its own film*. Ruiz speculated that films have the potential to become *living organisms*—that is, *completed systems*: you watch them while they watch you,[12] which is a shamanic take on cinema.[13] Ruiz concludes the second volume of his *Poetics* with a compelling "theoretical fiction" of the "filmic organism," which is "protean, filled with palpitations, as if breathing."[14] Films conceived as living organisms, however, demand a sovereign audience member[15]—"someone who goes to see films and establishes a personal and intense dialogue."[16] This poetic way of seeing films encourages our production of creative thoughts capable of transforming our disposition to *see*, an activity that, as has been implied, "requires the active movement of both the body and the mind."[17] In a context where our contemporary societies' mechanization has created "automatisms"[18] that pervade our daily routines, including the ways we see, which are propagated by the commercial film industry, a fresh disposition to watch films can potentially emerge with a new vision of the world with all its potential richness. Ruiz believed that *not* to "awaken our consciousness" through art is a "waste,"[19] and that the teaching of film should also be concerned with making students "conscious," arguing that this "is transmitted in a very strange way, it is never transmitted by concept, it isn't describable,"[20] as I shall explain further below.

One of Ruiz's foremost concerns about the current state of cinema (and which he felt the need to communicate to his students) was the impact that cinema's manipulation of the functions of vision has on our overall capacity to see. Ruiz argued that in order to sustain the central conflict narrative, mainstream cinema favors *foveal vision* (the frame's central field) rather than *general vision* (its background), thereby restricting the movement of our eyes. He pointed out that our fascination with the central-conflict narrative, reinforced by our eye operation, does not give us sufficient opportunity to detach ourselves from the film we are watching and see *our own* film. This meant for him that the "exercise entailed in the film itself is destroyed . . . which makes the film look like a cigarette: a drug, a passing entertainment with addictive elements."[21] This appeal to our sense of social responsibility and justice is made in the spirit of ethical-political duty that characterized Ruiz's classes at the University of Aberdeen. Through the simultaneous activation of multiple elements within a shot,[22] Ruiz the filmmaker seeks to privilege our general vision, encouraging our eyes to explore each shot's background detail. He invites us to see shots as "sovereign fragments"[23] that "mix" freely as part of an interactive process. Repeat viewings of Ruiz's films may play a part in this ocular exercise, which seeks to encourage our predisposition for a critical transition from "fascination" to "detachment" in order to "experience the film's events in their full complexity"[24] until eventually at a key moment it looks back at us. If, as physicists David Bohm and F. David Peat argue, "looking at a work of art is a creative act"[25] and "an artist teaches us to see the world in new ways,"[26] the learning transition Ruiz tries to forge within us challenges even critics, who can build up equally reductive sets of viewing automatisms rather than supporting the audience's creative viewing of its *own* films.

Ruiz's speculations about cinema were fueled by a profound desire to make sense of his filmmaking and to communicate his thoughts as well as to inspire fresh ones about a profession he had mastered, a duty that found meaningful expression in his pedagogical practice. His *Poetics* amount to a synthesis of such speculations, which have at their base a shared concern for humanity that he believed cinema has the potential to explore in order to give us the opportunity to learn about ourselves. The explorative strategy he used in this speculative endeavor consisted of borrowing and combining across the most diverse fields of knowledge to "metaphorically build paths leading to the apprehension of phenomena that try to escape us, cinema, for instance."[27] This starting point is reminiscent of Susanne K. Langer's assertion that cinema "seems to be omnivorous, able to assimilate the most diverse materials and turn them into elements of its own."[28]

Ruiz, the Joyful Speculative Bricoleur

Ruiz recommended that aspiring filmmakers study Spinoza's philosophy of affects as a framework for understanding "specifically cinematic emotions."[29] He speculated that "cinema can, with small elements, transmit the complexity of human emotions"[30] and liked to quote Antonio Damasio's work on the oft-neglected neurobiological component of ideas about the qualities of the thinking mind in Spinoza's *Ethics* (1677). *Joy* and *sorrow* were prominent concepts in Spinoza's attempts to comprehend human beings and suggest ways in which our lives could be lived better.[31] Damasio, drawing on the neurobiological component of these two concepts, states that "joy and its variants are preferable to sorrow and related affects, and more conducive to health and the creative flourishing of our beings."[32] Ruiz was aware of the impact of happiness on the filmmaking process and often speculated about his conscious striving for a happy mental state while creating, arguing that "the film won't be happy"[33] if its makers are unhappy. The notion that happiness "increases the fluency of ideation"[34] helps us to understand better the creative implications of a happy predisposition for Ruiz and, as we will see in the next section, it was mainly through the methodology of free "play" that he created the necessary conditions for the actualization of a joyful creative practice. For Ruiz, filmmaking was a joy, and he believed that every crewmember should partake in the collective joy that the making of a film signifies and make the best of the resulting creativity: "I don't just pay my technicians with money. They're artists. So I pay them through aesthetic challenges."[35] The use of aesthetic challenges as a form of payment attests to Ruiz's resistance to conform to the industry's mercantile orientation, which he believed destroys genuine love for cinema. The "sacralization of money" pervading the industry, he argued, has produced a mentality that "makes you measure everything by how much it costs," so when you want to make films "for the sheer joy of it" without thinking about making lots of money, people assume you are not "serious" about your work.[36] For Ruiz, this was evidence of the insidious power the industry has over the general perceptions and assumptions through which we unconsciously reinforce the interests and values of the industry itself. Lacking passion and love for cinema, the filmmakers' mind and body can only orchestrate to produce a type of film Ruiz characterizes as "mechanistic," a film that "can end up correct but mechanical."[37] Ruiz also asserted that, as a teacher, one of his concerns was to combat this mechanistic attitude, voicing his stringent criticism in the following terms: "You can't make films exclusively with people you've robbed of the desire to make them. You can't start the first day of shooting wanting to go on holiday."[38] Instead, by adopting an antimechanistic attitude, one can *learn* how to respond creatively to one's mechanized environment, a process that is essential to one's personal well-being and, as a consequence, that of the film itself if treated as an organism.

Spinoza argued that, as personal happiness occurs through the help of others, it is important to construct a democratic state in which we can all be free, acknowledging the importance of knowledge to this process. He suggested that the positive emotions that "social experience" is able to generate have the potential to awaken the "human decree" latent in society.[39] Ruiz's creative commitment was enacted at this juncture, where the personal and the collective converged, as he attempted to forge complex ways of filming, using all human imaginative potential at his disposal to create unique worlds capable of transforming each of us when we inhabit them.

Ruiz's cognitive predisposition could be summarized in the terms used by Damasio to characterize Spinoza's philosophical approach: "reason lets us see the way, while feeling is the enforcer of our determination to see."[40] In view of Spinoza's enthusiasm for intuition, it is relevant to point out that Ruiz also called his speculations on cinema *intuitions*,[41] referring to them as a "curious form of emotional lucidity."[42] Spinoza regarded intuition to be "the most sophisticated means of achieving knowledge,"[43] and while Ruiz perhaps uses the word in the Crocean sense, it clearly retains the qualities that Spinoza ascribed to it: the conscious process by which we use reason to analyze accumulated knowledge.[44] Ruiz articulated his cognitive and emotional levels of processing thus: "I try to work as an artist, which means to experience feelings and to make connections between what I learn and what I feel—which also involves my militancy—and to express these in artistic form."[45] In their research on the trajectory that our mind takes to think creatively and thereby contest its rigid orders, Bohm and Peat introduce the idea of "the flowing movement of intuitive reason" in order to attest to the dynamic interconnection between reason and intuition and argue that the creative perception responsible for thought takes place in "the broader context" of this movement.[46] Ruiz's autodidacticism,[47] grounded on critical cultural observation, allowed him to move freely between deductive and inductive learning processes, in a motion akin to the flowing movement of intuitive reason that Bohm and Peat discuss, an operation that facilitated his continuous assessment of established knowledge, freed him from rigid assumptions, and encouraged his engagement with creative thinking. This free movement of the mind was imbued by his natural predisposition to bricolage, a method for improvisation that ignited his imagination at all times and that he described thus:

> A small budget necessitates speed, but also what the French call "*bricolage*," improvising. I had never come across the concept until I came to France, although it was non-Frenchmen, like Picasso, who opened my eyes. What it means is making cinema using whatever you have to hand. You take a glass, you smash it, you create a light effect. That was Picasso's legacy, along with South Americans like Neruda. They applied the spirit of "*bricolage*" to poetry and to painting. I try to invoke that same spirit in cinema. It comes naturally to me. It's true, I think even in big-budget films, like, recently, *Time Regained*, or *Klimt*, there's still a lot of hand-made stuff,

people working with their hands. Props, effects, things you put in front of the camera. A lot of the poetry of cinema comes from doing things that way.[48]

The spirit of bricolage described here specifically in terms of a filming method can be applied to his wider creative practice. We can find, for example, traces of the invocation of the spirit of bricolage in his pedagogical work, most noticeably in the practical exercises he improvised with his students, in which he would creatively integrate the accidents and mistakes made during classes into the dynamic of improvisation itself. There are also traces of this method in the formulation of his theoretical speculations; for example, when in the middle of an explanation Ruiz introduces instances or exercises in which he is clearly experimenting with new paths through various combinations while encouraging us to use our own imagination to "fill in the gaps."

Ruiz's Poetic Pedagogy

Approach, Principles, and Intentions

Ruizian pedagogy addressed how cinema functions immanently, from a position of firsthand experience of the politics and technicalities of professional filmmaking but also from the perspective of an interdisciplinary critical thinker capable of detaching himself professionally and unveiling the poetic potential of his craft. For Ruiz, this entailed a shift from sociological, psychoanalytical, or anthropological approaches (that is, cinema as a terrain where the *symptoms* of a society manifest) to the arts themselves (that is, the understanding of how cinema works *from inside*). Ruiz undertook his teachings as an ethical-political duty to communicate to young people his ongoing speculations on cinema in order to empower students with creative awareness and to develop their expressive capacity and personal poetics. He believed that creativity could not be developed in the globalized film industry's context of standardization, which, through "the imposition of concepts," encourages "the death of original cinema."[49] The profit-driven logic of the industry imposes artificial boundaries not only on creativity but also on the joy of filmmaking, without which we cannot open our minds and consciousness to new perceptions of the world capable of dissolving the rigid assumptions that prevent us from transforming the ways we see it. Ruiz argued that with cinema as a mass product following the rules imposed by the market, "pupils learn a technique of fabrication but forget creation as madness, as shivering."[50]

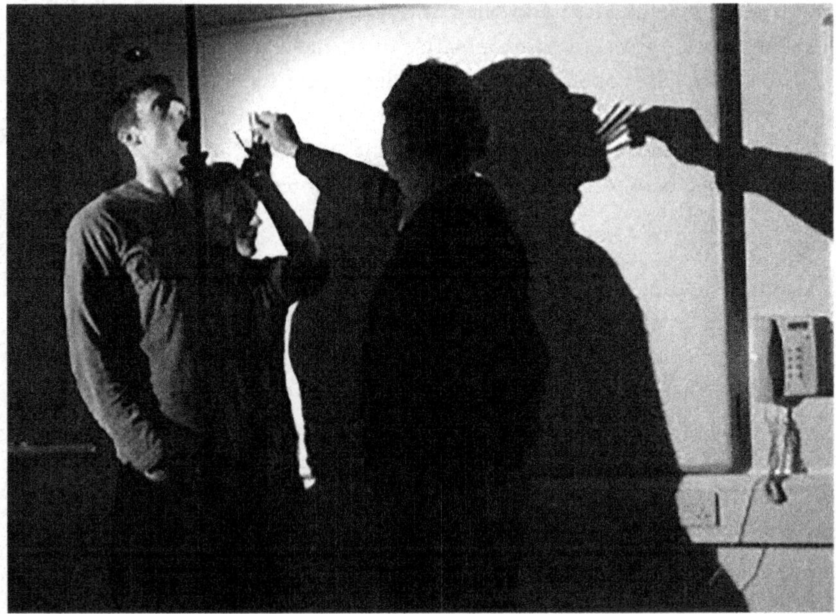

Ruiz orchestrates shadow play with Aberdeen University students in 2007. Courtesy of Lindsay Hodgson.

In the Spanish-language edition of the first volume of his *Poetics*, Ruiz devotes an extra final (as yet untranslated) eighth chapter to reflections on the teaching and learning of film.[51] He describes a teaching experience based on his understanding of cinema as a unique, mysterious phenomenon with its own poetic potential, and his awareness of the subjective quality of students' knowledge construction during the learning process. He warns of the side of filmmaking that can only be self-taught, arguing that "the transmittable portion of cinematic knowledge" is: "all that which is reducible to examples, to exercises, to experiments and to games. In sum, everything which along general lines precedes the making of a film."[52] During exercises designed to encourage students to develop their personal poetics, Ruiz the teacher identifies repeated objects, gestures, and camera movements and observes possible combinations; all of which indicate that a student's "personal trait has already been fixed."[53] He asserts that this process, "for the novice filmmaker is about marking a territory in which he will have to raise his imaginary cities and dictate his laws."[54] While this is happening, Ruiz minutely modifies his students' practical formulas as necessary, either by sharpening or broadening their scope. He argues it is frequently preferable to maintain these formulas' "vagueness, their mystery and their intimacy, and many other ingredients necessary for the free, sovereign practice of all the arts and of cinema above all."[55] Based on the collective and socializing aspect of education, characteristics it shares with filmmaking, Ruiz's poetic pedagogy privileges human interaction and an open dialogue that enriches his own learning, feeding into the speculative base of his praxis, as will be explained below.

The University of Aberdeen Case

1. Contents, Aims, and Delivery Strategy

Ruiz's classes at the University of Aberdeen consisted of a unique, eclectic flux of theory and practice aimed at developing students' personal poetics, which he regarded as the ability to make films with the spirit of bricolage; that is, using a mixture of one's own experiences, idiosyncrasies, ideas, and theories with everyday objects and friends as the main production value. It is little surprise that one who viewed cinema as a "military pursuit"[56] referred to himself as a general, trainer, or coach rather than a teacher: "Students of film seem to like that someone make a military strategy for them and also be a General."[57] The theoretical component of his military strategy, a Wellesian barrage of "general education" atypical of conventional film studies syllabi, which made several students voice doubts, took the shape of seminars-cum-lectures and miscellaneous class notes redolent of his *Poetics*. For the 2007 course, Ruiz concentrated on his provisional conceptualization of the six functions of the shot[58] and, in 2008, on an analysis of "Word and Image," the first chapter of Eisenstein's *The Film Sense* (1943).[59] Although the 2009 course was cut short by unforeseen circumstances, his class notes analyzed V. S. Ramachandran and William Hirstein's essay, "The Science of Art: A Neurological Theory of Aesthetic Experience" (1999) and his late theoretical speculations about five principles that can be used in poetic filmmaking: continuity, discontinuity, extension, synesthesia, and cryptesthesia.[60]

The filmmaking component consisted of supervised class exercises—generating narratives by reordering disparate photographs and combining seemingly disparate everyday objects (eggs and toothbrushes were particular favorites), and dramatizing and filming improvised scenarios and monologues devised by Ruiz—and unsupervised location shooting in groups of three or four. Ruiz forewarned the students that the general utility of this practical side had to do with their learning to be critical, rather than passive, spectators with some understanding of the effort involved in filmmaking. For each course, he presented a *general idea*, highlighting that it was possible to have an eclectic combination of ideas that provided a point of reference or "alibi" rather than a script within which the students created their own fiction films.

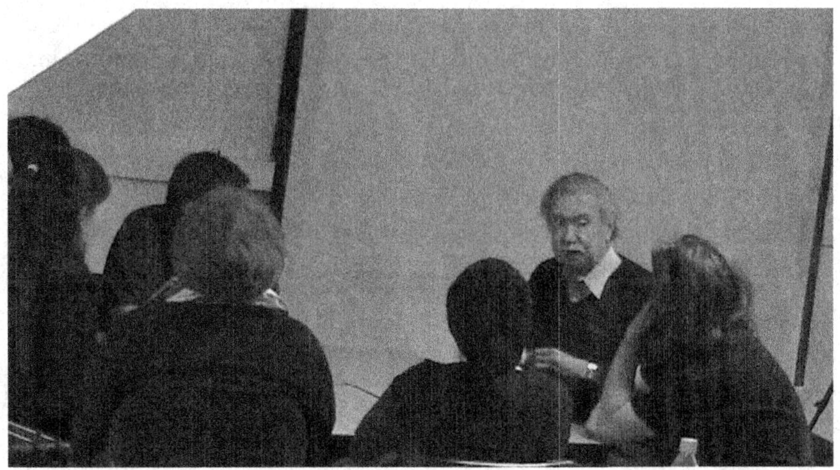

Ruiz initiates a game of pass the camcorder with Aberdeen University students in 2008. Courtesy of Lindsay Hodgson.

Ruiz's avowed keenness to deviate from, or shun entirely, the set-in-stone written screenplay was an obvious divergence from film industry norms, a strategy he summarized thus: "I have a clear structure at the beginning so the film can be imagined and then I can play inside it."[61] Playful improvisations during class involving the physical manipulation of objects, which Ruiz always tried to connect to people's everyday lives, offered students hands-on experience of what he meant by the notion of image determining narration. The manipulation of objects acquires a profounder meaning when we remember their importance to our apprehension of reality: "Knowledge of reality does not . . . lie in the subject, nor in the object, but in the dynamic flow between them."[62] Drawing on enigmatic images, each group invented its own story, what Ruiz called the macrofiction or macronarrative that communicates the official or explicit fiction, while he encouraged the students to combine freely in each shot objects and details in order to create microfictions or latent stories capable of *conspiring against* the macrofiction. This playful combination of objects, that are usually regarded as ornamental props in commercial cinema and are sometimes simply omitted because they add little to the central narrative or the audience's fascination, allowed the students to give expressive capacity to their films so as to activate an audience's creative viewings. The class notes Ruiz handed out, containing the latest theoretical speculations he intended to put into practice, and the various screenings he ran, as well as his direct supervision of students, were all synchronized to support the students' creation of their fiction films. The poetic flux of theory and practice behind Ruiz's provision of meaningful learning experiences defied the students' preconceptions about filmmaking, developing an awareness of the multiple orders of a film that they would not have found in the chronology of a conventional screenplay. The transmission of a poetic way of filmmaking thus demanded an equally poetic teaching strategy and set of activities, positioning *General Ruiz* as a facilitator who set the grounds for his students to construct their own learning consciously in continuous interaction with others.

2. Narrative Devices for Poetic Fictions

The general ideas suggested by Ruiz were *amnesia, senile dementia*, and a *house concealing an enigma* for the 2007, 2008, and 2009 courses respectively. The first two ideas called for the improvisation of fiction films, which involved the characterization of incoherent behavior within the context of university routines, having the oblique intention to encourage students to be critically aware of the rituals and schedules they took for granted and identify the automatized behavior that desensitized them to their academic environment. The third course's fiction films involved the dramatization of disconnected, discontinuous actions of living or dead inhabitants, visitors and doppelgangers, using cryptic references to folklore and playful voice-overs in order to give an inanimate object, in this case the students' invented house, life. The territories of memory, a mind in crisis, and concealed enigmas served as starting points for Ruiz's introduction of the poetic potential underlying incoherencies in narrative, materializing throughout the courses in a continuous move "from narrative evidence (what Greek rhetoricians referred to as *enargeia*) to visual doubt: am I seeing what I am seeing? And then from visual doubt working through itself on to a new narrative evidence."[63]

In his *Poetics*, Ruiz speculated about the rich world of images that "madmen and those who hallucinate inhabit, and perhaps not everyone is as fortunate"[64] and also used the idea of a "house" inhabited by amnesiacs as an illustration of how vicinity and resonance "come together to intensify a cinematic emotion."[65] The films he made contemporaneous to his time at Aberdeen give poetic treatments to the "house": *La recta provincia* and *Litoral* both prominently feature colonial Chilean haunted houses, and his camera keenly explores the enigmatic stately mansions and grounds that feature prominently in *Nucingen House* (2008) and *A Closed Book* (UK, 2010).

The use of allegories, dreamlike situations, and hallucinatory and nightmarish effect were common narrative devices used by all students to give

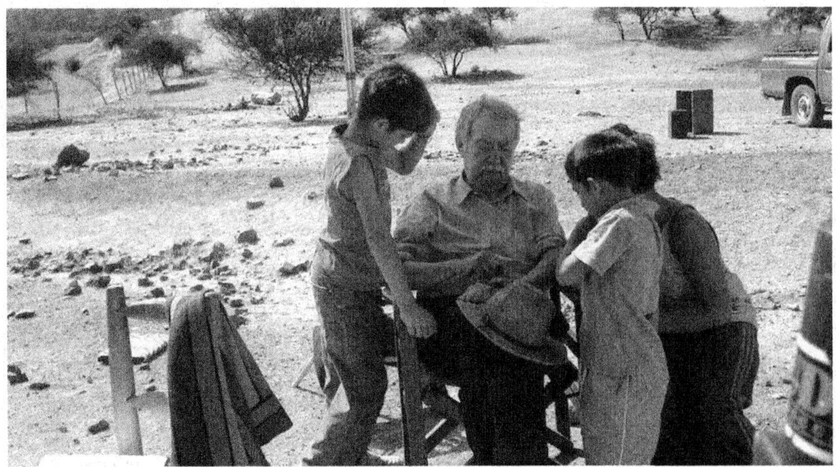

Ruiz interrogated by and interrogating curious locals while on location for *La recta provincia* in 2007. Courtesy of Inti Briones.

a poetic effect to their fiction films, for which Ruiz gave the following guidelines:

(a) Use enigmatic images (that is, unexplained images) as starting points for your fictions; the image precedes the narrative.[66]

(b) Use local reality, culture, and idiosyncrasy to make your videos personal. Allow the poetic potential of your backgrounds and immediate surroundings to translate into unforeseen cinematic possibilities.

(c) Play with details (for example, gestures, objects, sounds, music) via association/dissociation, appearance/disappearance, repetition/ juxtaposition. Make ambiguous and contradictory combinations in order to create misunderstandings.

(d) Play with time and space by altering the rhythm of images through repetitions with variations, making your videos last longer than seems necessary (that is, make them "boring" in order to encourage audience introspection and activate latent films).

The feedback that Ruiz and fellow classmates gave each group during weekly screenings of their video works-in-progress concentrated on identification of and critical reflection about the latent films within each video project. The course's poetic intentions necessitated this reflective attitude, a process Ruiz summarized as "a constant practice of both attention and detachment, an ability to enter into the act of filming and return an instant afterward to passive contemplation."[67] This dynamic exemplified group thinking about how to make the most of poetic resources and the building up of student confidence. Following Ruiz's principles, there were no "right" or "wrong" audiovisual projects.

The learning atmosphere Ruiz created through his class exercises challenged the ways in which pedagogical space and time are customarily organized at the university. For him, the conventional UK higher education course structure, consisting of four to six hours of class per week (condensed usually over a two-day period), allowed too much time to pass between sessions, diluting the participants' energies and holistic potential. The ideal Ruizian course would consist of three to four weeks of intensive collaboration, resembling a low-budget film shoot, working each day until a human lattice-like structure is formed. This is the "muscular level" of filmmaking that Ruiz advocated from the early 1970s onward: "It's about developing a series of instincts, of behaviors which lead to teamwork, like some sort of orchestra of cinema, in which you play a part and simultaneously you listen to it."[68]

3. Serio Ludere[69]

> Creative play is an essential element if forming new hypotheses and
> ideas. Indeed, thought which tries to avoid play is in fact playing
> false with itself. Play, it appears, is of the very essence of thought.[70]

Ruiz's pedagogical practice permitted him to play with new ideas in the spirit of the bricoleur and to try them out in collaboration with his students and then involve everyone in reflection about the implications of such a playful yet serious operation. Aware of the direct relationship between creative thinking and play, he intentionally located free play at the epicenter of his teaching methodology and his creative practice more generally. Free play, as a source of creativity, enabled Ruiz to refresh ideas through new combinations and to question certainties, challenging thus our tendency to "cling rigidly to familiar ideas," which is "the same as blocking the mind from engaging in creative free play."[71] Ruiz, by personally sustaining this attitude at all times during his teaching practice, became himself a (trans)formative living model to follow for his students. It is no surprise then that he saw in Aristotle, whose *Poetics* offers a certain questioning methodology that Ruiz drew upon to formulate his own poetics, "a model that one would have to keep practicing: to create, rather than certainties, uncertainties, and leave the certainties as a backdrop."[72] The pedagogical space then became a precious opportunity for Ruiz to take some critical distance from filmmaking in order to reflect about it and reapproach it afterward with fresh eyes. This activity involved a continuous search for the conceptual means needed to communicate his thoughts and reflections and lay the ground for an open dialogue that was always interdisciplinary in nature.

This helps us understand that the play Ruiz engaged in with his students, some of whom perceived the learning atmosphere created as more informal than traditional university courses, in order to stimulate creative thinking and therefore speculations, was in fact a most serious matter. We are reassured that poetic filmmaking is not "simply paying great attention and lots of imagination into inventing things at the last minute," because "there's a very considerable background of reading, personal obsessions, recurring themes, etc."[73] Johan Huizinga argues that civilization "arises *in* and *as* play, and never leaves it,"[74] and that the ludic and poetic capacity of play facilitates our "'imagination' of reality (i.e. its conversion into images)" that is rooted in a "primitive mode of thinking."[75] In his 1958 critique of Huizinga's research, Roger Caillois classifies play and determines its functions in various societies, asserting that "what is expressed in play is not different from what is expressed in culture"[76] and that, in fact, "play is a total activity" that "involves a totality of human behavior and interests."[77] Ruiz's interest in the Chinese tradition of thought and its *efficacy-oriented* way of working, which he regarded as an alternative creative filmmaking approach to the Western traditional *goal-oriented* way of working, proves relevant here: "Wisely and circumspectly, Chinese culture is less directed toward purposive innovation. The need for progress and the spirit of enterprise generally seem to them a kind of compulsion that is not particularly creative."[78] In the same way, the creativity behind Chinese games, mirroring the creativity of Chinese culture, as outlined below, applies to both Ruiz's films and pedagogy.[79] The Chinese feel that checkers and chess "train the mind to find pleasure in multiple responses, combinations, and surprises that continuously give rise to new situations. Aggressiveness is thus inhibited while the mind finds tranquility, harmony, and joy in contemplating the possibilities."[80]

Similarly, through childlike play (for "really to play, a man must play like a child"[81]), Ruiz invited his students to embrace fully the imaginative possibilities generated without feeling anxiety about what and where the experience was leading them. "Creativity is a natural potential," Bohm and Peat argue, yet "the urge to create fades as the human being gets older"[82] and the creative activity turns into something "mechanical" and "repetitive" due to external and internal "rewards" or "punishments."[83] In his discussion of university functions, Alfred North Whitehead (another Ruiz favorite) asserts that imagination is "a contagious disease" that "can only be communicated by a faculty whose members themselves wear their learning with imagination."[84] Ruiz himself was a model of imagination during his courses, generating ideas for and participating in every playful classroom improvisation.

Perhaps the main challenge that Ruiz's courses posed to the students, several of whom had not worked with high definition video before, was to understand the creative nature of their own discovery through play. Epstein summarizes: "Discovery always means learning that objects are not as we had believed them to be; to know more, one must first abandon the most evident certainties of established knowledge."[85] Ruiz's interdisciplinary approach was vital to this critical epistemological revision. As Whitehead, the mathematician who wrote about the "joy of discovery" in education,[86] counseled in his discussion of the need for mutual interaction between general and specialist knowledge: "You may not divide the seamless coat of learning."[87] For a profound understanding of creativity, interdisciplinarity appears to be the appropriate way forward, especially in light of Bohm and Peat's argument that creativity, "in its essence, cannot really be divided into different fields of specialization, for it is one whole."[88]

The playful learning experience that Ruiz planned for students and his dialogue with them fed into his own learning process and thus into the speculative basis of his praxis. He argued: "I believe in academia, in ancient Greek and Roman academia, which means that nobody—no teacher or master—can teach unless he learns from the one he's teaching; if that contact isn't established, the energy of teaching is lost."[89] As someone who understood how he constructed his own learning, Ruiz encouraged students to be conscious of their own, so as to attain an ever-greater degree of independence. As mentioned earlier, the pedagogical space provided a strategic opportunity for Ruiz to move from theory to practice and back again in a process he described as the "systole and diastole" of his creation.[90] Several of the ideas emerging from his experiments were to be replicated in Ruiz's commercial films. He argued: "I can't make cinema if beforehand I haven't made films where I have total freedom and there is no financial objective."[91] In this way, he positioned himself in a mobile state between the worlds of commercial and experimental cinema, that is, perpetually passing from one world to the other but never completely belonging to either: "I, like all exiles, am located on the borders."[92] Ruiz's passion for culture exudes from all his work, and the experience of exile alluded to here played an important part in exposing him to other ways of being and doing that he embraced with his usual autodidactic disposition, while Chilean culture regularly appeared in the middle of all this multicultural amalgamation as a recurrent referent against which he formulated his thoughts about cinema and world cultures more generally. The sustained reencounter with his motherland he went through during his last years while making a series of Chilean projects, however, took his speculations on Chilean culture to another level.

La recta provincia (2007) and *Litoral* (2008)

> I've often asked myself (and been asked) why I go there (so far away) to make films for Chilean television. And why I prioritize Chilean folklore, which isn't particularly rich compared with other Latin American countries and frankly poor if you compare it to the folklore of European or Asian countries. The answer I've given myself is very simple: it's because as a child I heard many of those tales that I want to film, I was told them by my grandparents from the Central Zone and from Chiloé.[93]

Ruiz used his own childhood memories as a creative source of inquiry to guide his reconstruction of a poetic sense of "Chileanness" in the Chilean projects he undertook during his creative return. These projects are made up of echoes from past history, filtered through the experience of childhood, and references to contemporary Chile, providing a poetic referent for the union of the Chile of yesterday and today. *Cofralandes* is the most emblematic example of this connective venture, filled as it is with miscellaneous images and sounds evoking school life through references to Chilean literature, stories, and play as well as the country's postdictatorial landscape. Awareness of one's own culture and its poetic potential, through which broader cultural connections can be made, was the spirit Ruiz the teacher passed on to his students when he encouraged them to identify spontaneous attitudes resulting from their own idiosyncrasies and turn them into a "permanent element of expression."[94] The TV series *La recta provincia* and *Litoral*, also framed within an evocation of "childhood" have, however, folklore as their central theme, a research area Ruiz had recently been absorbed in and that had echoed his parallel pedagogical work at Aberdeen. Ruiz took this opportunity to give Chilean television not only cultural depth by transmitting his latest research findings but also aesthetic value through their cinematic treatment: "I believe one should work towards television where one can introduce the maximum of resources of film. I think all genres and formats should be at the service of the performing arts."[95] Ruiz approached his televisual projects with the same playful seriousness, speculative thoughtfulness, and bricoleur's spirit with which he treated every bifurcation of his work.

Ruiz found in folklore creative possibilities for play to stimulate audiences' discovery of a parallel or latent film: "the popular element which is hidden in it, the fairy-tale or the children's story."[96] Folklore, legend, and myth—all forms that UNESCO seeks to safeguard for their role in transmitting values and collective memory, as "oral traditions and expressions" under its Intangible Cultural Heritage (ICH) rubric—had come to occupy a prominent place in the lower-budget work Ruiz did outside France in his later years. Ruiz outlined three areas of his folkloric research: Alexander Afanasiev's work on Slavic folklore's roots in pagan myth; Georges Perrot and Charles Chipiez's work on the theoretical reconstruction of ancient ruins; and the "folk poetry" improvised with a *guitarrón chileno*.[97] It is worth recalling Ruiz's attraction to Charles Dupuis's cryptic statement that "myth is born of science, science will explain it."[98] Ruiz speculated that Chile's popular folktales constitute the "echoes," "ruins," or "remains" of forgotten European, Arab, and Nordic cultures that cinema could potentially "reconstruct"; for him, cinema is "the art of organizing commonplaces around one or many stories."[99] Huizinga asserts that *ritual* shares the same characteristic of *play*, a key notion at the heart of Ruiz's creative and pedagogical process, especially in that they share the peculiarity of transporting the participants "to another world."[100] Here, for Huizinga, resides the connection between play, the mysterious, and the sacred. Rituals and fragments of memories form "the ideal place where divergent cultures can meet"[101] or "a common meeting territory for seemingly irreconcilable cultures."[102] Ruiz's *La maison Nucingen/ Nucingen House* (RO/FR/CL, 2008), originally conceived as a Mircea Eliade adaptation, exemplifies this exchange: a film Ruiz convinced his Franco-Romanian backers to shoot in Chile, "the only place where you can find German legends and folklore."[103] His theatrical play, *Amledi, el tonto* (2010), reimagined *Hamlet* through the folklore of Chiloé and Denmark. Ruiz's folkloric research points toward what he speculated was that *other* form of globalization, that "which is done through peoples, in which two countries search for elements in common."[104]

Again and again, Ruiz the auteur returned to Chile only to admonish it in terms so harsh that it becomes hard deciding where acrimony ended and affection began. He judged Chilean television to be "not bad but abject" and "subject to market rules imposed from outside."[105] In spite (and because) of this, he signed a three-year contract with TVN, Chile's national television channel, in August 2006 as part of the channel's 2010 national bicentennial celebrations, an initiative framed by a national cultural policy nominally intended to counteract the cultural desolation bequeathed by the neoliberal economic policies of the Pinochet military regime (1973–90).

This work for TVN can be seen as the official reencounter with the motherland so fundamental to the Ruizian ecosystem, a search for "the permanent Chile."[106] Both series shed new light on the Chilean (and *anti*-Chilean) aspects of Ruiz's exilic films, from the nostalgic wanderings of *Les trois couronnes du matelot/ Three Crowns of the Sailor* (FR, 1983), itself a direct antecedent of *Litoral*, to the traumatic desolation of *La ville des pirates/ City of Pirates* (FR/PT, 1983) and the inferno of *A TV Dante (Cantos 9–14)* (UK, 1991). *Cofralandes* and its forerunners *Lettre d'un cinéaste ou Le retour d'un amateur de bibliothèques/ Letter from a Filmmaker or The Return of a Library Lover* (FR, 1983) and *Las soledades* (UK, 1992) are semiethnographic essay-films made in Chile that creatively engage with the filmmaker's *saudade*, a Portuguese term signifying "a melancholy . . . nostalgia for what might have occurred."[107] Laleen Jayamanne remarks that the filmmaker's *saudade* on reencountering Chile in the 1980s "seems to create an affective register for turning toward tradition, toward a cultural memory, as a precondition for invention."[108]

Ruiz described his late Chilean productions as forming "part of a desire to retake Chilean reality, not as a critic of it, and far less as a business or a permanent job, but as an attempt to give present-day Chile a poetic dimension."[109] Ruiz chose to evoke the mysteries and paradoxes of the lost Chile of his childhood in both *La recta provincia* and *Litoral*, which he equated to "a sort of folkloric map of Chile,"[110] while explicit references to twenty-first-century Chile crop up more in his non-Chilean films. Some have argued that Ruiz's most avant-garde French films can be read "as reflections on the Chilean experience"[111] wherein Chileanness is insinuated as a "secret presence" or "subliminal wink."[112]

La recta provincia and *Litoral*, which evoke Chilean rural and maritime storytelling traditions respectively, received national broadcasts—four episodes of *La recta provincia* at 11:30 p.m. on Mondays in August and September 2007 and four episodes of *Litoral* at 10:00 p.m. on Saturdays in September 2008—and garnered higher-than-feared (though admittedly unexceptional) ratings. TVN's delayed, late-night transmission of the first episode of *La recta provincia* was roundly criticized, and repeated calls for DVD releases of *La recta provincia* and *Litoral* have fallen on deaf ears. Of the first series, Ruiz noted:

> It's almost a miracle something that atypical can be shown on television, albeit at midnight. Things shown on television have a certain rhetoric characteristic of television. It isn't that this work is so intellectual or difficult, it's simply very country. In fact, the people the film interested most were rural folk or people who'd lived in the countryside, who'd go on holiday there.[113]

In *La recta provincia*, shot in high definition during a month on location in Putaendo, Rancagua, and the outskirts of Santiago, a mother and her adult son in rural Chile find a flute-like human bone and, in their quest to bury it with its rightful skeleton, encounter rural angels and devils.[114] In *Litoral*, shot on Digibeta over two months in and around Santiago (Melipilla), Valparaíso (Quilpué), and Chiloé Island with the support of the Chilean Navy, the sailors of the ghost ship *Lucerna* recount variations of stories to one another in nightly assemblies. The sizeable casts of each series are populated by Ruiz's friends and past collaborators (among them, veteran actress Bélgica Castro and documentarian Ignacio Agüero)—some of whom are not professional actors—and also, most particularly in the case of *Litoral*, numerous young actors making their television debuts. Key crewmembers on both projects were Ruiz's long-term accomplices, wife and editor Valeria Sarmiento and composer Jorge Arriagada. While *La recta provincia* is characterized by Ruiz's self-confessed "obsessive conservation"[115] of pastoral tales and Chilean folklore, of which the "scattered body" (*cuerpo repartido*)[116] is perhaps the most prominent, *Litoral* draws attention to the heuristics—"as both 'mirror of the creative process' and as 'theatre of the theatre of the world'"[117]—of the production of tales:[118]

> there are immortal stories in the sense that they are like birds of prey which devour people, oblige them to act out the same stories, with the same central elements. It isn't necessarily certain that those stories happen, it's very possible, simply, that they are repeated.[119]

The sailors in *Litoral* are the protagonists both of the stories they tell (and retell, with variations) and of the very comics they read. Their tales are archetypal Ruizian vignettes: one sailor is hired to father a child[120] but finds he has been hired by ghosts; another is taunted by murdered triplets named Amelia; another marries a girl whose fiancés die in accidents only to find that she has a "brother" who inhabits her body; the cuckolded captain's "human horns" continue to grow even after he saws them off, and so on. Ruiz, on the process of inventing the tales in *Litoral*: "there's an interesting theme which is under discussion by anthropologists: do the popular roots or high culture come first?"[121] The antitelevisual poetic dimension is brought to the fore through play with language and the "condensation" of scenes into often beautiful long takes that are often devoid of close-ups and that Ruiz hoped produced "an otherworldly element that is dreamlike."[122]

La recta provincia explores the uniqueness of the Spanish language of rural Chile, still spoken today as in Ruiz's childhood, while *Litoral* brings back to life the archaic Chilean urban Spanish of the 1950s, in both cases giving insight into the Chilean national character, punctuating the specificity of its urban and rural condition. Ruiz speculated that, in order "to develop a mode of production with Chileans' way of being," it is necessary to "make the Chilean's way of speaking expressive again and I'm not referring to the accent but to the syntax, which is very particular."[123] His playful investigation into Chilean syntactical and behavioral eccentricities unveils hidden, unconscious orders pervading this culture. The contemplative encounter with this idiosyncratic concoction, Chile's plurality, should mark the beginning of the audience's creative perception and open dialogue, in the sovereign mode discussed earlier, freed of the fixed assumptions that underlie Chilean "cultural conditioning."[124]

Both series' matter-of-fact oneirism poses challenges to the industry that produced them. While neither can be considered the most radical of Ruiz's Chilean films—this honor would doubtless fall to *Cofralandes*, which he described as "the film which has most to do with the film theories that I've invented"[125]—he makes no significant concession to the mainstream in either series. Of *La recta provincia*, Ruiz stated: "There are certain things which verge on provocation . . . in the first chapter, there's a scene which is a single take lasting over four minutes, which is filmed in long shot. In France I am forbidden that."[126] The contract afforded TVN the opportunity to capitalize on the director's international reputation (following decades of apparent indifference), but Ruiz was granted a measure of creative freedom to resume his pre-exilic attempts at "*converting* and *creating* Chile, making it artistic."[127]

Final Thoughts

Forays into British film studies and Chilean television provided Ruiz in the final years of his life with a meaningful opportunity to pursue further his long-held interests in teaching film and in Chilean culture. The former entailed communicating his poetic message to new generations, as well as his engagement in new experimental practice and free creative reflection, or *speculation* as he preferred it, which informed his work outside education. The latter produced a cinematic, televisual exploration of the universal and poetic value of folklore that he had tapped into in his recent research in order to enhance the complexity of his filmmaking.

Ruiz's efforts to test the limits of his creative practice translated into an organic flow of teaching and learning imbued by his combinatory disposition. In line with his poetic speculations about films as living organisms, I would argue that his pedagogy is also "living." It promotes formative experiences that transcend the boundaries of educational institutions. Like his ideal audience's personal transformation when one of his films evokes new cinematic emotions, Ruiz's students' sense of empowerment after developing their personal poetics enabled them to spread the poetic seeds beyond the space of the classroom. Ruiz's pedagogy, far from being disruptive to or disconnected from his filmmaking, in fact permeates and feeds directly into his creative work.

What Ruiz the master bricoleur learned from one project fed into future projects in a continuous process of exchange that sheds light on our understanding of cinema's relationship with the other arts and their place within humanity. At no point did Ruiz shrink from issuing his stringent challenge to the hegemonic order of culture-industry theory and practice, as the televisual and educational ruptures presented here have shown. We are left with his childlike recurrence to *play*, laughing at this world we live in, but always in so serious and speculative a way that we anchor ourselves within it with insight and creativity.

Notes

1. Macarena García G., "Raúl Ruiz: Contra la inmediatez; 'El capitalismo se extendió al arte y la cultura,'" *Mercurio*, April 30, 2006. Website. Accessed April 12, 2013.

2. James Norton, "The Mystery, as Always: Raúl Ruiz, Klimt, and the Poetics of Cinema," *Vertigo* 3, no. 6 (2007): 10.

3. Ruiz, interview by Armando Casas, "Raúl Ruiz: El cine como guerra de guerrillas," *Reflexiones Marginales* 16 (2005). Website. Accessed August 31, 2014.

4. Ruiz, interview by Nick James, "Mexico Rising: Interview," *Sight and Sound* 14, no. 4 (2006): 177–82. Website. Accessed April 11, 2013.

5. Raúl Ruiz, *Poetics of Cinema 2*, trans. Carlos Morreo (Paris: Dis Voir, 2007), 22.

6. Ian Christie, "Disbelieving Documentary: Rouch Viewed through the Binoculars of Marker and Ruiz," in *Building Bridges: The Cinema of Jean Rouch*, ed. Joram ten Brink (London: Wallflower, 2007), 267–76, at 273.

7. Norton, "Mystery, as Always," 10.

8. Raúl Ruiz, *Poetics of Cinema 1* (Paris: Dis Voir, 1995), 88.

9. Ruiz, interview by Jaime Natche and Diego León Ruiz, "En compañía de Raúl Ruiz," *Miradas: Revista del audiovisual*, EICTV San Antonio de los Baños, Cuba, March 30, 2001. Website. Accessed May 6, 2004.

10. Ruiz, interview by Casas.

11. Ruiz, *Poetics of Cinema 1*, 58.

12. Ruiz, interview by Antonio Becerro, "Raúl Ruiz: 'Los perros son seres extraordinarios,'" Perrera Arte blog, January 15, 2006. Website. Accessed April 11, 2013.

13. See Ruiz, *Poetics of Cinema 1*, 73–90, and Ruiz, *Poetics of Cinema 2*, 38–39.

14. Ruiz, *Poetics of Cinema 2*, 107 and 110.

15. See Ruiz interview by Octavio Crespo, "Entrevista: Raúl Ruiz y sus imágenes del 'Chile permanente'; 'En Chile, la elegancia es monopolio de los pobres,'" *Mercurio*, August 5, 2007. Website. Accessed April 12, 2013.

16. Ruiz quoted in Cooperativa, "El cine chileno no existe según Raúl Ruiz," July 25, 2001. Website. Accessed April 11, 2013.

17. David Bohm and F. David Peat, *Science, Order, and Creativity* (1987; London: Routledge Classics, 2011), 54.

18. See Ruiz, interview by Juan Andrés Salfate, "Un tal Raúl Ruiz," *Mercurio*, August 8, 2002. Website. Accessed October 2, 2008.

19. Ruiz interview by Orlando Milesi, "Raúl Ruiz: 'Sobreproducción de imágenes' en el mundo," *Ansa*, July 9, 2008. Website. Accessed January 30, 2011.

20. Ruiz, interview by Casas.

21. Ruiz, interview by Salfate.

22. The "minimum of complexity" he alluded to in Carole Anne Klonarides, "Raúl Ruiz," *BOMB* 34, no. 4 (1991): 177–82. Website. Accessed April 12, 2013.

23. Ruiz, *Poetics of Cinema 2*, 93.

24. Ibid., 36–41.

25. Bohm and Peat, *Science, Order, and Creativity*, 167.

26. Ibid., 168.

27. Ruiz, *Poetics of Cinema 2*, 107.

28. Susanne K. Langer, *Feeling and Form: A Theory of Art Developed from Philosophy in a New Key* (London: Routledge and Kegan Paul), 412.

29. Helen Bandis, Adrian Martin, and Grant McDonald, eds., *Raúl Ruiz: Images of Passage* (Melbourne, Australia: Rouge Press, 2004), 59.

30. Ruiz, interview by Santiago Rubín de Celis and Andrés Rubín de Celis, "Entrevista Raúl Ruiz: 'La historia es una hábil coordinación de sospechas,'" *Miradas de cine*, March 11 and 14, 2011. Website. Accessed April 11, 2013.

31. Antonio Damasio, *Looking for Spinoza: Joy, Sorrow, and the Feeling Brain* (London: William Heinemann, 2003), 8.

32. Ibid., 271.

33. Geoffrey Macnab, "Pursuit of Happiness," *Daily Tiger Rotterdam International Film Festival*, January 25, 2009. Website. Accessed April 11, 2013.

34. Damasio, *Looking for Spinoza*, 101.

35. Raúl Ruiz and Jérôme Prieur, "Un voyage fantastique," *Three Crowns of the Sailor*, DVD, directed by Raúl Ruiz (1983; France: Blaq Out, 2006).

36. Ruiz, interview by Daniel Sandoval, "Entrevista a Raúl Ruiz," Asociación de Amigos del Arte y la Cultura de Valladolid, 1997. Website. Accessed April 11, 2013.

37. Ruiz, interview by Casas.

38. Ibid.

39. Damasio, *Looking for Spinoza*, 173–74.

40. Ibid., 277.

41. Ruiz, *Poetics of Cinema 2*, 10.

42. Raúl Ruiz, *Poética del cine* (Santiago: Editorial Sudamericana Chilena, 2000), 145.

43. Damasio, *Looking for Spinoza*, 274.

44. Ibid.

45. Julianne Burton, *Cinema and Social Change in Latin America: Conversations with Filmmakers* (Austin: University of Texas Press, 1986), 183.

46. Bohm and Peat, *Science, Order, and Creativity*, 142.

47. See Ruiz, interview by Luis Carlos Muñoz Sarmiento, "Entrevista con Raúl Ruiz: La poética de la desconfianza," *Mil Inviernos*, 2012. Website. Accessed August 12, 2014.

48. Ruiz and Prieur, "Un voyage fantastique."

49. Ruiz, interview by Sandoval.

50. Ruiz, interview by DPA, "Raúl Ruiz prefiere que lo pirateen si así se ven sus películas," *Mercurio*, March 29, 2009. Website. Accessed April 11, 2013.

51. Ruiz, *Poética del cine*, 139–57.

52. Ibid., 140.

53. Ibid., 141.

54. Ibid., 142.

55. Ibid., 151.

56. Ruiz, *Poetics of Cinema 2*, 9.

57. Ruiz, interview by DPA.

58. See Bandis, Martin, and McDonald, *Raúl Ruiz: Images of Passage*, 57–68.

59. These seminars and writings were integrated with screenings illustrative of a wide scope of poetic approaches to filmmaking, including Wojciech Has's *Rekopis znaleziony w Saragossie/The Saragossa Manuscript* (PL, 1965); Allan Dwan's *Tennessee's Partner* (US, 1955); Cavalcanti et al.'s *Dead of Night* (UK, 1945); Carl Theodor Dreyer's *Gertrud* (DK, 1964); Chris Marker's *La jetée* (FR, 1962); and clips from Ruiz films (sometimes in rough-cut form, as were the cases of *La recta provincia* and *Litoral*).

60. See Michael Goddard, *The Cinema of Raúl Ruiz: Impossible Cartographies* (London: Wallflower, 2013), 176–82. Screenings included Jacques Tourneur's *Cat People* (US, 1942); Robert Wise and Gunther von Fritsch's *The Curse of the Cat People* (US, 1944); Josef von Sternberg's *Anatahan* (JP, 1953); Sacha Guitry's *Le roman d'un tricheur/Confessions of a Cheat* (FR, 1936); André Delvaux's *Rendez-vous à Bray* (BE, 1971); and the *Twilight Zone* episodes: Robert Stevens's "Walking Distance" (US, 1959); John Brahm's "Young Man's Fancy" (US, 1962); and John Brahm and Paul Lynch's versions of "Shadow Play" (US, 1961 and 1986 respectively).

61. Ruiz, interview by James.

62. Bohm and Peat, *Science, Order, and Creativity*, 57.

63. Ruiz, *Poetics of Cinema 2*, 33.

64. Ibid., 31.

65. See ibid., 62–64.

66. Ibid., 10, 22, and 44.

67. Ruiz, *Poetics of Cinema 1*, 90.

68. Ruiz, interview by Enrique Lihn, "Diálogo con Raúl Ruiz por Enrique Lihn," *Revista Atenea* 500 (2009): 265–79.

69. Ruiz refers to cinema as *serio ludere* (Ruiz, *Poetics of Cinema 2*, 69).

70. Bohm and Peat, *Science, Order, and Creativity*, 37.

71. Ibid., 40.

72. Ruiz, interview by Casas.

73. Ruiz, interview by Muñoz Sarmiento.

74. Johan Huizinga, *Homo ludens: A Study of the Play-Element in Culture* (London: Hunt, Barnard, 1949), 173.

75. Ibid., 174.

76. Roger Caillois, *Man, Play, and Games* (London: Thames and Hudson, 1962), 64.

77. Ibid., 175.

78. Ibid., 33.

79. Ruiz, *Poetics of Cinema 2*, 109.

80. Caillois, *Man, Play, and Games*, 84.

81. Huizinga, *Homo ludens*, 199.

82. Bohm and Peat, *Science, Order, and Creativity*, 230.

83. Ibid., 231.

84. A. N. Whitehead, *The Aims of Education and Other Essays* (London: Ernest Benn, 1970), 145.

85. Jean Epstein, "Magnification and Other Writings," *October* 69, no. 3 (1977): 21.

86. Whitehead, *Aims of Education*, 3.

87. Ibid., 18.

88. Bohm and Peat, *Science, Order, and Creativity*, 189.

89. Ruiz, interview by Casas.

90. Ruiz, interview by Salfate.

91. Ruiz, interview by Milesi.

92. Ruiz, interview by Sandoval.

93. Ruiz, interview by Yenny Cáceres Seguel, "Capitán Ruiz," *Qué Pasa*, September 7, 2008. Website. Accessed September 8, 2008. Specifically, Ruiz is thinking of the town of Mulchén and Chiloé Island in southern Chile.

94. Eduardo Sabrovsky, ed., *Conversaciones con Raúl Ruiz* (Santiago: Ediciones Universidad Diego Portales, 2003), 102.

95. Waldemar Verdugo Fuentes, "Semblanza de Raúl Ruiz," 2011. www.letras.s5.com: Página chilena al servicio de la cultura. Accessed September 14, 2013.

96. Ruiz, interview by Diego Brodersen, "¿Por qué no jugar con el cuento infantil?" *Página 12*, April 3, 2009. Website. Accessed April 11, 2013.

97. Raúl Ruiz, "The Invention of a Film: *Recta Provincia*," lecture, University of Aberdeen, May 1, 2007.

98. Ruiz, *Poetics of Cinema 1*, 104.

99. Ruiz, *Poetics of Cinema 2*, 106.

100. Huizinga, *Homo ludens*, 18. Huizinga's assertion seems to echo Sheldrake's theorizations about the "cosmic resonance" of rituals, an idea Ruiz finds pertinent to poetic filmmaking (see Ruiz, *Poetics of Cinema 2*, 40).

101. Leonardo Núñez, "Raúl Ruiz cautiva en presentación oficial de 'Recta Provincia,'" *Mercurio*, August 8, 2007. Website. Accessed April 11, 2013.

102. Soledad Gutiérrez, "Raúl Ruiz en TVN: 'La recta provincia' tendrá secuela inspirada en el mar," *Mercurio*, March 29, 2007. Website. Accessed October 2, 2008.

103. Ruiz, interview by Antonio Reynaldos, "Ruiz: 'Ser chileno es una enfermedad incurable,'" *Nación*, January 27, 2009. Website. Accessed April 11, 2013.

104. Ruiz, interview by Yenny Cáceres, "Raúl Ruiz: 'Chile me duele menos que un lumbago,'" *Mabuse*, October 10, 2005. Website. Accessed April 11, 2013.

105. Ruiz, interview by Jorge Garrido, "Diálogo abierto: Una conversación múltiple con Raúl Ruiz," *Revista Chilena de Antropología Visual*, 9, 2007. Website. Accessed April 11, 2013.

106. Ruiz, interview by Crespo.

107. Ruiz, *Poetics of Cinema 1*, 108.

108. Laleen Jayamanne, *Toward Cinema and Its Double: Cross-Cultural Mimesis* (Bloomington: Indiana University Press, 2001), 172–73.

109. Ruiz, interview by Cáceres Seguel, "Capitán Ruiz."

110. Ruiz, interview by Brodersen.

111. Ignacio López-Vicuña, "Raúl Ruiz's 'Lost' Chilean Film: Memory and Multiplicity in *Palomita blanca*," *Studies in Hispanic Cinemas* 6, no. 2 (2009): 120.

112. Jacqueline Mouesca, *Plano secuencia de la memoria de Chile: Veinticinco años de cine chileno (1960–1985)* (Madrid: Ediciones del Litoral, 1988), 123.

113. Ruiz, interview by Rodrigo Acuña Bravo, "Mundo Placeres conversó con Raúl Ruiz: 'Todas las películas están condenadas a ser fantasmas,'" Radio Placeres, March 28, 2008. Website. Accessed April 11, 2013.

114. "Recta Provincia" was the name given to a secret society of pagan sorcerers on Chiloé that underwent judicial condemnation in 1880 (see Ruiz, *Poetics of Cinema 1*, 97–101). Ruiz's *La recta provincia* came in for criticism in some quarters as its narrative bore little relation to this piece of Chilean history.

115. Ruiz, interview by Patricia Carbonari, "Entrevista a Raoul Ruiz: El problema de los guiones de hierro es que se oxidan," *Extrabismos*. Website. Accessed January 15, 2009.

116. This chimes with Ruiz's use of "a legend that relates the gathering up of the scattered limbs of Osiris's body" as a "useful metaphor" during his speculations about how actors can build their worlds poetically (Ruiz, *Poetics of Cinema 2*, 93).

117. Ibid., 56.

118. See Ruiz, interview by Brodersen.

119. Ruiz, interview by Carbonari.

120. Like in Karen Blixen's "The Immortal Story" (1958), filmed by Orson Welles for French television in 1968.

121. Ruiz, interview by Brodersen.

122. Raúl Ruiz and Erwan Lozachmeur, "*Ce jour-là* raconté par Raoul Ruiz," *Ce jour-là*, DVD, directed by Raúl Ruiz (2003; France: Gemini Films, 2006).

123. Ruiz, interview by Salfate.

124. Bohm and Peat, *Science, Order, and Creativity*, 252.

125. Ruiz, interview by Crespo.

126. Ruiz, interview by Romina de la Sotta and Christian Stüdemann H., "Raúl Ruiz: 'Que la serie exista es un milagro,'" *Guachacas*, August 25, 2011. Website. Accessed April 11, 2013.

127. Alejandra Rodríguez-Remedi, "*Cofralandes*: A Formative Space for Chilean Identity," in *Visual Synergies in Fiction and Documentary Film from Latin America*, ed. Miriam Haddu and Joanna Page (New York: Palgrave Macmillan, 2009), 87–103, at 88.

Inter-*auteurial* Itineraries and the Rekindling of Transnational Art Cinema

Raúl Ruiz and Orson Welles

Catherine L. Benamou

Para Raúl

Las Maletas

This chapter is an attempt to understand how Orson Welles and Raúl Ruiz, both enfants terribles at the beginning of their film careers, opened up the possibility for new forms of authorship through a practice focused on creative collaboration and transnational production. For Welles, this transnationalism began with the making of the film *It's All True* (1941–42) in Mexico and Brazil; for Ruiz, it was as much a part of his early career attempting to produce films in Argentina, then in Chile, as it was of his years in exile. Yet, thanks to a critical emphasis on authorship as a singular activity, the effects of transnationalism upon, and resulting transculturation coursing through the work of both directors has yet to be fully grasped. Instead, until recently, their oeuvre has been subjected to a geocultural bifurcation in criticism.[1] Best known for his contributions to the development of a globally oriented art cinema in Europe,[2] Ruiz has also been recognized within Hispanophone circles for his vital role in helping to build Chilean national cinema in the 1960s and early 1970s. Based mainly on his Chilean career, Ruiz has been critically aligned with the "new Latin American cinema," although it is questionable as to whether the term can be applied consistently to his films after 1974, when he began working, out of necessity, in Europe.[3] Among other attributes, Ruiz's later films—like those of other exilic filmmakers— involve an exploration of the ways in which cinema, as anthropologist David

MacDougall has observed, bears a "disconcerting resemblance to memory," even though this raises the conundrum of "how to represent the mind's landscape."[4] Ruiz chose to tackle this not by way of explicitly autobiographical revelation and revisitation, but, as Fabrice Revault d'Allonnes has suggested, by tapping into and cultivating the "collective imaginary."[5]

Ruiz's margin of distance from the dominant aesthetic (whether branded as industrial or stemming from alternative waves, whether working in Chile or in France), combined with his unwavering political, or at the very least, intensely skeptical engagement with the world *at heart* is reflected in an unrelenting formal search for uncanny or peripheral angles and viewpoints, a decentering (or at least destabilization) of narrative authority, and the historical relevance of films produced at pivotal moments for the Chilean as well as the French and broader European sociopolitical spheres. Paradoxically, his pliability in strategy, along with the treatment of spectatorship as a matter of *ethics*, and the embrace of difference (both for himself as "outsider" and with regard to the intratextual interweaving of cultural sources and historical contexts) brought Ruiz closer to previous generations of cineastes, including those whose careers were launched in the United States, such as Orson Welles, even as these same traits set the tone for postexilic generations of Chilean filmmakers.[6] The attention to spectatorial ethics involves not so much the fashioning of a particular type of message as giving the viewer handles with which to begin critically unpacking a film, by shaping performances and manipulating narrative structure, delivery, and form in such a way that the element of illusion or of confabulation can be recognized as such.[7] This freeing up and simultaneous critical grounding of spectatorship helped to expand Ruiz's abovementioned pursuit of the collective imaginary, and, in the case of Welles, arguably increased the effectiveness of intersubjective point-of-view and heterodiegetic narration.[8]

No express study of Ruiz's multifaceted relationship to Orson Welles has been undertaken to date, even though open references to Welles's films have surfaced frequently in interviews with Ruiz and analyses of his work.[9] Ruiz himself mentioned being engrossed in reading a Welles biography while teaching at Duke University in the mid-1990s, and in interviews he has acknowledged Welles's influence on specific films.[10] There are biographical parallels: even though Ruiz and Welles made bold aesthetic contributions to their respective national cinemas, they struggled to get their work produced at the start of their careers, then went into exile (for Welles, this began in 1947, during the editing of the film *Macbeth* [1948]), at which point their projects became transnational in substance, if not always in sponsorship or production process. In spite of limited or intermittent access to global theatrical distribution, both directors were, each in their own right, "public intellectuals," expounding their views on film aesthetics and cultural politics in extended interviews on screen and in print. Critical appreciation of their greater filmographies has been far more prevalent in western Europe and Latin America, as contrasted with the United States. (Interestingly, both were recognized for their artistic accomplishments by the French government.)[11]

In each case, the circumstances attached to exile contributed to a penchant for the baroque, lending a melancholic tone to some of their most significant films: *Touch of Evil* (US, 1958); *F for Fake* (FR/IT, 1974); *Chimes at Midnight* (FR/ES/CH, 1967) for Welles; *Les trois couronnes du matelot/ Three Crowns of the Sailor* (FR, 1983); *Mémoire des apparences/Life Is a Dream* (FR, 1986); *Le temps retrouvé/Time Regained* (FR/IT/PT, 1999) for Ruiz. A humanist, self-reflexive premise, a departure from straightforward realism, open narrative discourse (facilitated by the baroque),[12] uneasy plot endings, and a creative exploration of sociocultural displacement suffuse much of their mature work.

At the textual level, Ruiz and Welles often trod the boundary between documentary and fiction film, where they each planted seedlings of allegory.[13] It can be argued that these allegories were animated by the fact that both filmmakers went from working in a position at the epicenter of national production to an exilic trajectory, an experience that creates a frame with which to reveal meaningful differences as well as study their common ground. Both were attentive to the built environment (whether using "found" locations or specially constructed sets), and, drawing upon their backgrounds in theater, they cultivated ensemble acting (including the casting of theatrical and nonprofessional actors rather than trained screen actors). Both directors were also attracted to "B" cinema, even though their own films could hardly be labeled as such. Averse to the wide screen, both found in television a flexible terrain of creative possibility.

It would be a mistake to simply bundle these signs of cultural flexibility and departures from contemporary industrial practice under the label of "postmodern." Instead, as I hope will become clear, Welles and Ruiz retained at least one foot firmly in modern cinema as a means of innovating, of exploring the legendary or fantastic, and indeed, even of *critiquing* the modern without erasing a sense of the historical real. Through their neobaroque take on modern construction, we can see the possibility of transforming viewers' perceptions of historical events, along with new interpretations of well-known source texts authored by Cervantes, Picasso, Mondrian, Tarkington (Welles), Shakespeare, Kafka, and Dinesen (Welles and Ruiz), Calderón de la Barca, Klossowski, Klimt, Racine, Proust (Ruiz). As Denilson Lopes has suggested in the case of Welles, which can easily be extended to include Ruiz, these filmmakers dwelt in the realm of the neobaroque, a strategy that "seeks to avoid isolations between modern and post-modern cinema, which could take the latter in the direction of a regressive pre-modern, pre-vanguardist posture."[14]

In what remains of this chapter, I will attempt to bring into greater relief aspects of Ruiz's creative relationship to the cinematic oeuvre of Orson Welles, first by way of a brief review of openly acknowledged "citations" of Welles's film work, then through a broader, multiperspectival gleaning of salient points of resonance, divergence, and tension in their aesthetic orientations as "maverick *auteurs*." Two caveats prior to embarking on this exercise: first, there is the tangible way in which Ruiz, a voracious cinephile, was influenced by, and admired, not only Welles, but also Luis Buñuel, the short stories of Jorge Luis Borges, the self-reflexive novels of Marcel Proust (treading the threshold between cinema and literature), and even, sporadically, the work of Alfred Hitchcock, Marcel Carné, and F. W. Murnau.[15] In highlighting affinities with and traces of Welles's work in Ruiz's films, I will only be foregrounding one important tributary among several to be discerned in the Ruizian intertext (some of these other affinities actually help to bring him closer to Welles). Second, while I wish to momentarily align Welles and Ruiz as artists, I do not intend to minimize meaningful differences arising from gaps in generation (Ruiz was born the year *Citizen Kane* was released), industrial habitus, and geocultural origin.

Direct Citations

There are a number of audiovisual "quotations" of Welles (both self-conscious and unwitting) in Ruiz's work. For example, it is difficult not to notice the parallel between the construction in depth in scenes of *Het dak van de Walvis/On Top of the Whale* (NL/FR, 1982) featuring the protagonists conversing inside the house with the child playing, or indigenous characters waiting, in the expansive backyard, and the deep focused shot that pierces through various planes of construction in the snow sled scene from *Citizen Kane* (US, 1941), where the young Kane is outside playing while his parents discuss his future with Thatcher inside the boarding house. The opening shot of *Time Regained*, although evenly lit, shows the steeple of the cathedral of "Combray" (actually Illiers-Combray), which holds a special significance for Proust, and the opening shot of the fortress Xanadu, looming in the distance behind a forbidding fence in *Citizen Kane*. There are similarities between the nostalgia of the Combray scene and that attached to the large Victorian house that is shown before we meet the main characters (other than Eugene) in Welles's *The Magnificent Ambersons* (US, 1942). It is also difficult not to sense the resemblance between the roving, traveling shots in *Time Regained* and the long-winded traveling shot through the streets of the industrializing town in *The Magnificent Ambersons*, both revealing to us the society in transition in which the main characters lived. All three films are about loss and the circuitous paths of personal memory, reaching beyond the scope of the protagonists' individual consciousness to encompass the intersubjective, which permits a dialogue with the spectator regarding a past that is beyond their reach. Moreover, Ruiz himself acknowledged a debt to Welles's *The Lady from Shanghai* (US, 1947), with its lonely sailor who finds himself entrapped in a plot he did not bargain for, and the fateful quest in the story of the sailor in *Three Crowns of the Sailor*, as well as unintended parallels (because he had not yet viewed the film) with the labyrinthine search for the past of magnate Gregory Arkadin in Welles's *Mr. Arkadin/Confidential Report* (FR/ES/CH, 1955)[16] with its not-so-likeable protagonist Guy seeking monetary gain, much like the young adventurer who meets the sailor at the beginning of Ruiz's film. Again, these citations are not overtly inscribed as a winking gesture of postmodern appropriation, but rather occur in subtle homage to Welles, suggesting creative and philosophical affinity; meanwhile, each inscription makes perfect sense to the organic character of Ruiz's "sister" films.

Further resemblances can be noted between Ruiz's love of voice-over narration, exemplified in *On Top of the Whale, Three Crowns of the Sailor*, and *L'hypothèse du tableau volé/The Hypothesis of the Stolen Painting* (FR, 1979) and that of Welles in *Magnificent Ambersons, The Lady from Shanghai, Ghost Story* (dir. Hilton Edwards, IE, 1950), *Othello* (US/FR, 1952), and *F for Fake*. It is interesting to consider the effects of musical counterpoint and even dissonance in *On Top of the Whale* and *Time Regained*, as compared to Welles's *Citizen Kane, The Lady from Shanghai*, and *Othello*. However, there are meaningful differences: Welles's narration is either detached, uttered from the omniscient position of a "storyteller," and hence heterodiegetic, providing an authorial segue into the body of the diegesis, or it is anchored in the individual consciousness of a character in the film (diegetic), following the conventions of documentary (*F for Fake, Filming Othello* [DE, 1978]) or *film noir* (*The Lady from Shanghai*). In Ruiz, the narrational subject is much less stable, such that the voice-over narration is either: (a) subverted as the subject is displaced by the psychological or ideological perspective of other characters (*On Top of the Whale, Three Crowns of the Sailor*), (b) shown to be grounded in "immateriality" as the narration is delivered by a ghost (*Three Crowns of the Sailor, Memories of Appearances*), or (c) is rendered ambiguous by life changes or changes in our reception of the characters (*Time Regained, Hypothesis of the Stolen Painting*). In *On Top of the Whale*, the anthropologist's viewpoint (and corresponding worldview) is displaced by that of his daughter, his anthropological subjects, the Yaghanes Indians,[17] and his wife on both the soundtrack and in the focalization of the narrative through camera positioning and angle. In *Three Crowns of the Sailor*, we find ourselves listening to the sailor's voice, even though the heterodiegetic narration is being offered by the young Polish adventurer; similarly, in *Memories of Appearances*, we slip from an "objective" voice-over narration into the ghostly navigation of Ignacio's, the political prisoner's, dream.[18] In *Time Regained*, a different actor delivers Proust's voice-over narration as the actor who plays Proust in the diegesis, and there is considerable ambiguity (echoing Proust's writing) in the latter part of the film as to whether the narration is contemporaneous to the events or delivered from Proust's deathbed, as images of characters shift in age and appearance through superimposition, and the older Proust meets the young Proust at seaside. In *Hypothesis of the Stolen Painting*, we are left to wonder whether the actor delivering the voice-over narration is the same as the actor playing the role of the art collector, whereas the discourse of the collector regarding the logic of the missing painting becomes increasingly fanciful and far-fetched, paralleling in a Ruizian paradox the "flesh and blood" performance of the paintings' characters in *tableaux vivants*. As a result, we come to question the reliability of the narration and are left to contemplate the ways in which memory becomes entangled in the boundary between real and (partly) imagined events.

Architecture as Metaphor, the Mirror

Thanks to Welles's anticipation of and Ruiz's embrace of neorealism[19] and the French New Wave, we see ample use in their films of traveling shots of conversations in outdoor spaces that allow for the geohistorical real to seep into the diegesis, and at times, for the dialogue to be jostled by ambient sounds, as if to hold the drama in check. Yet whereas Welles uses the street as a narrative site of gendered and class tensions and sociocultural shock (*The Magnificent Ambersons, Touch of Evil, The Trial* [FR/DE/IT, 1962], *F for Fake*), for Ruiz, the street provides another opportunity for spectatorial voyeurism (or at least, narrative insight), plot pivots (and an attendant sense of loss or disillusionment), and transculturation. The built environment, meanwhile, is not just the locus of the mise-en-scène in their films, but is transformed through lighting, camera angle, and choreography into an expression of the characters' existential states. Whereas Welles's use of architecture has been celebrated for its contributions to realism (see, for

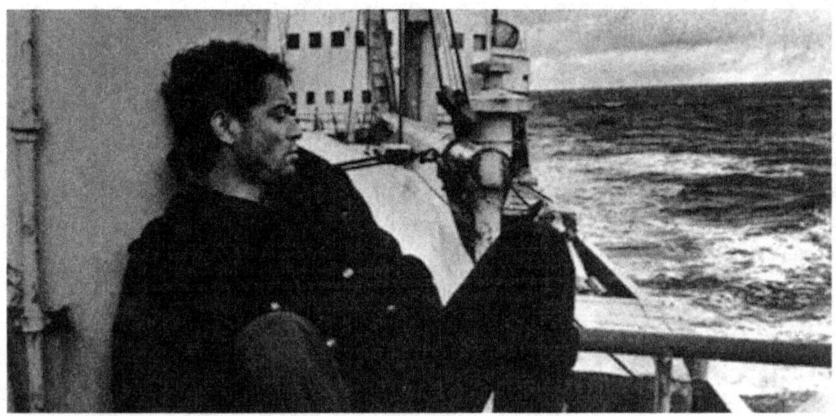

Production photograph from *Three Crowns of the Sailor*, dir. Raúl Ruiz, 1983. Copyright François Ede/ Cinémathèque Française.

example, *Citizen Kane* cinematographer Gregg Toland's remarks on the subject),[20] the exaggeration in both Welles's and Ruiz's films of ambient sound (especially the sound of the human body, such as footsteps, moving through architectural space) often has a boomerang effect: syncopation rather than synchronization is suggested even though the sound index-ically pertains to the actual bodies we follow on screen. The sound of a teacup breaking in *Time Regained* is too loud to be merely descriptive, like the shriek of the cockatiel in the Xanadu sequence of *Citizen Kane*; each sound instead marks a plot turning point, as well as a shift in affect. Like-wise, both directors (probably with Ruiz following Welles's example) place objects in the extreme foreground, or, by revealing corners of architectural space, show objects in exaggerated proportion to their surroundings. This is exemplified in Welles's foregrounding of the bottles of medicine after Su-san's suicide attempt; Kane's pant leg, which appears in the foreground at the *Inquirer* office after Jedediah's bad musical review in *Citizen Kane*; Ia-go's cage in the opening sequence of *Othello*; the burlesque dancer's fishnet legs, which form a framing device in one of the early investigation scenes in *Touch of Evil*; or the chandelier looming large from the ceiling in Ruiz's *The Hypothesis of the Stolen Painting*, the pock-marked leg aboard the ship in *Three Crowns of the Sailor*. Welles and Ruiz reveal ceilings in interior shots and attend to structural elements, such as door and window frames, that are ordinarily left out of, or kept at the remote periphery of, the frame.[21] This not only situates performers in "real space," but it also gently removes the spectator from intense immersion in the diegesis.

As part of this general, shared interest in architectural form and detail, each director shows a preference for specific elements that open up channels of focalization for scenes, and by extension, interpretations of characters and plot trajectories. For Welles, hallways and foyers are transformed into main stages for the action in his films—most dramatically in *Citizen Kane* and *The Magnificent Ambersons*, yet, rather than conduits for transiting domestic space, hallways are sites for breeding conflict and conspiracies (*Citizen Kane, The Magnificent Ambersons, Touch of Evil, Mr. Arkadin, The Trial*), whereas foyers are the locus for insults, indignation, and the seeds of marital discord (*Citizen Kane, The Magnificent Ambersons*). Similar tensions are to be found in Ruiz's use of doorways and doors. In *Diálogos de exiliados/Dialogues of Exiles* (FR, 1974), the opening and shutting of doors is used almost comically to transition among interlocutors in political conversation, as if to relativize ideological differences (given the loss of a historical-political context in which they might have made more sense). A window is used as a door to "smuggle" someone into the Paris apartment where numerous Chilean exiles are lodged, and, near the end of the film, doors are opened to a sunny exterior that is geographically ambiguous enough that it could represent either Chile or France. However, we are unable to accompany the protagonists into this world that lies just beyond the interiors where many Chilean exiles have confined themselves—perhaps because this outer world represents a virtual horizon of a change in fate that can only be hoped for, and has yet to materialize. Less dramatically, yet just as intriguingly, in *Hypothesis of the Stolen Painting*, a character's passage through doors that are "invisible" because decorated with the same covering as the walls, serves as a turning point or an intrashot editing device, as well as a hint that all is not entirely well with the art collector who is our guide to the paintings: that his seemingly coherent, rationally coded discourse veils irrational musings and an irrepressibly passionate investment in the story alleged to be accessible in crystallized form in the missing painting (which may not be stolen after all, but merely concealed from our view). Through this play on the missing painting, Ruiz removes from our contemplation the core of a conventional dramatic narrative depicted in the group of paintings, along with the possible solution to the mystery of disappearance, and instead converts the alleged disappearance into narrative excess through the depiction of the painting's content by live bodies in a *tableau vivant* and the collector's obsessive monologue. In Ruiz's France-based work, it is possible to convert these material transoms into allegorical thresholds, pointing to the disappearance of living beings, the unrecuperable losses attached to exile, and at the same time, the possibility that hope might take root in the very place that marks the spot of disappearance.

We see this trope again in *Time Regained*, as Proust (Marcello Mazzarella), on his deathbed, pushes through French doors to find himself on the Atlantic beach of his childhood.

Aside from their individual predilections, both Ruiz and Welles incorporate mirrors as portals for narrative insight. One of the first images of *Citizen Kane* is of the nurse reflected in the snowy globe that Kane has let fall upon uttering his last words. The image is quite distorted, shot with a fish-eye lens as if to paradoxically convey the subjective viewpoint, with fading eyesight, of Kane himself, but also the division between the inner world of the globe (Kane's childhood) and the cold, institutionalized "outer" world (because populated only by professional care, devoid of intimate human company) of the bedchamber. A decade later in *Othello*, two scenes shot inside the regiment headquarters include shots of Othello viewing himself and his surroundings through a mirror. In the first, Othello sees Desdemona (Suzanne Cloutier) advancing toward him from behind in deep space to confess that she has lost her handkerchief. We view her not with suspicion as Othello might, but as she responds to his questioning with an expression of distress and concern. In the second, Othello is talking to Iago (Micheál MacLiammóir) about his lieutenant, Michael Cassio (Michael Laurence), whom Iago will accuse of having an affair with Desdemona—here Welles positions the mirror in front of Othello to denote a blank space in the frame where Desdemona has been previously, with the back of the mirror facing Iago, "blinded" by his thirst for power, ethically and spatially separated from Othello and Desdemona's shared "space."

Ruiz uses the mirror sparingly in most of his work, yet meaningfully in two films. In *On Top of the Whale*, the mirror is one of the remnants of Western civilization found in the backyard of Narciso's (Fernando Bordeu) farmhouse. In what seems to be a surreal parody of the Lacanian "mirror phase," Ruiz equates looking in the mirror with becoming pregnant with child, and Ana, the child character, undergoes a physical transformation resembling pregnancy.[22] In *Time Regained*, Ruiz uses the mirror to show not the protagonist but how other characters (Proust's home care nurse, his friend Gilberte [Emmanuelle Béart]) view Proust.[23] In resisting the use of conventional reverse shots, and using the mirror to reveal the protagonist directly, both Ruiz and Welles avoid its use as a tool of transparency, duplicity (as in film noir) or simple reflection; instead, like the introduction of other optical instruments (such as the magnifying glass in *Mr. Arkadin* or *Time Regained*), it is used reflexively to refract our attention away from the character's viewpoint to an undefined, yet meaningful space in between the protagonist and their interlocutors.[24] Only we (together with the chambermaid Emilia [Fay

Compton]) in *Othello* can notice the eclipsing of Desdemona; only a child can notice the special power of the mirror in *On Top of the Whale*, and only a caring housekeeper can notice that the bedridden Proust is dying in *Time Regained*. These gazes disrupt that of the narcissistic subject, even if only momentarily. Perhaps Ruiz was thinking of the final sequence of *The Lady from Shanghai* when he stated, "The cinema is a mechanical mirror endowed with memory. . . . One would be surprised by the number of ways of entering this mirror that contains other mirrors, and through which one can follow all kinds of itineraries, and all sorts of things!"[25]

The metaphoric dimensions and para-narrational uses of these elements, along with the reflexive attention (beyond mere description) given to architecture in both Welles's and Ruiz's films, is intricately connected to the importance of baroque aesthetics to their work.

The (Neo)Baroque and Melancholia

More than one critic, such as Christine Buci-Glucksmann,[26] has commented on the baroque as a specific point of resonance between Ruiz's work and the films of Orson Welles. Here, it is worth noting not only the manifestations of baroque construction in their films, especially as it affects narrative interpretation, but also the fact that the baroque is not the predominant aesthetic model in either the United States or Chile, even as it might shape and define national representational discourse in other countries, such as Brazil.[27] Hence, its embrace can be seen as a means whereby Ruiz and Welles differentiated themselves from their filmmaking contemporaries and compatriots and were able to connect with audiences beyond the initial borders of their productions. Whereas in the United States Welles lost the Oscar for best film of 1941 to Ford's *How Green Was My Valley*, in 1942 he received first prize for the baroque *Citizen Kane* in both Argentina and Brazil, and Argentine screenwriters soon thereafter began adopting nonlinear, "puzzle" structures in their screenplays.[28]

To begin with, baroque narrative frameworks are evidenced in Welles's and Ruiz's adaptation of seventeenth-century texts to twentieth-century settings and circumstances (Miguel Cervantes's *Don Quixote* by Welles, and Pedro Calderón de la Barca's *La vida es sueño/Life Is a Dream* by Ruiz). The baroque is visually conveyed by the alternation between black-and-white with color stock in the same film (Welles's *It's All True* [1941–42] and Ruiz's *The Suspended Vocation* [1978]), and aurally palpable in the contrapuntal use of sound as well as unconventional sound bridges (a good example is Ruiz's *On Top of the Whale*, in which swells on the orchestral soundtrack stoke suspense, while the acting in the same scene is deadpan or nonchalant, or the echoing mambo jazz track in *Touch of Evil*, which is used not for entertainment but as an anempathetic backdrop for Grande's murder). It is implicit in the set design of films such as *Citizen Kane*, where classical and medieval elements are combined into a single fireplace,[29] not to mention the aesthetic hodgepodge evoked by Kane's vast art collection, and in the shifts in costume design in *Time Regained*, extending from the late nineteenth to early twentieth centuries and timed independently of the narrative timeline. The baroque also thrives on the building of expressionist (Welles) or surreal (Ruiz) elements into scenes that are otherwise phenomenally realist in style and tone. This is most skillfully done in *Citizen Kane* (the burning sled), and *Lady from Shanghai* (Grisby's unruly motorboat) and in Ruiz's *Time Regained*, with the shattered teacup scene being only one example. It thrives as well as on the use of mirrors or reflective surfaces, and noticeably unconventional camera movements. The latter are achieved through the counterintuitive editing of camera angles (breaking the 180-degree rule in *Three Crowns of the Sailor*, or the insertion of canted close-ups in the evening yacht scene in *The Lady from Shanghai*), or the narrative reliance on continuous and curvaceous panning, tilting, traveling shots, as in Welles's *Touch of Evil* and Ruiz's *Time Regained*.

At times, shifts in style are linked to shifts in cultural sensibility and temporal register. Although Welles and Ruiz were involved in making art cinema, often from literary adaptations, they also freely referenced popular culture and adopted residual techniques and technologies from the silent era (with Welles serving as partial inspiration for Ruiz).[30] These elements are often woven into a frictive interplay of cultural opposites, relativizing the "classic" or the "modern,"[31] and at times creating kinesthetic "magnets" in the mise-en-scène, which can yield absurd or darkly comic results. Such is the case of the bishop who is pursued by a flock of young novitiates as though he were a rock star in *The Suspended Vocation* (Ruiz), or the initial search for criminal evidence in *Touch of Evil*, which leads from a burlesque cabaret hosted by Zsa Zsa Gabor to a candy bar and a pianola repeating antiquated tunes at the brothel owned by Tania (Marlene Dietrich), their real-life stardom offset by the tawdriness of their characters. A magnifying glass can be used to defamiliarize or confuse the subjects in photographs (*Time Regained*), or to bring us uncomfortably close to a flea circus performed on the Professor's (Mischa Auer) forearm in *Mr. Arkadin*, in marked contrast to the use of wide angles and tracking shots in these films.

Less obvious, but equally important, is the manner in which the baroque is closely tied to various types or registers of melancholia. For example, there is the melancholia that is linked to loss experienced by the characters (of homeland for the sailor in *Three Crowns*, of a way of life in *The Magnificent Ambersons*), but also that which results from the loss of "nation" (both directors had been involved in national politics prior to leaving for Europe), loss of a working method and framework that was disrupted by exile, and continued to be disrupted as the directors respectively entered into an interstitial mode of production.[32] As Denilson Lopes has observed, "Melancholy is not simply a vague sadness or prostration, fruit of amorous disillusionment, of any type of psychological problem. Its gentle force originates in the perception of the passage of time, of the ruins that are accumulating, even in the history of sentiments."[33] In other words, unlike nostalgia, melancholy signals an awareness of loss even as affective attachment to the lost object continues: the regretful, allegorical speech of Lucy (Anne Baxter) to her father, Eugene, in *The Magnificent Ambersons* about Georgie Amberson's drift away from his community, and her.[34] Welles's avoidance of nostalgia for the past in this film is facilitated by the fact that he does not depict the agrarian era of the Midwest, with its class divisions, political clientelism, strict gender norms, and social ostracism, in an entirely sympathetic light. The entitlements that Georgie (Tim Holt) associates with his privilege are precisely the social traits that will be challenged by, and somewhat superseded in, the turn-of-the-century modern age. For Ruiz, the avoidance of nostalgia, and corresponding lapses into melancholia, are critical to maintaining political honesty and realism in representations of exile; melancholia also permits the exploration of aesthetic idioms other than those of verisimilitude and naturalism.

One of the narrative correlates of neobaroque melancholia is the inscription and articulation of tensions and fusions among temporalities, which can—and does—take the form of an evanescent line, even a conversation between, the living and the dead in the films of Ruiz and Welles. This occurs in Ruiz's *Three Crowns of the Sailor*, which is narrated by a ghost, his *Memories of Appearances*, which brings the dead back to "life" through an exercise in mnemonic and cinematic remembrance,[35] and Hilton Edwards's (heavily guided by Welles) *Return to Glennascaul* (1951), in which a young Irishman (Michael Laurence) whose car has stalled on the highway is received at the home of a mother and daughter of his grandmother's time (Shela Richards and Helena Hughes) who are ghosts. As a presence that visibly lingers, yet is immaterial, the ghosts that haunt Welles's as well as Ruiz's films are portals into baroque melancholia, as are the shadows found throughout their mise-en-scènes. The latter are used not merely for a doppelgänger effect, following noir convention, but as a trace of a partially inaccessible past, as well as an unforeseeable diegetic future: the darkened silhouettes of Isabel (Dolores Costello) and Eugene (Joseph Cotten) in the vestibule after the homecoming ball in *Magnificent Ambersons*, or the playful shadows on the wall, reminiscent of Indonesian shadow puppets, but also indicative of the child's creative, metaphysical powers, which travel from the margin to the center of the diegesis in Ruiz's *On Top of the Whale*. Whereas the mirror provides us with a palimpsest of viewpoints within individual shots, the shadows and superimpositions of figures (in *Three Crowns of the Sailor* and *Time Regained*) help to produce a multiplicity of temporalities.

Fabrice Revault d'Allonnes has perceived "in betweenness," here facilitated by the transiting between presence and absence by way of spectral images and melancholia, as a prelude to "disnarration . . . 'tensions' or distortions between text and image; the famous 'two films in one,'"[36] that characterize Ruiz's approach to film aesthetics. For both Welles and Ruiz, the baroque (or neobaroque, historically speaking) does not just harbor passageways into memory; it is also a means of loosening the sutures in the narrative as it progresses, revealing the cyclical nature of time, the multidimensionality of narrative subjectivity.[37]

Adaptation as the Woof for the Weft of History and Memory

Je reste un tout petit peu un néorealiste.[38]

Girding the fragile boundary between the symbolic and the experiential is the explicit act of storytelling (through narration, or in conversation), which is at once the fulcrum, or root, the vessel for subject formation and remembrance, and the by-product of many of Welles's and Ruiz's films. *The root*: both directors, expert oral storytellers in their own right, took inspiration from strong storytellers (Cervantes, Tarkington, Melville, Dinesen, Kafka, Klossowski, Proust) to develop their film plots, understanding cinematic adaptation as a process of translation, transmutation, and transposition,[39] while retaining most of the characters, the lure of the plotline and inferring the presence of a literary source through voice-over narration. Rather than filter out their own ideas to subordinate theme and style to the shape of the hypotexts, they each selected stories that resonated, literally or metaphorically, with their own concerns, transforming the adaptation into an active conversation with the authors of the original. Hence the identity of both authors, literary and cinematic, is reflected in the new work.[40]

The fulcrum, the vessel: even though they both produced documentaries, Ruiz and Welles remained skeptical of the degree to which the experiential could be captured on film. On the other hand, the symbolic dimensions of film could only emerge in partnership with the historically situated spectator,[41] leaving storytelling as the most reliable and productive avenue of representation. For Ruiz and Welles, adaptation took on the function of not only testing their mettle as *auteurs*, but also serving as a kind of refuge through which it became possible to allegorize historical events and personal experiences. However, owing to the degree of fragmentation and open-ended narration in several of Welles's, and especially Ruiz's films, it is not possible to extract any latent content in one uniform sheaf: allegorization (with a small "a") is limited in duration and in scope, and it may also have more than one referent, whether personal or sociopolitical in origin. For example, *The Trial* seems to be alternately about contemporary life in the Soviet Union under the KGB and the deportation of European Jews and progressives under the Nazis: Welles shot several scenes at the abandoned Gare D'Orsay in Paris, where files and debris still remained from the occupation, which might help to explain the genuine look of dismay and anxiety on Anthony Perkins's face as he finds himself (as Joseph K.) entangled in its corridors. However, Welles would probably discourage us from limiting our interpretation to these historical regimes, pointing the vectors outward instead to include life under any kind of modern totalitarian society in which the status quo of the institution is placed above the interests and rights of the individual (Ruiz probably would have agreed.) Specific scenes in Ruiz's *The Suspended Vocation* (the interrogation and penitence) and *Time Regained* (Proust's meeting with Morel [Vincent Perez] in an enclosed space after the latter has defected from the French army, the blood-stained bed resulting from the sadism of de Charlus [John Malkovich]) point to the torture and hiding of political prisoners following the 1973 Chilean coup d'état, even though the plotlines correspond to Francophone films ostensibly set in Europe. Thus, Welles and Ruiz were able to create narrative content that remains relevant to audiences that can relate to their concerns, while appealing to a broad audience versed in western European literature. *By-products*: the episodic, at times personal nature of the allegory (as contrasted with "national" allegories elsewhere in Latin American or French cinema), and the general unsuturing of the narrative as a result of baroque construction, especially in Ruiz's films, invites viewers to draw their own conclusions. In the course of interpretation, we are able to plug our own story into the unease or pathos of the characters, the half conversations or unspoken events that we only catch a glimpse of at the edge of the diegesis.

This viewing dynamic complements, rather than precludes, the kind of spectatorial realism with a "Bazinian premise," so celebrated in Welles, that stems from the stylistic maximization of available architecture, available light, and nonprofessional actors. That is, deep focus shots and long takes in their films are capable of momentarily eliciting contemplative engagement informed by the spectator's recognition—and impression—of the real. In this respect, it is worth noting that Welles was the more "authenticist" of the two, while Ruiz cultivated voyeurism beyond what is stoked by the hallway conversations of Welles's *Magnificent Ambersons*, the crane shots in *Touch of Evil*, or the speedboat scene in *The Lady from Shanghai*. Nevertheless, both insisted on a measure of intersubjectivity through the transfer of focalization from one character to the next, thereby offsetting the omniscience of voice-over narration and impeding the unwavering centering of narration around the most socially powerful characters.

The Oneiric, the Fabular, and the Performative Body: Points of Contrast

The cure for anything is salt water: sweat, tears, or the sea.[42]

As a last exercise, I would like to briefly compare Welles's and Ruiz's adaptation of short stories by Isak Dinesen (Karen Blixen) in *Histoire immortelle/The Immortal Story* (FR, 1968) and *Three Crowns of the Sailor*, respectively, which were produced over a decade apart. There are uncanny resemblances in plot and theme between these adaptations, even though there are important stylistic differences, and neither adaptation can be traced to just one of Blixen's stories. Set in Macao, yet shot mostly in Spain, *The Immortal Story* is a medium-length film using minimal sets and cast. It narrates the story of a French woman, Virginie (Jeanne Moreau), whose father's fortune, life, and house were laid waste by an American, Mr. Clay (Welles), who has come to take economic (and it is implied, political) control of the island. Clay is assisted in this endeavor by his accountant, Levinsky (Roger Coggio), who uses Clay's last ambition to see a fabular prophecy actually come to life, as a means of distributing part of his fortune to Virginie, so that she may buy her freedom from prostitution, and to an unwitting Danish sailor, Paul (Norman Eshley), who has become stranded in the port. As a condition for the compensation, Paul and Virginie must mate, and Virginie bear the offspring, thereby providing Clay not only with voyeuristic pleasure but also the progeny he lacks. In an ironic twist, Clay expires before the plan comes to fruition, and Paul has fallen in love with Virginie, yet the lovers separate, and Paul, in an act of moral rectification and in defense of pure love, refuses to tell the story.

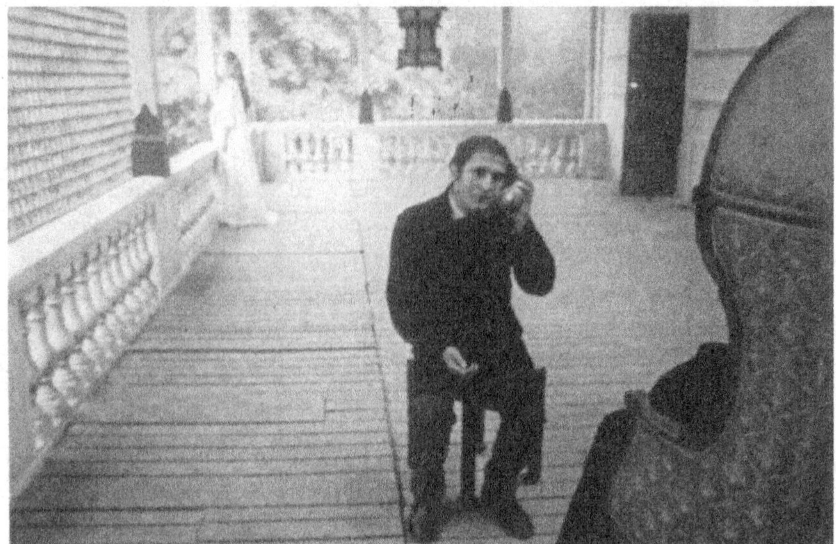

Frame enlargement from *The Immortal Story*, dir. Orson Welles, 1968.

Ruiz's adaptation, *Three Crowns of the Sailor*, is considerably more complex in narrative structure and aesthetic tone than *The Immortal Story*, which, as a "minor" film, is depicted in straightforward, linear fashion even though Virginie, Paul, and Levinsky narrate their pasts in flashback as diegetic interlocutors in the present. Ruiz's version provides us with an extended flashback in a story told by a sailor (Jean-Bernard Guillard) in need of three Danish crowns that he owes a boat captain, stretching from his departure from Valparaíso, Chile, to his eventual demise in Europe after winning the freedom of his lover, a young prostitute (Nadège Clair), and bringing his mother and "son" (an aging Asian man who looks like a child) to live with him in France. They are the original "three" missing pieces of the sailor's life. The sailor's interlocutor, and the voice-over narrator at the beginning of the film, is a young Polish student, who, in Freudian fashion, has just killed his mentor and taken money to travel on a ship when he meets the sailor and urges the sailor to tell his story and get him aboard a ship before helping him out with three crowns (one of which has to be wrenched from the fist of his dead mentor). The film has a bloody ending before the student is able to board the ship and tell the story.

Both films contain elements of more than one story written by Dinesen: "The Dreamers," from *Seven Gothic Tales* (1934), involves an opera singer, Pellegrina Leon, who travels with an older Jewish man and a male servant (whom Welles has conflated as the accountant Levinsky), while "The Young Man and the Carnation" and "The Sailor-Boy's Tale," from *Winter's Tales* (1942), involve the search for love, the transformation of loved ones upon return ("The Young Man"), and a sailor protagonist. The ambiguity in the adaptations allows each director to explore themes that are personally meaningful to them (for Welles, the tyranny of greedy individuals, for Ruiz, transatlantic migration, and through circumnavigation, a portrayal of merchant marine life at sea), as well as allegorize larger conflicts. Both directors use the quotation from the "Book of Isaiah" (Levinsky recites this for Clay in *The Immortal Story*, the ungrateful student finds a written version in the opening scene of *Three Crowns*) that portends destruction. Even though Welles averts the destruction of all but Clay in *The Immortal Story*, it is not difficult to see in the ragged sailor an image of a US soldier exhausted from combat in Vietnam, or in the sailor's narrative in Ruiz's film the story of exiled Chileans unable to return, or of the massacre that took place in Ruiz's birthplace, Puerto Montt, in 1969 (the sailor returns to Valparaíso to find a ghost town), and the World War II Holocaust, which is referenced in both films. The differences, both obvious and subtle, between these films are indicative of philosophical differences in the directors' approach to representing the past. Briefly, Ruiz is able to give much freer rein to the oneiric dimension in the sailor's tale (such that the content and appearance of people and objects in the mise-en-scène reach surreal proportions), whereas Welles chooses to avoid representing the "fantastic" aspects of the sailors' legend related by Levinsky, opting for evenly lit (or at most, chiaroscuro) realist scenes. This difference might be rooted in the fact that Welles, as a radio host, actor, and theatrical director, was more attached to verbal language than Ruiz, who invested a great deal of narrative energy in the image. Still, Ruiz embarks on explorations of the fantastic in the Todorovian sense, such that surrealism (in the mise-en-scène, in dialogue or character-based narration) never transports us entirely (as, for example, in Hollywoodian sci-fi) into an imaginary universe.[43] Both directors give us a foothold in the real despite the apparent self-containment of the adaptation, with one (Ruiz) pursuing the psychoanalytic and the other (Welles) emphasizing the phenomenal. A second difference involves the treatment of the performative body. Ruiz incorporates many images of abjection, of the grotesque, or the freakish, including the androgynous dancer the sailor chooses to pursue his "happiness." Through the oneiric in combination with casting and bodily representation, Ruiz bends the boundaries of gender difference in *Three Crowns*, just as he pursues the topic of homosexual desire in *Time Regained*. Welles chooses to use his own body as an object of aversion in *The Immortal Story*, much as he did in *Touch of Evil* and *The Trial*, which can only produce ambivalence in a spectator trained to engage in what Anne Friedberg has called "extra-cinematic identification" with Welles's off-screen or cross-platform persona, as contrasted with the "villains" that he plays on screen.[44]

Notes on Exilic Production and Transnational Authorship

On est tous des éxilés. C'est un des premiers effets de la globalization.[45]

Sadly, even though their geographical itineraries coincided briefly in Paris in the mid-1970s, Welles's and Ruiz's paths probably didn't cross enough to permit a Parisian conversation owing mainly to a gap in circumstances and artistic habitus: Ruiz, fresh off the boat and based in Belleville, was attempting to get support for the Chilean community and his own film projects, as depicted in the introspective *Dialogues of Exiles*; Welles, lodged at the Georges V hotel, was shooting and editing *F for Fake* in collaboration with French documentary filmmaker and art collector François Reichenbach, while struggling to get his last massive project, *The Other Side of the Wind*, back on track. A few years later, he would return to shoot a few scenes for the ironically self-reflexive and melancholic revisitation of the early 1950s production of *Othello* in *Filming Othello*. He was also trying to produce, without success, an adaptation of Shakespeare's *King Lear* in France, around the time that Ruiz was working on *Three Crowns of the Sailor* and *La ville des pirates/City of Pirates* (FR/PT, 1983). In an ultimate twist of irony, Ruiz offered, by way of a mutual acquaintance, to facilitate, thanks to his own working relationship with the French Ministry of Culture and the INA, access to production soundstages in Paris for Welles's project; however, it is unknown whether Welles ever responded to this offer.[46]

There are important differences in circumstance that brought them to Paris: Welles's initial departure from the States was largely self-imposed, whereas Ruiz was part of a diaspora of Chilean émigrés seeking to escape imprisonment or death at the hands of the military dictatorship.[47] These contrasts led to differences in approach to the "interstitial mode of production" (Naficy) that each of them encountered in exile: Ruiz had little trouble, after initial hardship, in securing support through France's INA and Antenne 2 for his films, as France was his adoptive country of residence, and this provided the material basis in his films for transculturalism across the Atlantic. Welles struggled to obtain private backing for his projects, sporadically achieved thanks to his collaborators and the symbolic capital of his public persona. Despite his conflicts with and departures from the mold of Hollywood filmmaking, it was still a foundational experience (Welles learned basic découpage from John Ford's *Stagecoach*), and he still sought a largely Anglophone audience despite the transnational character of his exilic projects. That is to say, there is a trace of the hegemonic in Welles's cultural discourse, and a bit more of the iconoclastic in that of Ruiz, who cut his teeth on Cinema Nôvo and the French New Wave. While neither director shied away from the excess that accompanies the baroque, Ruiz (following Buñuel) was willing to cultivate the abject to the point of alienating the viewer.

These differences in circumstance and strategy lead us to delve further into the origins of, and directions taken by, the transnational in the oeuvre of Welles and Ruiz, neither fitting easily into the "cosmopolitan" or "auteurist" definitions of transnationalism described by Mette Hjort.[48] What both Ruiz and Welles accomplished was an ability to work *through* (rather than simply assimilate into) the transnational in their insistence on developing nonconformist approaches to making films while remaining consistent with their creative methods and concerns. Upon closer scrutiny, it is possible to see how, through their mobile authorship and efforts at adaptation, national cinema could be and has been sustained by a "transnationality that overflows and unfolds across all borders,"[49] especially when it is nourished by an attention to memory and place. Whereas Ruiz bore a greater *social* burden of representation given his participation in an exilic diaspora, Welles bore the baggage of having apprenticed in one of the largest industrial apparatuses in film history. The greater edge given to the surreal, the blurring of the reality/fantasy boundary in Ruiz's films might very well be linked to the double conditions of exile, along with an interest in psychoanalysis and the creative freedom allowed by INA as a producing organization. In addition to its capacity for representing a general "epistemological crisis" that Ruiz encountered in the wake of the Chilean coup, as Bliss Cua Lim has observed, the "fantastic," here taking the form of the surreal or the fabular, might help one to find "an appropriate way of knowing and of taking one's bearings when the certainties that govern the known, familiar world suddenly appear limited or questionable."[50] This is especially illustrated in *Memories of Appearances*.

Finally, thanks to a difference in generation, as well as in personality, Ruiz appears to have been able to live more easily with technical imperfections and other "flaws" or shortcuts associated with "minor" cinema. Welles never ceased to lament the constraints imposed by others who held the institutional—and purse—strings, "I've got problems with my distributor," he puns when his car breaks down in *Return to Glennascaul*. Ruiz, on the other hand, gave a philosophical answer to the question of whether imperfection resulted from "choice" or "circumstance": that his films were most often the product of an effort to adapt to and accommodate the inevitable unpredictable, and that he (as a quasi-surrealist at heart), fully embraced this challenge.[51] One would do well in either case to avoid literal, or teleological, readings, and to appreciate instead the multi-strandedness and spiraling vectors of their films and career trajectories.

Notes

1. Exceptions for Ruiz include some of the essays in Helen Bandis, Adrian Martin, and Grant McDonald, eds., *Raúl Ruiz: Images of Passage* (Melbourne, Australia: Rouge Press; Rotterdam: International Film Festival Rotterdam, 2004), and Miguel Marías, "El futuro de Raúl Ruiz," in *Raúl Ruiz*, ed. Miguel Marías, Adrian Martin, Jonathan Rosenbaum, François Margolin, Jorge Arriagada, and Andrés Claro (Madrid: Cátedra/Filmoteca Española, 2012), 7–70.

2. Arguably, most if not all "art cinema" is globally oriented in that it is the product and the beneficiary of the transnational circulation of aesthetic and political discourse linked to the post–World War II flow of films into and out of Europe and Asia. However, not all "art cinema" can be said to speak to a global constituency through either hybrid, multilingual constructions (as is the case for Ruiz, and occasionally, Welles) or the search for a language and configuration of screen space that can transcend the national (just shy of a hegemonic commercial form that might be termed Euro or Asian, and more recently, Latin "pudding").

3. See for example Richard Peña, "Images of Exile: Two Films by Raoul [*sic*] Ruiz," in *Reviewing Histories: Selections from New Latin American Cinema*, ed. Coco Fusco (Buffalo, NY: Hallwalls Contemporary Arts Center, 1987), 136–38; and Zuzana M. Pick, *The New Latin American Cinema: A Continental Project* (Austin: University of Texas Press, 1993), 23, 161, 176–85. On the gradual distanciation of Ruiz from Latin American–focused cinema, see Peña, "Images of Exile," 138–39.

4. David MacDougall, *Transcultural Cinema* (Princeton, NJ: Princeton University Press, 1998), 231. Cf. Raymond Bellour on cinema as a "memory-screen," in Raymond Bellour and Guy Rosalato, "Dialogue: Remembering (This Memory of) a Film," trans. Thomas Y. Levin, in *Psychoanalysis and Cinema*, ed. E. Ann Kaplan (New York: Routledge, 1990), 211.

5. See Fabrice Revault d'Allonnes, "Pour R. R., il y a réel et réel," in Christine Buci-Glucksmann and Fabrice Revault d'Allonnes, *Raoul Ruiz* (Paris: Dis Voir, 1987), 76–81.

6. For the contemporary impact of Ruiz's cinema and cultural politics, see Andreea Marinescu, "The Dream of Memory in Raúl Ruiz's *Memories of Appearances: Life Is a Dream*," *Framework* 55, no. 1 (2014): 9.

7. The ethical notion of empowering the spectator, cultivating their "free will" to decipher the filmic image, is aligned with Bazin's theory of realism, as delineated

in his cinemark essay, "L'évolution du langage cinématographique," in André Bazin, *Qu'est-ce que le cinéma?* (Paris: Les Éditions du Cerf, 1985), 63–80, especially 75–76.

8. The challenge to the spectator is what Andrew proffers as a defining characteristic of art cinema: "Purportedly outside the system, they must teach us how to deal with them. . . . The effort they demand of spectators to learn a new system, one suitable for a single film, places the film outside standard cinema where it may be either ignored or given special, even lasting, attention." In Dudley Andrew, *Film in the Aura of Art* (Princeton, NJ: Princeton University Press, 1984), 6.

9. This is particularly the case in Francophone criticism; see, for example, Buci-Glucksmann and Revault d'Allonnes, *Raoul Ruiz*, 11, 52, 74.

10. Raúl Ruiz, personal conversation with the author, October 1996.

11. Welles was awarded the Chevalier d'Honneur in 1982; Ruiz was able to obtain support for his projects through Institut national de l'audiovisuel (INA) in France.

12. For an explanation of "open discourse" as a category of film narration, see Richard Neupert, *The End: Narrative and Closure in the Cinema* (Detroit: Wayne State University Press, 1995), 111–33.

13. A distinction needs to be made between "allegory" with a small "a" and "national Allegory" with a capital "A," as elaborated upon below.

14. Denilson Lopes, *Nós os Mortos: Melancolia e Neo-Barroco* (Rio de Janeiro: Sette Letras, 1999), 14; my translation from the Portuguese.

15. For Ruiz's own comments on Proust, see Raúl Ruiz, "À Propos du *Temps retrouvé*," in *Raoul Ruiz: Entretiens*, ed. Jacinto Lagueira (Paris: Éditions Hoëbeke, 1999), 79–80; for Carné, see Pascal Bonitzer and Serge Toubiana, "Entretien," in Lagueira, *Raoul Ruiz: Entretiens*, 15; for Mürnau, see Michel Ciment, Hugo Niogret, and Paulo Antônio Paranaguá, "Entretien," in Lagueira, *Raoul Ruiz: Entretiens*, 49–50; for Proust and the cinema, see Sara Danius, *The Senses of Modernism: Technology, Perception, and Aesthetics* (Ithaca, NY: Cornell University Press, 2002), 95–107, 117–21.

16. Ruiz said that he had not yet seen *Mr. Arkadin* at the time he scripted and directed *Three Crowns of the Sailor*, but was struck by the resemblance between the two films; in Bonitzer and Toubiana, "Entretien," 15.

17. The Yaghanes were a hunting-gathering tribe inhabiting the steppes of Patagonia; see the 1989 interview with Raúl Ruiz in this volume.

18. See Marinescu, "Dream of Memory," 10–11, 25.

19. See Catherine L. Benamou, *It's All True: Orson Welles's Pan-American Odyssey* (Berkeley: University of California Press, 2007), 86–119, 167–72, 206–10, for Welles's use of neorealist techniques in the unfinished *It's All True*, especially in the Brazilian episodes.

20. Gregg Toland, "Realism for *Citizen Kane*," *American Cinematographer* (February 1941), reprinted in *American Cinematographer* 72, no. 8 (1991): 37, 39.

21. Ruiz's use of ceilings, echoing that of Welles's, is most obvious in films such as *The Suspended Vocation* and *Three Crowns of the Sailor*.

22. See Jacques Lacan, "The Mirror Stage as Formative of the I as Revealed in Psychoanalytic Experience," in his *Écrits*, trans. Alan Sheridan (New York: W. W. Norton, 1997), 1–7.

23. Again, here, and elsewhere in this film, a possible nod to Lacan, "From the outset, we see, in the dialectic of the eye and the gaze, that there is no coincidence, but, on the contrary, a lure. When, in love, I solicit a look, what is profoundly unsatisfying and always missing is that—*You never look at me from the place from which I see you.*" Jacques Lacan, *The Four Fundamental Concepts of Psychoanalysis*, ed. Jacques-Alain Miller, trans. Alan Sheridan (New York: W. W. Norton, 1978), 102–3.

24. For more on the complexity of the play of viewpoints in Ruiz's work, see Christine Buci-Glucksmann, "L'œil baroque de la caméra," in Buci-Glucksmann and Revault d'Allonnes, *Raoul Ruiz*, 25.

25. Raúl Ruiz, "Miroirs du cinéma," in Lagueira, *Raoul Ruiz*, 67.

26. Buci-Glucksmann, "L'œil baroque de la caméra," 11.

27. On this latter point, see Lopes, *Nós os Mortos*, 9; and Ismail Xavier, *Allegories of Underdevelopment: Aesthetics and Politics in Modern Brazilian Cinema* (Minneapolis: University of Minnesota Press, 1997), 16–28.

28. See Claudio España, "Emergencia y tensiones en el cine argentino de los años cincuenta," *Nuevo Texto Crítico* 21/22 (January/February 1998): 53.

29. See Robert L. Carringer, *The Making of Citizen Kane* (Berkeley: University of California Press, 1996), 60.

30. For the combination of "literate" and "popular" culture in Ruiz, see Jacinto Lagueira, "Présentation: Cinéma majeur et mineur," in Lagueira, *Raoul Ruiz, Entretiens*, 9; for multiple time frames and baroque construction in *Citizen Kane*, see Lopes, *Nós os Mortos*, 34–36; for these components in Ruiz's films, see Revault d'Allonnes, "Pour R. R.," 74.

31. On Ruiz's search for an alternative beyond the "classical" or "modern" in cinema, see interview with Fabrice Revault-d'Allonnes, cited in Buci-Glucksmann and Revault d'Allonnes, *Raoul Ruiz*, 57 and 69.

32. According to Hamid Naficy, this mode corresponds to filmmaking that is undertaken outside the confines of a national, state-driven or commercial industry; see Naficy, *An Accented Cinema: Exilic and Diasporic Filmmaking* (Princeton, NJ: Princeton University Press, 2001), 40–62.

33. Lopes, *Nós os Mortos*, 15.

34. For more on the distinction between nostalgia and melancholia, see Celeste Olaquiaga, *The Artificial Kingdom* (New York: Pantheon Books, 1998), 68–76.

35. See Marinescu, "Dream of Memory," 10–13.

36. Revault d'Allonnes, "Pour R. R.," 65. My translation from the French.

37. Andreea Marinescu mentions the "de-suturing" of the (political) subject in Ruiz's *Memories of Appearances: Life Is a Dream*; Marinescu, "Dream of Memory," 7.

38. "I am still just a little bit neorealist." Raúl Ruiz, in Bonitzer and Toubiana, "Entretien," 19.

39. See Robert Stam, "Beyond Fidelity: The Dialogics of Adaptation," in *Critical Visions in Film Theory*, ed. Timothy Corrigan and Patricia White with Meta Mazaj (Boston: Bedford/St. Martins, 2011), 549.

40. By contrast, for a concise description of how adaptation was commonly achieved in the golden age of the Hollywood industry, see Hortense Powdermaker, quoted in Imelda Whelehan, "Adaptations: The Contemporary Dilemmas," in

Adaptations: From Text to Screen, Screen to Text, ed. Deborah Cartmell and Imelda Whelehan (New York: Routledge, 1999), 7. See also Stam, "Beyond Fidelity," 547–50.

41. For Welles on this point, see Orson Welles and Peter Bogdanovich, *This Is Orson Welles*, ed. Jonathan Rosenbaum (New York: Da Capo Press, 1995), 82.

42. Originally in Isak Dinesen [Karen Blixen], "The Deluge at Norderney," *Seven Gothic Tales* (New York: Harrison Smith and Robert Haas, 1934), 39.

43. For Todorov, see Bliss Cua Lim, *Translating Time: Cinema, the Fantastic, and Temporal Critique* (Durham, NC: Duke University Press, 2009), 102. For Ruiz's approach to the baroque and surrealism, see Laleen Jayamanne, *Toward Cinema and Its Double: Cross-Cultural Mimesis* (Bloomington: Indiana University Press, 2001), 161–78, especially 171.

44. Anne E. Friedberg, "A Denial of Difference: Theories of Cinematic Identification," in *Psychoanalysis and the Cinema*, ed. Ann E. Kaplan (New York: Routledge, 1990), 42.

45. "We are all exiles. It's one of the first effects of globalization." Raúl Ruiz, in an interview by Jérôme Prieur in *Un voyage fantastique*, dir. Jérôme Prieur (2006) on a DVD of *Three Crowns of the Sailor* (Facets Video, 2006). Translation by author.

46. Bill (William) Krohn to Orson Welles, TLS, 1981, Welles-Kodar Collection, Orson Welles Manuscripts, Special Collections Library, University of Michigan, Ann Arbor.

47. For an excellent overview of the Chilean exilic experience, see Thomas C. Wright and Rody Oñate Zúñiga, "Chilean Political Exile," *Latin American Perspectives* 34, no. 4 (2007): 31–49.

48. Mette Hjort, "On the Plurality of Cinematic Transnationalism," in *World Cinemas: Transnational Perspectives*, ed. Nataša Ďuričová and Kathleen Newman (New York: Routledge, 2010), 20–24.

49. Ana M. López, "Historia nacional, historia transnacional," in *Horizontes del segundo siglo*, ed. Julianne Burton-Carvajal, Patricia Torres, and Ángel Miquel (Guadalajara: Universidad de Guadalajara; Mexico City: Instituto Mexicano de Cinematografía, 1998), 81.

50. Lim, *Translating Time*, 102.

51. See Raúl Ruiz, interview with the author, December 1989, in this volume.

Filming Vienna 1900

The Poetics of Cinema and the Politics of Ornament
in Raúl Ruiz's *Klimt*

Janet Stewart

"The Café Central," observed Alfred Polgar in 1926, "lies on the Viennese latitude at the meridian of loneliness. Its inhabitants are, for the most part, people whose hatred of their fellow human beings is as fierce as their longing for people, who want to be alone but need companionship for it."[1] This evocative description aligns the famous Viennese coffeehouse with the modern metropolis itself, the inhabitants of which, as Georg Simmel pointed out in his 1903 lecture on "The Metropolis and Mental Life," cultivated an attitude of outer reserve that masked a general aversion toward others.[2] The Café Central, of course, was one of a number of prime locations of modernity in metropolitan Vienna around 1900, providing a meeting place and performance space for poets, artists, musicians, theorists, and others. This being the case, it is hardly surprising that when the prolific Chilean film director, film theorist, and artist Raúl Ruiz set out to make a feature film focusing on Gustav Klimt—*Klimt* (AT/FR/DE/UK, 2006)—he would assign to the Café Central a prominent supporting role. Ruiz's apparently predictable choice of location feeds into one of two main criticisms commonly leveled at his film: that it does little more than rehearse well-worn clichés about Klimt and his Vienna. While this suggests that Ruiz was guilty of producing a work that is unsurprising and unoriginal, another school of thought declares itself critical of Ruiz's commitment to "art-house" cinema. Writing in the *Sunday Times*, for example, Cosmo Landesmann criticizes the film for being "unnecessarily difficult to follow."[3] This chapter sets out to counter these paradoxical

Originally published in the *Journal of Austrian Studies* 46, no. 2 (2013): 49–79. Reprinted with permission from the journal editors.

claims, arguing that far from remaining in thrall to what Marjorie Perloff calls "seductive Vienna,"[4] Ruiz's *Klimt* offers a sophisticated attempt to translate aspects of the visual art theory of the period around 1900 into cinematic form. Recognizing this allows us to read the film alongside Ruiz's *Poetics of Cinema*, his unorthodox two-volume work of film theory, and so to counter the reductive suggestion that the film is willfully obtuse by demonstrating its contribution to wider debates on the politics of film aesthetics.[5]

Ruiz's Vienna: Filming the Art World

Approaching *Klimt* in this way allows us to understand Ruiz's decision to locate parts of the action in the Café Central not as a reiteration of the "tourist gaze" but as representative of the film's commitment to engage creatively with visual art theory of the early twentieth century. The Café Central, then, stands in for the institution of the coffeehouse, which was one of a number of representative sites of urban modernity Walter Benjamin presented in his unfinished *Arcades Project*.[6] Many such sites are found in *Klimt*; in addition to the coffeehouse, key locations include the exhibition site, the clinic, and the art gallery.[7] The modernity of these spaces—and therefore, as I shall argue, their interest to Ruiz—lies, in part at least, in their embodiment of the new way of understanding space and spatial relations being theorized by August Schmarsow and others around 1900, which was predicated on the productive dissonance between the experiential dimension of architecture as a phenomenon to be perceived by bodies in motion and the cognitive dimension of architecture as an entity to be gazed upon from a fixed and distanced perspective.[8]

Alois Riegl drew upon these ideas in his *Spätrömische Kunstindustrie/ Late Roman Art Industry* (1901) to make the distinction between optic and haptic vision that was later to be taken up by so productively by influential thinkers including Walter Benjamin, Gilles Deleuze, and Félix Guattari.[9] Optic visuality, according to Riegl, provides a distant view, taking in "a synoptic survey of objects in space," while haptic perception centers on near vision; it is analogous to "the sense of touch in the way that it must synthesize mentally a number of discontinuous sensory inputs."[10] While Riegl employed new understandings of the experience of space to develop a theoretical account of art history, architects, artists, filmmakers, and others were producing artworks that engaged with similar ideas. As Massimo Cacciari perceptively argues with reference to the work of the Viennese architect and cultural critic, Adolf Loos, the dissonance between lived experience and the distanced gaze, between haptic and optic perception, expressed itself in a struggle between interior and exterior, in the "endless contradiction between the thought-out space of calculation, the equivalence of exteriors, and the possibility of place, the hope of a place."[11] In Loos's work, this "exterior-interior relationship" was played out at the interface between exterior and interior, at the level of the surface.

Loos, of course, is best known as the author of "Ornament und Verbrechen"/"Ornament and Crime," his polemical contribution to debates about the status of the modern ornament, and indeed it is in this context that Ruiz first introduces him in *Klimt*.[12] The Café Central provides Ruiz with the ideal setting to stage a programmatic confrontation between Klimt and Loos, which begins with Loos delivering a set piece, explaining his thoughts on "Ornament and Crime" with reference to a mirror. He invites members of his audience to look into the mirror, urging them to acknowledge its use value. He then asks them to recognize that the frame's only purpose is to give "pointless, unproductive work to craftsmen." He concludes: "The frame is useless, therefore inexpressive. The mirror is useful, therefore functional, therefore expressive and therefore beautiful." Klimt's response to Loos is composed and emphatic. He slowly and deliberately rubs his slice of cake in Loos's face, telling him, as he does so: "What you were just saying was merely ornamental. Therefore it's useless and therefore it's ugly. However, this cake has allowed me to shut your mouth. Therefore it's useful, it's expressive and, above all, it's beautiful." Loos replies with dignity, "You I forgive, Herr Klimt, because at least all your paintings are sexual, as all art should be." On hearing this, Klimt produces his handkerchief and carefully wipes the cake from Loos's face, apologizing as he does so.

This scene serves the diegetic function of establishing the identity and artistic disposition of two central figures in the Viennese art world around 1900. At the same time, however, the staged encounter also offers the attentive viewer a clue to understanding Ruiz's cinematic engagement with Klimt's Vienna. The seminal cultural histories that sought to construct "Vienna 1900" as an object of study—most notably, Carl Schorske's *Fin-de-Siècle Vienna* and Allan Janik and Stephen Toulmin's *Wittgenstein's Vienna*—were inflected by the concerns of their own time and by their particular research interests: historiography for Schorske, the philosophy of language for Janik and Toulmin.[13] Just as Schorske was a historian reflecting upon the writing of history, so Ruiz was a filmmaker who writes about the possibilities of the cinematic form. *Klimt* offers him a vehicle through which he can demonstrate the relevance, for his "poetics of cinema," of the important debates about ornament, space, and surface taking place in Vienna's art world in the late nineteenth and early twentieth century.

What did Ruiz understand by the "poetics of cinema?" This is not a simple question to answer, for although deceptively short, his *Poetics of Cinema* is a work that defies easy categorization. Proceeding in poetic fashion allows Ruiz to retain his focus on a series of relations that, he proposes, make up any film: relations between "the visible and hidden events, the implicit and the explicit, the explicable and the inexplicable."[14] His thinking about these sets of relations is guided by three "intuitions or metaphors," each of which suggests connections between his thinking and directions in contemporary film theory. The first of these accords the image priority over narrative as a structuring device, which is, of course, a central theme for Gilles Deleuze as he develops his writing on cinema's capacity to transform thought; the second, refracting work by Paolo Cherchi Usai on the materiality of film and the death of cinema, makes a claim for cinema being "decomposed" by a given set of shots, rather than composed of them; while the third aligns itself with phenomenological approaches, such as that offered by Vivian Sobchack, to suggest that aesthetic validity is dependent on the film "view[ing] the spectator as much as the spectator views the film."[15] Where Ruiz departs from existing theoretical positions is in his approach; often anecdotal, always elliptical, it draws upon a range of sources that go far beyond the canon of film theory while remaining rooted in his practice of filmmaking.

Early twentieth-century Vienna presents him with some of these sources, and is also a site that he renders cinematic through his practice. In line with his thinking in *Poetics of Cinema* on the nature of history as "*terra incognita*" (in the sense that Paul Valéry employed the term) Ruiz appears to have identified Vienna 1900 as a time in which, "there are still things to be explored."[16] The kind of exploration he has in mind here is indebted to Benjamin, whose writings are referenced throughout the *Poetics of Cinema*, invoking the work of memory to reject notions of linear time in favor of the productivity of discovering new constellations of events and ideas. Ruiz's return to Vienna around 1900, then, is not the result of a seductive nostalgia, but a productive repetition that draws knowingly upon the twin logic of fascination and detachment that, he argues, is a central formal aspect of cinema.[17]

Klimt takes up these ideas most obviously in its structure, which is derived from the act of remembering Vienna around 1900. The film begins in the sterile if rather surreal environment of a clinic, following Egon Schiele as he goes to visit Klimt on his deathbed, in the throes of advanced syphilis. This provides the framing narrative for the series of loosely connected memories that transport the viewer back to early twentieth-century Vienna, and to the considerable controversy pertaining to the reception of Klimt's *Fakultätsbilder/*

Faculty Paintings, a set of large-scale murals that he had been commissioned to produce for the Faculties of Law, Medicine, and Philosophy at the University of Vienna.[18] Rather than following a clear narrative trajectory, Klimt's memories of this period are linked visually through the double trope of mirror and water, which offer a set of "memory-images." Here, as in earlier major works directed by Ruiz, such as *Mémoire des apparences: La vie est un songe/Memory of Appearances: Life Is a Dream* (FR, 1986) and *Le temps retrouvé/Time Regained* (FR/IT/PT, 1999), Ruiz shows an explicit concern with memory-images, which are accessed through a fragmented or even suspended narrative.[19] While in *Time Regained,* Ruiz engages with Proust's literary reflections on memory, in *Klimt,* the examination of memory is given credence by embedding it in the discoveries and artistic techniques of Klimt's age, allowing Ruiz to engage with ideas gleaned from Sigmund Freud and Arthur Schnitzler, among others. As Ruiz tells us in the second volume of *Poetics of Cinema,* the "actual film is called *Klimt, a Viennese fantasy in the manner of Schnitzler*"[20] and indeed, in Ruiz's film, Klimt's wanderings through a series of key interior-exterior spaces of early twentieth-century Vienna and Paris, framed through a number of devices that question the boundary between the real and the imaginary, owe no small debt to the spatial practices of navigating Vienna that Schnitzler constructed in his *Traumnovelle* of 1926.

In addition to modeling itself formally upon Schnitzler's fictional work, *Klimt* demonstrates extensive knowledge of the "art world" of Vienna around 1900 and of the struggles among competing visions of "the modern" that defined that world. Setting out not merely to film art but also to reconstruct a particular art world on celluloid, the film foregrounds a large number of important voices in these debates, including Hermann Bahr, Emilie Flögge, Egon Friedell, Friedrich Jodl, Oskar Kokoschka, Alois Riegl, Egon Schiele, Franz Wickhoff, and Bertha Zuckerkandl, as well as Loos and Klimt. The manner in which these characters are identified in the film can appear clumsy and without diegetic justification, as in the scene where a waiter in the Café Central is called upon to identify a series of characters, in response to one of his colleagues repeatedly asking: "And who is that?" Yet I would argue that this "hyperrealism" is not accidental; it serves to offer an example of what Ruiz calls the "excess of faithfulness" through which an artist can "distort an original work."[21] Through this device, paradoxically, Ruiz is able to distance *Klimt* effectively from the standard "heritage film."[22] As we will see, rather than presenting the past as pastiche, Ruiz's film draws together history and theory, casting the art world of early twentieth-century Vienna as the source and repository of materials through which he can articulate a set of reflections on the "poetics of cinema."

Ornament

Prominent among the "materials" that Ruiz draws upon is ornament, a recurrent and contested concept in artistic circles around 1900. The most striking visuals employed in the film are highly ornamental, and at first glance appear rather predictable, owing much to a conventional rendition of Klimt's work. In one scene, for example, set in Klimt's studio, the artist is seen at work with gold leaf in a space bathed in golden sunlight. A slammed door releases a shower of gold leaf into the room, which rains down on Klimt and his half-completed canvases. Yet there is more to this scene than a representation of Klimt's so-called golden phase. Before the door slams, Klimt is engaged in conversation with "Midi" (Emilie Flögge, his long-term partner). As they talk, we see only Klimt's mirror image against a background of golden art nouveau ornament, while Midi's body provides a projection screen for the art nouveau patterning that clads the wall behind her. Here we see Ruiz playing with the relationship between painting and cinema as he elucidates it in the first volume of his *Poetics of Cinema* with reference to Shih-T'ao's eighteenth-century enumeration of six central techniques of Chinese painting. One of these techniques involves making the background dynamic and drawing attention toward it,[23] an effect that Ruiz achieves here by blurring the boundary between body and surface, and by setting the art nouveau patterning in motion.

The film's main aesthetic concern, of course, is with art nouveau, and the form of ornament presented in this scene appears throughout the film, in paintings and textiles of all kinds, but the film does not limit its engagement with ornament to the way in which it was taken up and used in the work of the Viennese Secession. The bugbear of the Secession movement, nineteenth-century historicism and its forms of ornamentation, are also referenced here, both in the sumptuous bourgeois interiors frequented by Klimt and in the playful reproduction in cake form of the monumental Ringstrasse, the buildings of which Loos castigated as a "Potemkin City" in an article of the same name published in 1898 in *Ver Sacrum*, the journal of the Secession. Loos's critique of false ornamentation articulated in this piece was part of his ongoing crusade against ornament in all forms of culture, including food. In "Ornament and Crime," for example, Loos states his preference for plain roast beef, instead of the opulent stuffed "peacocks, pheasants, and lobsters" that characterized the "show dishes of past centuries."[24] Ruiz's decision to cast the buildings of the Ringstrasse in cake form, then, is an indirect allusion to Loos's writings, suggesting that the film's engagement with his work might go beyond the initial staged encounter between Klimt and

Loos. Notwithstanding the alignment between these figures that encounter seems to offer, the film's sustained engagement with "Ornament and Crime," as we shall see, actually functions to rethink the import of Klimtian ornament through the critical perspective offered by Loos's essay.[25]

In "Ornament and Crime," Loos draws together a number of disparate threads, including reference to Socrates, Voltaire, and Beethoven, the tattooed people of Papua New Guinea, Goethe's use of language, and the uniform of the Austro-Hungarian infantry, in order to offer a set of reflections that would connect wider debates on ornament to his concern to shape the nature of the modern and define "modern man." Drawing on insights offered by the then prevalent doctrine of Social Darwinism, Loos sought to demonstrate that a process of cultural evolution would see ornament lose its relevance for modern design, a move that was entirely in line with economic rationalization of the kind diagnosed at the time by Max Weber and others. In focusing on ornament, Loos's essay was embedded in two related fields of debate: first, an ongoing debate on ornament, which was being carried out in the early twentieth century in the nascent fields of art history and architectural history, in work by writers such as Riegl, Joseph August Lux, and Herman Muthesius; and second, in wider anthropological, cultural historical, and sociological accounts of ornamentation, as seen in works by Max Nordau, Caesaro Lombroso, Ernst Haeckel, and others. Loos's essay, in which he "attempted to settle scores . . . and speak the final word in the ornament debate" came relatively late to these discussions.[26] Although his essay may have allowed him to settle some scores, the ornament debate was far from closed after its publication. Instead, "Ornament and Crime" provided the catalyst for further discussion. Ruiz's return to the question of ornament a century after Loos had presented his ideas to audiences across central Europe performs a kind of Nietzschean repetition, restoring the possibility of what was, rendering it possible anew. Rather than simply continuing the debate on ornament on its own terms, or regarding it as a closed historical phenomenon to be recounted, Ruiz reactivates the textual images from which Loos's argument proceeds, translating them into filmic images in order, finally, to employ them as an elaboration of his contribution to film theory.[27]

Loos's essay opens with a particularly arresting set of images. In line with Ernst Haeckel's then popular "recapitulation theory," the essay establishes a rhetorical link between phylogenetic and ontogenetic development, connecting the perceived developmental "gap" between the "tattooed natives of Papua New Guinea" and "modern man" with the gap between the child and the adult.[28] In both cases, the development in question is characterized by increasing self-awareness, or, as Loos would have it, morality. Regarding the gap in this fashion allows him to maintain that: "A child is amoral. A Papuan too, for us."[29] He then proceeds to establish connections between arrested cultural development and ornament, and between ornament and sexuality, encapsulated in his claim that "all art is erotic."[30]

The constellation of art, sexuality, gender, and race that Loos presents in the first three paragraphs of "Ornament and Crime" is reflected in *Klimt* in two main ways. First, the film historicizes these ideas, seeking out events that would allow them to be visualized within the economy of the film in its fidelity to the cultural and intellectual history of Vienna around 1900; second, however, the film also defamiliarizes Loos's ideas through the use of cinematic devices, placing them in the new constellation of Ruiz's *Poetics of Cinema*. Although Ruiz claims that the point of *Klimt* is to shed light on "certain aspects of Viennese life and . . . certain particularities of its social life,"[31] in the film we actually find something more than this. Ruiz accepts the entry point that Loos's essay offers into the filmic reconstruction of patterns of misogyny and colonialism around 1900, but as we shall see, also develops his cinematic response in a different direction, as he takes up the challenge of thinking about ornament in a set of related theoretical contexts: spatiality and "surface effects," reproducibility, and optic and haptic vision.

Spatiality and "Surface Effects"

In "Ornament and Crime" Loos qualifies his critical claim that "all art is erotic" with the observation that the cross was the first erotic ornament. He justifies this comment with reference to spatial relations, arguing that the cross's vertical axis stands for the man, who penetrates the reclining woman, represented by the horizontal axis.[32] Significantly, Ruiz chooses to dwell on this image in his staging of Loos's essay. The confrontation between Klimt and Loos, described at the outset of this chapter, takes place against the backdrop of a leaded glass window that creates the illusion of a row of crucifixes. The climax of the exchange comes when Loos states that all art should be sexual and then poses the rhetorical question: "The crucifixion, for example, now what could be more sexual than the crucifixion?" The misogynistic overtones of the image of active man and passive woman offered by Loos in "Ornament and Crime" and reiterated in Ruiz's *Klimt* are redolent of an attitude prevalent in Vienna around 1900. It is this worldview, for example, that permeates works such as *Geschlecht und Character*, Otto Weininger's influential diatribe against feminism, in which he contends that "man possesses sexual organs, her sexual organs possess woman."[33] And it is this worldview that gave rise to a general dismissal of ornament as not only degenerate but also resolutely feminine.[34]

Loos, as Hal Foster argues, shares this perspective, which, Foster claims, offers him the basis from which to articulate a modernism based on the domination of the "phallic order."[35] Yet this is not Loos's last word on the subject. While the tenor of his writings does not accord with Ruiz's characterization of him as an art critic responding approvingly to Klimt's erotic use of ornament, neither do his arguments suggest a stance that is simply against ornament. Instead, Loos's critique functions in part by attempting to construct an alternative to the penetrative ornament of the cross. In his architectural work, as Hélène Furján points out, ornament is linked not to depth, but to surface, a position that allowed him to respond critically to both historicism and art nouveau:

> Loosian ornament was no longer the attached supplement of classical ornament, or the figural additions of the Secessionists, an ornament applied to the surfaces of a building. It was instead an ornament that could no longer be detached from the surface it was to adorn: it had *become* the surface.[36]

Furján does not draw out the gendered dimension of this stance, but this becomes apparent if we regard Loos's equation of ornament with surface as a rejection of the cross as penetrative ornament. Since the cross is representative of existing gender relations, the ornament as surface can be read as a critique of the status quo. And indeed, even as they continue to underscore uneven gender relations, Loos's writings also offer glimpses of an opening up to the possibility of alternative constellations.[37]

Like Loos, Ruiz is drawn to exploring the tension between depth and surface as a way of visualizing and criticizing social relations, but while Loos's creative medium was architectural surfaces, Ruiz works with the projection screen. In *Klimt*, the physical meeting of the central protagonist with Lea de Castro is preceded by a screened encounter, in which Klimt, apparently, is confronted with filmic evidence of his relationship with a mysterious and attractive young woman. This presentation of "documentary evidence" takes place during Klimt's visit to the Paris 1900 exhibition and is soon revealed to be a filmic illusion, constructed for the occasion by none other than the pioneering French filmmaker, Georges Méliès.[38] Later, we see Klimt engaging in penetrative relations with de Castro, and later still, we observe him attempting to touch her, but instead, only being able to lay his hand upon a projected image on the surface of a cinema screen. Having this relationship begin and end as a projection, and indeed, having it exist in the economy of the film as the projection of the mind of a dying man, allows Ruiz to suggest the primacy of surface over depth. In this way, he can question the penetrative logic of early film that, according to Ella Shohat, is both the product and depiction of the gendered and colonial perspectives that informed knowledge construction around 1900. Her description of Freud's epistemology holds also for the work of Weininger, or indeed, Loos's description of the cross as ornament; all assume "the (white) male as the bearer of knowledge, one who can penetrate woman and text, while she, as a remote region, will let herself be explored till truth is uncovered."[39] The conflation of misogyny and colonialism identified here, Shohat points out, is also typical of early film; in Méliès's *Le voyage dans la lune/A Trip to the Moon* (FR, 1902), for example, "the 'last frontier' to be explored is first seen in the rocket's phallic penetration of the rounded moon."[40]

In *Klimt*, Ruiz addresses these connections among early twentieth-century epistemology, cultural production, and colonialism, displaying colonial culture through the presentation of a "cannibal show" ostensibly as part of the 1900 Paris Exposition. Here, he reconstructs the practice of staging popular anthropological shows (*Völkerschauen*), which was prevalent throughout Europe around 1900.[41] His foregrounding of the figure of the "cannibal" also offers another allusion to "Ornament and Crime," in which Loos invokes the otherness of the Papuan, for him the very epitome of premodern man, by describing him as one who "slaughters his enemies and devours them."[42] While Loos sought to reify the distinction between modern Western man and premodern cannibal, however, Ruiz sets out to question the essentialist underpinnings of this view. He does this, primarily, by foregrounding spatial relations.

The scene begins with an exterior shot of the building in which the "cannibals" are on display, with the camera placed behind a fence to produce the effect of looking out from behind the bars of a cage.[43] Over a soundtrack that mimics the disjunctive sounds of Schoenberg's twelve-tone music, a voice states "cannibals here." As it does so, the camera pans down the fence to reveal Klimt standing in the shadows looking off screen at something lying beyond the fence, before he turns to mount the steps and enter the building. The scene then cuts to the interior of the building, with the camera located at the bottom of a set of steps. It takes up a position next to the caged "cannibals," gazing upward at the visitors descending to take in the central attraction of the mini-exhibition that also includes display cases and information panels. As the visitors are exhorted in French, German, and English to "not touch the cannibals," the camera pans around to reveal the cage and its inhabitants, then tracks around the exterior perimeter of the cage, its gaze trained toward the inside, until it meets Klimt who has been approaching the cage from the opposite side. As Klimt moves toward the cage, the attendant indicates how dangerous it is to get too close, and the Schoenbergian soundtrack reiterates this threat. Ignoring these comments, Klimt appraises two of the "cannibals" at close range, both of whom meet his gaze with the same curiosity that he displays. This encounter appears to offer a moment of recognition, signaled by a change in the music from the discordant to the melodic. The camera then cuts away from this encounter to take up a position within the cage; moving through the cage's interior, it monitors the behavior of the visitors outside. As it does so, the whir of a film projector can be heard that, it is then revealed, has been set up just outside the cage. Here, Ruiz references Eadweard Muybridge's pioneering work on *Animal Locomotion* by projecting a film of moving horses onto a screen suspended in the middle of the room.[44] More than merely reminding the viewer of a particular historical phenomenon that witnessed the construction of human zoos and ethnographic shows in the name of scientific progress, this scene, by spatializing relations between self and other and placing the projected image in the museum/exhibition display space, serves to comment on cinema's own complicity in displaying otherness to the Western spectator in a way that produces and reproduces colonial structures. Ruiz's film provides critical commentary on the way in which cinema "transform[ed] the initially unknown *mappa mundi*, through its popularizing mimetic apparatus, into a comprehensible and palpable world."[45] It does so through the simple device of highlighting the relationship between exterior and interior by shifting the perspective from the Western viewpoint (outside the cage looking in) to the viewpoint of the Other (inside looking out) and so demonstrating the constructedness of perception, and its dependence on spatial relations. This revelation is compounded by having Klimt and the "cannibals" each gaze upon the face of the Other.

Reproducibility: Copying and Coupling

In this initial encounter with the "cannibals," Klimt remains on the outside of the cage looking in, while the camera takes up a position inside the cage. In the next scene, however, he finds himself cast in a role akin to that of the cannibal, as the object of another's gaze. Apparently captured on film by Méliès, Klimt ostensibly encounters himself on show in the Paris exhibition, alongside his own artistic work. Méliès, whose filmography, as Shohat notes, included a number of films related to colonial explorations, including *Le*

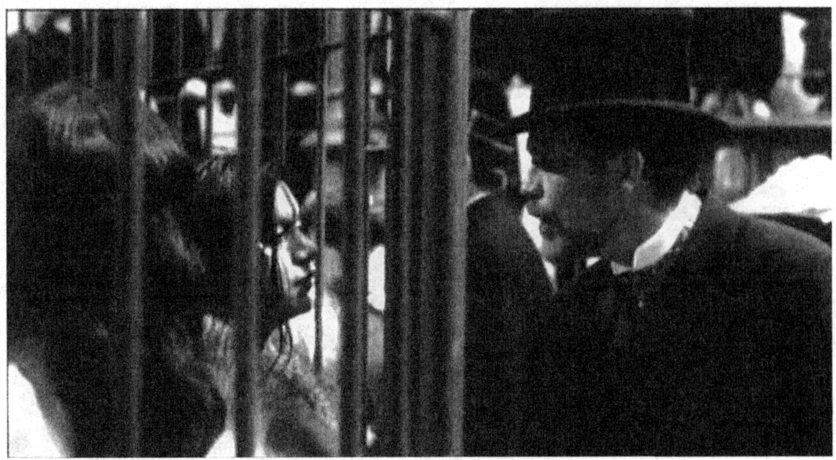

Klimt and the caged "cannibals" gaze upon one another in *Klimt*.

fakir, mystére indien (1896), *Vente d'esclaves au harem* (1897), *Cleopatre/Cleo-patra's Tomb* (1899), *La fontaine sacrée ou la vengeance de Bouddha/The Sacred Fountain* (1901), *Les aventures de Robinson Crusoé/Robinson Crusoe* (1902), and *Le palais des milles et une nuits/The Palace of Arabian Nights* (1905), con-structs Klimt as research object, placing him in the context of those late nineteenth-century technological developments that allowed for what Jean-Louis Comolli terms the "geographic extension of the field of the visible."[46] The connection between Klimt and the geographic Other is clearly suggested in Ruiz's film: the first time that Klimt appears on screen within the film is in the scene discussed above, where his encounter with the Other in the shape of caged cannibals gives way to an uncanny encounter with the Self as Other.

Observing the film of running horses projected on the screen beside the cannibals, the spectator is aware of the shadows of a number of visitors cast on the screen, before Klimt emerges from behind it to engage in conversa-tion with a young girl. When she leaves, he stands up in front of the screen, hesitantly reaching out to touch it and apparently, in so doing, casting his shadow upon it. Almost immediately, however, it becomes clear that this is not his shadow, but instead that of the elusive figure who appears through-out the film as Klimt's double, engaging him in discussion and commenting upon his actions. Klimt greets the figure with an ambiguous, "you again," suggesting both recognition and distance. And indeed, this is not the first time that Klimt has encountered this figure. Their initial point of contact comes in an early scene in the Café Central, as Klimt excuses himself briefly

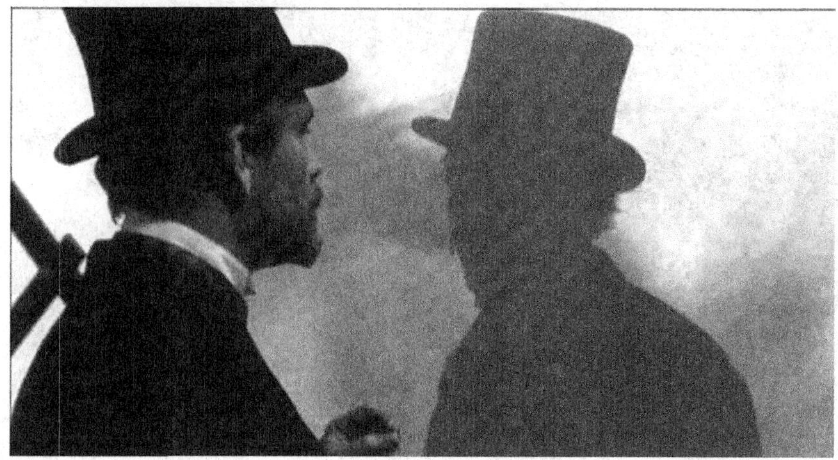

Klimt encounters the Minister as a shadow on screen in *Klimt*.

from a group of intellectuals and artists engaged in heated discussion about modern art. The figure appears as a reflection in a mirror in front of which Klimt is standing. The mirror then shatters, offering us a view of Klimt on his deathbed, the shadowy figure in his hospital room with him, before returning to the previous timeframe. On their second meeting, the figure introduces himself as "secretary to the consular service of the Austrian embassy . . . third secretary." On their next meeting, where he appears casting his shadow on the screen, he whispers to Klimt, "I am your shadow," after mocking Klimt's wonder at the film projection: "Oh, don't tell me you've never seen an electric theater show."

It is perhaps inevitable that a film indebted to Schnitzler and Freud, and invoking Méliès, would take up the idea of the uncanny. *Klimt* does so, not only by confronting the central protagonist with his doppelgänger in the shape of the minister, but also through the device of filming film itself. Intimately connected to the figure of the doppelgänger, the filming of film itself, as the media theorist Friedrich Kittler (who, like Ruiz, was fascinated by the cultural history of early cinema) points out, demonstrates "what happens to people who are in the line of fire of technological media."[47] Ruiz shows this by having Klimt react with fear and horror to being confronted with his own image on film. Here, Klimt is expressing the fear of being in the eye of the other that is famously described by Freud in his essay on "The Uncanny."

Yet Ruiz's use of the device of doubling goes beyond reiteration of the Freudian uncanny to focus instead on the "inventiveness of copying," a theme upon which he expounds at length in his writing.[48] In his chapter on "Images of Images," he extends the discussion of doubling to a wider set of reflections on reproduction, taking up his commentary on Walter Benjamin's essay, "The Work of Art in the Age of Its Technological Reproducibility"[49] and contextualizing it, in typical Ruiz style, with reference to Antonio Tabucchi, Canaletto's Warsaw paintings, Thomas Aquinas, Auguste Blanqui, George the Monk, André Breton, Friedrich Nietzsche, Aby Warburg, and others. Ruiz begins by taking the reader through various imaginary examples of copying through processes of enlarging details of a particular work, discussing various ways in which an "excess of faithfulness can distort an original work."[50] Here, he is covering similar ground to that discussed in Benjamin's reflections in "The Task of the Translator,"[51] transposing that discussion to the realm of the image. And indeed, as Ruiz's argument progresses, this connection becomes ever clearer. Toward the end of the chapter, he employs a long anecdote centering on the trajectory of a fifteenth-century painting produced by a blind painter dictating a system of numbers to his disciples in order to "mak[e] it plausible that every image is but the image of an image, that it is translatable through all possible codes, and that this process can only culminate in new codes generating new images, themselves generative and attractive."[52] Ruiz's emphasis on the "translatability" of the image reveals his debt to Benjamin, as does his insight that the process of translation has at its core the production of "new codes generating new images," for Benjamin's essay foregrounds the creativity of translation in breaking down the "decayed barriers of [its] own language" in order to extend its expressive possibilities.[53] Meanwhile, Ruiz's description of "every image [being] but the image of an image" might be read productively alongside Benjamin's claim for an ideal pure language, a "predestined, hitherto inaccessible realm of reconciliation and fulfillment of languages."[54] Translation, maintains Benjamin, signals the direction to be taken if such an ideal is to be realized. In this reading, the "but" in Ruiz's claim ("every image is *but* the image of an image") is suggestive of an ineluctable, as yet unattainable "pure image," akin to the idea of the "never-seen" that cinema might reveal, as discussed in "For a Shamanic Cinema."[55]

In *Klimt*, Ruiz explores the idea that every image is already but an image of an image through the technique of film filming film itself. The film of Klimt that Méliès presents for the edification of the assembled guests at the Paris exhibition is offered to the viewer in the form of an image of an image, a film of a film. The viewer is then challenged to make sense of these images through processes of translation. They could be read in terms of Ruiz's reiteration of the uncanny, but they could equally be grasped through taking up Ruiz's fascination with film history and early film, or indeed understood as commentary upon his own reflection on reproduction and the "inevitable association" that he sees between copying and coupling.[56] Méliès's film apparently offers evidence of Klimt's liaison with a beautiful young woman, only for it to become clear that the copy precedes the event; the relationship exists first on screen and is only consummated after the film has been viewed. In this example, the physical relationship itself might be regarded through the prism of translation as the manifestation of a "new code" that generates new images. This "new code," this manifestation of the relationship between copying and coupling, is itself imbricated in a set of reflections on the gaze as a structure of control.

Optic and Haptic Visuality

Throughout *Klimt*, when sexuality is put on display through the depiction of the act of coupling, the camera often takes up the gaze of a third party, and so reproduction becomes associated with the question of the voyeuristic gaze and the imposition of the structures of control that operate through processes of seeing and being seen. These, of course, are the same structures of control that are encapsulated in the iconography of the cage (which gestures toward Max Weber's comments on the control mechanisms of modern rationalized bureaucracy).[57] They are also the structures of control that shaped other sites of modernity that appear in *Klimt*, such as the asylum, a form of building designed, as Foucault points out, for the containment of madness and the irrational. It is, then, perhaps not surprising to find that the first instance of coupling observed in Klimt takes place in the asylum. As Schiele goes to visit Klimt on his deathbed, he stops to watch a copulating couple, the man having discarded his prosthetic limb before engaging in the sexual act.[58] Similarly, Klimt's sexual relations with the two Lea de Castros (the "real" one and the "false" one) are viewed through the device of the two-way mirror, while Schiele's voyeurism, which he recognizes with hysterical laughter, appears accidental and remains fleeting; for those watching Klimt, the voyeurism is thoroughly premeditated. Both instances, however, are markedly de-eroticized.

The lack of eroticization in the staging of these encounters is tied to the way in which the couples under observation find themselves the object of quasi-scientific surveillance, viewed from the distanced perspective of optical vision. In this way, Ruiz draws attention to the role of cinema and other forms of technologized vision in controlling and conditioning new bodies, and in containing the irrational, again suggesting connections between Ruiz's evocation of early cinema and Kittler's approach to the subject.[59] Ruiz takes up the theme of control and containment from the outset of the film, which opens with a view of Klimt's *Medizin/Medicine* (1901–7), which was exhibited to great controversy at the tenth exhibition of the Secession in 1901, with its critics denouncing its presentation of pathological bodies.[60] Maintaining this thematic, the film's opening sequence cuts from the pathological figures depicted in *Medizin* to the sanitized environment of the modern clinic, where a white-coated doctor is seen at work, sitting at a desk stamping what at first appear to be pieces of paper, but are then revealed to be photographs of near-naked pathological bodies. As the camera looks over the doctor's shoulder, he picks up a magnifying glass and examines the photograph in front of him, which shows a one-legged man leaning back on a desk, the muscles on his remaining leg bulging, while his stump is pulled upward by means of a rope. In connecting these photographs to the iconography of *Medizin* through the juxtaposition of painting and photography, Ruiz could be simply reiterating Klimt scholarship, which suggests that he painted his portraits from photographs.[61] But more importantly, he is also constructing a connection to artistic work on changing forms of perception enabled by Muybridge's artistic and scientific photographic work, which had been published in 1872 and, as Marlowe-Storkovich points out, was used by professors at the Vienna Academy of Fine Arts in their teaching.[62]

In *Animal Locomotion*, Muybridge also examined the movements of "abnormal bodies"; as well as amputees, he also studied people suffering from conditions such as epilepsy or hydrocephalus.[63] Similarly, other scientific photographers were becoming interested in the insight afforded through photography into nervous disorders. Work of this kind was carried out at the Salpêtrière in Paris by Jean-Martin Charcot and his associates and published in journals such as *Iconographie photographique de la Salpêtrière* (1876–80) and its successor, the *Nouvelle iconographie de la Salpêtrière: Clinique des maladies du systéme nerveux* (1888–1918). Gemma Blackshaw connects the vitriol to which Klimt's *Medicine* was subjected in reviews to the early twentieth-century's desire to understand "madness" through images, arguing that "such criticisms brilliantly—though unwittingly—underline the aims of the Salpêtrière's *NIS* [*Nouvelle iconographie de la Salpêtrière*] journal: to highlight the invasion of pathology into art, and art into the imaging of pathology."[64] In other words, what was seen here was a belief in the close connection between art and detection, a relation that Kittler takes up with specific reference to cinema in his investigation into film and madness.[65] "Madness," he

133

tells us, "is cinematographic not only in motoric and physiognomic terms; cinema implements its psychic mechanisms itself."[66]

The question of the relationship between art and detection is one that Ruiz found enthralling; *L' hypothèse du tableau volé/The Hypothesis of the Stolen Painting* (FR, 1979), for example, had already seen him combine elements of the detective film and the art documentary.[67] In *Klimt* he develops this focus to dwell upon relations between technologized vision and forms of detection. This can be seen in the doctor's careful examination of photographs to reveal physical and mental pathologies, and in Ruiz's repetition of the doppelgänger function to reiterate cinema's role in transforming life "into a form of trace detection."[68] It can also be seen in Midi's presentation of photographic evidence that proves Klimt to have carried out the theft of his own paintings and in the use of a microscope to make visible his syphilis infection at an early stage, before the symptoms could reveal themselves to the naked eye. Uniting these examples of the relations between technologized vision and detection is the idea of the camera's ability to see more than the naked eye, an idea that is taken up and developed by Benjamin in his reflections on the "optical unconscious," which are contained in his "Little History of Photography"[69] and extended in "The Work of Art in the Age of Its Technological Reproducibility."[70]

As R. L. Rutsky points out, Benjamin's discussion of the "optical unconscious" takes technologized vision beyond the realm of the purely optical vision: "Benjamin's optical unconscious is not . . . entirely 'optical'; through it, images are 'taken in' not only at an unconscious level, but also at a tactile, bodily level."[71] In *Klimt*, Ruiz takes up the challenge of depicting the dialectical relationship between optic and haptic perception, allowing Klimt to reach out and touch the screen onto which an image of his object of desire, Lea de Castro, is being projected. Here the de-eroticized forms of voyeurism depicted earlier in the film give way to an eroticized relationship with the screen. Klimt, in this scene, stands in for the spectator. We identify with him as he seeks what Laura U. Marks, in a discussion of video erotics, has described as "an embodied perception [responding] to the screen as another skin."[72] Significantly, in making this point, Marks emphasizes the importance of the surface; as well as foregrounding embodied perception, she argues, the erotic capacities of haptic visuality "push[es] the viewer's look back to the surface of the image."[73]

Admittedly, Marks is making an argument about video in particular, the "electronic texture" of which, she maintains, denies depth vision in favor of a "multiplication of surface."[74] While she sees in video a denial of depth, film might more usually be equated with depth. T. J. Clark, for example, couches the distinction between film and painting in terms of depth and surface, arguing:

> Cinema's formal raw material is depth—depth without surface, depth inhabited by bodies capturing a moving, puncturing play and fall of light which lures us always further forward and across, deeper into the illusion, never back to the plane of projection. It's not just that there is no picture surface in cinema, it's that powerful cinema depends on exorcizing even the ghost of surface, and conjuring away the picture plane as well.[75]

In Ruiz's *Klimt*, depth may not be denied, but neither, I argue, is the surface "exorcized" in the manner imagined by Clark. The film's engagement with the idea of haptic visuality ensures a space for the play of "surface effects," which we could gloss, drawing upon work by Andrew Benjamin, as that which the surface enables or produces. This claim is staked in the film's opening sequence, which involves the camera traveling across the surface of Klimt's *Medizin*, to produce a view of work based on "near vision."[76] Here, the spectator is treated to something akin to the form of embodied perception later encapsulated by Klimt reaching out to touch the projected image of Lea de Castro. The film opens with a blank screen accompanied by the sounds of lapping water. This then cuts to a panning shot of art nouveau ornament, which is gradually revealed, as the camera moves further across the painting, to be a close-up of the figure of Hygieia, the central element of Klimt's *Medizin*. Reaching Hygieia's face, the camera lingers on a close-up. Maintaining this near view, the camera rotates on its own axis, giving the illusion that the painting itself has been set in motion. After one full rotation, the camera resumes its journey over the surface of the work to reveal *Medizin*'s collection of "delirious and diseased bodies spiraling around 'the pale skeleton of Death.'"[77] The movements of the camera, then, echo central formal features of the painting itself.

As Siegfried Kracauer pointed out, tilting and panning have long been integral to the filming of artworks,[78] but the technique of the camera circulating together with the objects or figures upon which it is trained is less common in the filming of art. This is a method employed by Ruiz at a number of points in *Klimt*, such as in the coffeehouse scene in which Klimt encounters Loos. Here, Ruiz makes use of a mobile camera to emphasize the kinesthetic perception of space called for by early twentieth-century architectural theorists such as August Schmarsow and rendered tangible at that time in the architectural experiments of innovators such as Oskar Strnad

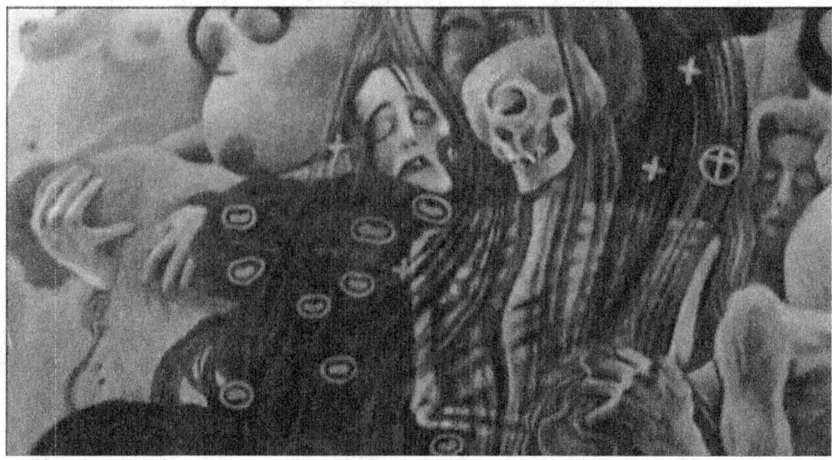

Medizin, as filmed by Ruiz, showing details of "pathological bodies" in *Klimt*.

and Friedrich Kiesler, who sought to bring movement to the audience's experience of the theater.[79] As part of the International Exhibition of New Theatre Techniques held in Vienna in 1924, Kiesler developed the concept of a "Railway-Theater," which, he suggested, might employ the technology of the roller coaster to set both the stage and the auditorium in motion, allowing the audience to experience the theatrical effect of space and speed for themselves.[80] A cartoon commentary upon Kiesler's design by L. Tuzynsky that appeared in *Der Goetz von Berlichingen* in 1924 bearing the motto, "Everything turns—everything moves,"[81] sought to depict the dizzying effects of his planned construction. Something similar to the sense of vertigo depicted here is induced in the spectator of the coffeehouse scene in *Klimt*, and is also invoked at other points in the film, emphasizing the experience of moving through other elements of the filmscape, including the exhibition site, the art gallery, and the clinic.

Ruiz's method here can be illuminated with reference to the "principles of cinematography" discussed in his manifesto "For a Shamanic Cinema," which he develops with reference to the writings of Shih-T'ao, an eighteenth-century Chinese painter. Three of the six ways of dealing with the visible world suggested by Shih-T'ao concern themselves with mobility: one, alluded to earlier in this chapter, involves "mak[ing] the background dynamic and draw[ing] the attention towards it," another "entails adding scattered dynamism to immobility," while the sixth and final process "is known as vertigo. We enter the painting. The multiplicity of events becomes an organic whole to which we belong in body and in gaze."[82] Combining these processes, as Ruiz does in *Klimt*, allows him to produce a form of cinema the haptic nature of which we might seek to describe, drawing on Giuliana Bruno's work on hapticality, in terms of its "architectural itinerary related to motion and texture."[83]

"Surface Effects" and Theoretical History

In discussing the haptic nature of cinema, Bruno seeks to distinguish "motion and texture" from "flatness."[84] In Ruiz's *Klimt*, on the other hand, his cinematic engagement with "motion and texture" is combined with a fascination with "flatness" and the idea of the surface. Resisting the penetrative logic of early cinema, Ruiz's *Klimt* takes up the question of the surface of the painting, the picture plane, and its relationship to cinema and architecture. In so doing, he makes a connection between surface and motion, taking up a position that might be usefully illuminated with reference to Andrew Benjamin's reflections on the nature of "surface effects" in architecture. Drawing on the work of Loos, among others, Benjamin puts forward the argument that once the idea of surface can be distinguished analytically from the tectonic wall "instead of its being attributed a static quality, the surface will henceforth have a dynamic one."[85] He then proceeds to demonstrate the way in which this understanding of surface is important for the development of "theoretical history," which he defines as the attempt to "examine the detail of architecture's history that is guided by the attempt to discern potentiality."[86] Potentiality, he maintains, must be understood in terms of the generative rather than the representative. By this, he sets out to describe the relationship of past to present, where the past is not understood as something "simply given" to be rediscovered, but as something to be "activated by the present."[87]

Benjamin's central concern in this article, then, is to think through the relationship between architectural history and architectural theory, making a strong claim for the creativity of "theoretical history." Similarly, Ruiz's *Klimt* is a product of his ongoing concern to address the relationship between film and visual art *history* and film and visual art *theory*. His commemoration of Vienna around 1900, then, can be regarded as a work of "theoretical history" that attempts to discern the generative and critical potentiality of works produced at that time. "Theoretical history," as Andrew Benjamin employs the term, demonstrates an ambivalent relationship to the past, which is entirely in keeping with Ruiz's own thinking and theoretically-informed practice. He begins his reflections on "The Cinema: Traveling Incognito" by simultaneously denying and invoking history,[88] a stance that is also evident in *Klimt*. It is precisely this ambivalence, however, that allows him to see in Vienna around 1900 as a particular constellation of ideas and events that reveal the potentiality of his "poetics of cinema" and its central pillars of the priority of the image and the nature of spectatorship. These concerns are taken up in the dialectic of optic and haptic visuality that is explored in *Klimt*. Writing on "haptical cinema," Angela Lant observes:

> The illusion of moving photographic pictures on a plane, and the cutting of diverse spaces against one another in multishot films suggested, in its early reception, a pressing out into and back into space, a claiming of new space, a movement between haptical and optical, entailing specific interactions with a viewer. If we could document concrete contiguities between filmmakers and art theorists on this point, the place to look would be Vienna during the early decades of this century.[89]

In *Klimt*, Ruiz plays out this meeting in imaginary form, bringing together "theoretical history" and artistic production as a way of exploring the possibility of reinvigorating cinema, which he describes as currently "dead or in its death throes."[90] His encounter with Loos and Klimt, by way of Méliès, is part of his search for the "secret film,"[91] the film "traveling incognito within every film,"[92] the film "gifted with infinite polysemia,"[93] the importance of which lies in its generation of new codes based on "intuitive thinking" that (re)-assign to cinema a central role in constructing "a politics for the arts and a language of the world."[94]

At a basic thematic level, Ruiz is attracted to Klimt because of the opening that his struggles offer for extended reflection on the relationship between politics and aesthetics. Beyond this, however, Ruiz has constructed a work that engages with elements of Klimt's aesthetics and with early twentieth-century debates on the nature of art in order to think through ways of potentially reconceiving the relationship between politics and cinema. He does this by exploring the possibility of constructing a new cinematic language, which prioritizes image over narrative and foregrounds the existence of the embodied spectator at whom the film looks back. In his desire to discover a third way for cinema, rejecting both the mainstream and the "avant-garde," he turns to a defense of poetics and the "decorative image," which, in part, has its roots in the debates about ornament taking place in Vienna around 1900. Ruiz's *Klimt* offers extended reflection on this "politics of pretty,"[95] combining theory and practice to provide a unique perspective on current debates on the political potential of film aesthetics being played out in works by Rosalind Galt and others.

Notes

1. Christoph Grafe and Franziska Bollerey, eds., *Cafes and Bars: The Architecture of Public Display* (New York: Routledge, 2007), 91–93.

2. Georg Simmel, "The Metropolis and Mental Life," in *Georg Simmel on Individuality and Social Forms*, ed. Donald N. Levine (Chicago: University of Chicago Press, 1971), 324–39.

3. Cosmo Landesman, "Klimt," *Sunday Times* (London), June 3, 2007.

4. Marjorie Perloff, "Seductive Vienna," *Modernism/modernity* 10, no. 2 (2003): 221.

5. This chapter refers to the director's cut of *Klimt*, available on DVD, rather than the shorter commercial release.

6. Walter Benjamin, *The Arcades Project*, trans. Howard Eiland and Kevin McLaughlin (Cambridge, MA: Harvard University Press, 1999).

7. The coffeehouse, the art gallery, and the exhibition site are locations explored by Benjamin in his extensive investigation of the modernity contained in his unfinished *Passagenwerk/Arcades Project*. On the relation of such sites to cinematic history, see Anne Friedberg, *Window Shopping: Cinema and the Postmodern* (Berkeley: University of California Press, 1993), 47–94. In *Madness and Civilization*, Michel Foucault devotes time to considering the asylum as a site of modernity (London: Routledge, 2001), 229–64. For a discussion of the asylum in early twentieth-century Vienna, see also Nicola Imrie and Leslie Topp, "Modernity Follows Madness? Viennese Architecture for Mental Illness and Nervous Disorders," in *Madness and Modernity*, ed. Gemma Blackshaw and Leslie Topp (Farnham, UK: Lund Humphries, 2009), 76–99.

8. On Schmarsow's theory of space in the context of German architectural theory around 1900, see Mitchell M. Schwarzer, *German Architectural Theory and the Search for Modern Identity* (Cambridge: Cambridge University Press, 1995).

9. Alois Riegl, *Die Spätrömische Kunstindustrie* (Vienna: Verlag der Kaiserlich-Königlichen Hof- und Staatsdruckerei, 1901). Benjamin draws upon Riegl's concept of haptic perception in "The Work of Art in the Age of Its Technological Reproducibility" (*Selected Writings, Vol. 3*, 101–33) and elsewhere. For an overview of Benjamin's use of art history, including Riegl, see Thomas Levin, "Walter Benjamin and the Theory of Art History," *October* 47 (1988): 77–83. See Margaret Iversen's *Alois Riegl: Art History and Theory* (Cambridge, MA: MIT Press, 1993), 16–17, and Angela Dalle Vacche, ed., *The Visual Turn: Classical Film Theory and Art History* (New Brunswick, NJ: Rutgers University Press, 2002), for commentary upon Benjamin and Riegl in the context of film theory. Gilles Deleuze and Félix Guattari take up Riegl's concepts of the haptic and optic as a way of explaining their distinction between the nomadic space of thought and the striated space of state power in *A Thousand Plateaus: Capitalism and Schizophrenia* (London: Continuum, 2004), 543–51.

10. Margaret Iversen, *Alois Riegl: Art History and Theory* (Cambridge, MA: MIT Press, 1993), 9.

11. Massimo Cacciari, *Architecture and Nihilism: On the Philosophy of Modern Architecture*, trans. S. Sartarelli (New Haven, CT: Yale University Press, 1993), 172.

12. Adolf Loos, "Ornament and Crime," in *Ornament and Crime: Selected Essays*, ed. Adolf Opel, trans. Michael Mitchell (Riverside, CA: Ariadne Press, 1998),

167–76. "Ornament and Crime" existed first only in the form of a public lecture, first given around 1908. It was not published in any form until 1913, when it appeared in abridged French translation in *Cahiers d'Aujourd'hui*. It was subsequently published in its entirety, again in French, by Le Corbusier in the second issue of his journal *L'Esprit Nouveau* in 1920, but did not appear in German until 1929, when it was published in the leading German broadsheet, the *Frankfurter Zeitung*. For a detailed account of the article's genesis and publishing history, see Christopher Long, "The Origins and Context of Adolf Loos's 'Ornament and Crime,'" *Journal of the Society of Architectural Historians* 68, no. 2 (2009): 200–223.

13. See Carl Schorske, *Fin-de-Siècle Vienna: Politics and Culture* (New York: Vintage Books, 1981), and Allan Janik and Stephen Toulmin, *Wittgenstein's Vienna* (New York: Simon and Schuster, 1973). For an overview of cultural and intellectual histories of Vienna 1900, see Allan Janik, "Vienna 1900 Revisited: Paradigms and Problems," in *Rethinking Vienna 1900*, ed. Steven Beller (New York: Berghahn, 2001), 27–56.

14. Raúl Ruiz, *Poetics of Cinema 2*, trans. Carlos Morreo (Paris: Dis Voir, 2007), 11.

15. Ruiz, *Poetics of Cinema 2*, 10. See Vivian Sobchak, *The Address of the Eye: A Phenomenology of Film Experience* (Princeton, NJ: Princeton University Press, 1992).

16. Ruiz, *Poetics of Cinema 1*, 2nd ed., trans. Brian Holmes (Paris: Dis Voir, 2005), 54.

17. Ruiz, *Poetics of Cinema 2*, 109–11.

18. See Schorske, *Fin-de-Siècle Vienna*, 208–78.

19. Ignacio López-Vicuña, "Raúl Ruiz's 'Lost' Chilean Film: Memory and Multiplicity in *Palomita blanca*," *Studies in Hispanic Cinemas* 6, no. 2 (2009): 120.

20. Ruiz, *Poetics of Cinema 2*, 41.

21. Ibid., 44.

22. The European heritage film emerges as a genre that develops from the British heritage film. Scholars such as Higson argue that such films do little more than present the past as postmodern pastiche. See Andrew Higson, "Re-presenting the National Past: Nostalgia and Pastiche in the Heritage Film," in *British Cinema and Thatcherism: Fires Were Started*, ed. L. Friedman (London: UCL Press, 1993), 112. Others, however, have argued for their critical potential in revising the past. See Lutz Koepnick, "Reframing the Past: Heritage Cinema and the Holocaust in the 1990s," *New German Critique* 87 (2002): 56.

23. Ruiz, *Poetics of Cinema 1*, 86.

24. Editors' note: This line is missing in the 1998 translation of Loos's essay used here, but can be found in Loos, "Ornament and Crime," in Ulrich Conrads, *Programs and Manifestos on Twentieth-Century Architecture*, trans. Michael Bullock (Cambridge, MA: MIT Press, 1970), 21.

25. Loos did, however, admire Klimt, as demonstrated in a sketch for his American Bar, which he had considered naming the Klimt-Bar (Adolf Loos Archive, Graphische Sammlung der Albertina, Vienna 260).

26. Long, "Origins and Context of Adolf Loos's 'Ornament and Crime,'" 218.

27. Galt offers a compelling overview of the "trajectory of the ornament from art into film" in eloquent defense of her recuperation of the pretty based on a

careful critical account of "the political imaginary of pretty films" in Rosalind Galt, *Pretty: Film and the Decorative Image* (New York: Columbia University Press, 2011). She does not, however, take up the specific example of Ruiz's *Klimt* in this work.

28. Loos, "Ornament and Crime," 167. On Haeckel's theoretical writings on Darwinism and their influence in Vienna around 1900, see Doris Byer, "Evolutionistische Anthropologien. Zur Ambivalenz eines hundertjährigen Fortschrittsparadigmas," in *Wissenschaft, Politik und Öffentlichkeit*, ed. M. G. Ash and C. H. Stifter (Vienna: WUV, 2002), 185–206.

29. Loos, "Ornament and Crime," 167.

30. Ibid., 167.

31. Ruiz, *Poetics of Cinema 2*, 41.

32. This line is missing from the version of "Ornament and Crime" published in the Frankfurter Zeitung in 1929.

33. Cited in Claude Cernuschi, *Recasting Kokoschka* (Madison, NJ: Fairleigh Dickinson University Press, 2002), 82.

34. Wagner and Dijkstra both take up the question of sexuality and the subjugation of women in Vienna around 1900 in Nike Wagner, *Geist und Geschlecht: Karl Kraus und die Erotik der Wiener Moderne* (Frankfurt am Main: Suhrkamp, 1982), and Bram Dijkstra, *Idols of Perversity: Fantasies of Feminine Evil in Fin-de-Siècle Culture* (Oxford: Oxford University Press, 1998). For an overview of Loos's view of women's fashion and female sexuality, see Janet Stewart, *Fashioning Vienna: Adolf Loos's Cultural Criticism* (London: Routledge, 2000), 112–16. On the gendered dimension of "Ornament and Crime," see also Galt, *Pretty*, 121–29.

35. Hal Foster, *Prosthetic Gods* (Cambridge, MA: MIT Press, 2004), 75–87.

36. Hélène Furján, "Dressing Down: Adolf Loos and the Politics of Ornament," *Journal of Architecture* 8, no. 1 (2003): 116.

37. Stewart, *Fashioning Vienna*, 119–24.

38. The appearance of Méliès must also be understood in the context of Ruiz's ongoing engagement with early cinema. In his film adaptation of Proust's *In Search of Lost Time*, for example, Ruiz depicts the young Proust as a film projectionist, whose face is "alternately obscured and illuminated" by images from films by Méliès, drawing a connection between Méliès's innovative filmic language and Proust's innovative writing. See Melissa Anderson, "In Search of Adaptation: Proust and Film," in *Literature and Film: A Guide to the Theory and Practice of Film Adaptation*, ed. R. Stam and A. Raengo (Oxford: Wiley-Blackwell, 2005), 105.

39. Ella Shohat, "Imaging Terra Incognita: The Disciplinary Gaze of Empire," *Public Culture* 3, no. 2 (1999): 64.

40. Ibid., 49.

41. Anne Friedberg provides detailed information on the anthropological shows that were part of the Paris 1900 exhibition, including a "Tour de Monde," which re-created Africa, South America, and Asia with dioramas and plaster reproductions in *Window Shopping: Cinema and the Postmodern* (Berkeley: University of California Press, 1993), 84. For an overview of the Völkerschau phenomenon in Europe around 1900, see Raymond Corbey, "Ethnographic Showcases, 1870–1930," *Cultural*

Anthropology 8, no. 3 (1993): 338–69. Peter Altenberg's *Ashantee* (Berlin: S. Fischer, 1897) offers a literary take on one particular Völkerschau in Vienna.

42. Loos, "Ornament and Crime," 167.

43. Although ostensibly part of the Paris 1900 exhibition, the building that Klimt enters is clearly the Burgtheater in Vienna. This is signaled in the narrative itself; that building had featured in the previous scene as part of a discussion between Klimt and his mysterious "shadow" about art, architecture and monumentality.

44. Muybridge began his experiments on "zoopraxography" in 1872, reproducing in photographic form the movements of animals and humans and setting these in motion with the help of the Zoöpraxiscope. His work gained wide recognition through the publication of sets of photographic plates under the title Animal Locomotion in 1872, through his lecturing activities in educational institutions in Europe and the United States, and through a set of public lectures given as part of the World's Columbian Exposition in Chicago, 1893 (for which a dedicated zoopraxographical hall was erected) and described in detail in Muybridge's *Descriptive Zoopraxography*. See Eadweard Muybridge, *Animal Locomotion: An Electro-Photographic Investigation of Consecutive Phases of Animal Movements* (Philadelphia: University of Pennsylvania Press, 1887).

45. Shohat, "Imaging Terra Incognita," 43.

46. Jean-Louis Comolli, "Machines of the Visible," in *The Cinematic Apparatus*, ed. Teresa de Lauretis and Steven Heath (New York: St. Martin Press, 1980), 122–23.

47. Friedrich Kittler, *Gramophone, Film, Typewriter*, trans. G. Winthrop-Young and Michael Wutz (Stanford, CA: Stanford University Press, 1999), 149.

48. Ruiz, *Poetics of Cinema 1*, 43–55.

49. Walter Benjamin, "The Work of Art in the Age of Its Technological Reproducibility," in *Selected Writings, Volume 3 (1935–1938)*, ed. Howard Eiland and Michael W. Jennings (Cambridge, MA: Harvard University Press, 2002), 101–33.

50. Ruiz, *Poetics of Cinema 1*, 44.

51. Benjamin, "The Task of the Translator," in *Selected Writings, Volume 1 (1913–1926)*, ed. Marcus Bullock and Michael W. Jennings (Cambridge, MA: Harvard University Press, 1999), 253–63.

52. Ruiz, *Poetics of Cinema 1*, 53.

53. Benjamin, "Task of the Translator," 261.

54. Ibid., 257.

55. Ruiz, *Poetics of Cinema 1*, 90.

56. Ibid., 47.

57. In *Der protestantische Ethik und der Geist des Kapitalismus* (1905; Munich: C. H. Beck, 2004), Max Weber describes machine production and mechanization as sitting on the shoulders of the individual as a "stahlhartes Gehäuse." This metaphor was mistranslated by Talcott Parsons as "iron cage," but has since, as Bhaer argues, taken on its own trajectory as a "traveling idea." See Peter Bhaer, "The 'Iron Cage' and the 'Shell as Hard as Steel': Parsons, Weber, and the *Stahlhartes Gehäuse* Metaphor in *The Protestant Ethic and The Spirit of Capitalism*," *History and Theory* 40 (2001): 168–69. It is in this latter sense that I invoke Weber here.

58. The discarding of the prosthetic limb is important in continuing the thematic of pathological bodies established from the outset of the film. It is also a reference to

Schiele's self-portraiture. On Schiele's self-portraits and the idea of the pathological body around 1900, see Gemma Blackshaw, "The Pathological Body: Modernist Strategising in Egon Schiele's Self-Portraiture," *Oxford Art Journal* 30, no. 3 (2007): 377–401.

59. Kittler, *Gramophone, Film, Typewriter*, 136.

60. Blackshaw, "Pathological Body," 399. For a detailed iconography of *Medizin*, see Tina Marlowe-Storkovich, "'Medicine' by Gustav Klimt," *Artibus et Historiae* 24, no. 47 (2003): 231–52.

61. Marlowe-Storkovich, "'Medicine' by Gustav Klimt," 238–39.

62. Ibid., 239–40.

63. Muybridge, *Animal Locomotion*, vol. 8, plates 549, 561.

64. Blackshaw, "Pathological Body," 389.

65. Kittler, *Gramophone, Film, Typewriter*, 140–75.

66. Ibid., 159.

67. See Goddard for an analysis of Ruiz's *Hypothesis of the Stolen Painting* and its reflection on the relationship between thought and image, in Michael Goddard, "Hypothesis of the Stolen Aesthetics," *Contretemps* 3 (2002): 75–84.

68. Kittler, *Gramophone, Film, Typewriter*, 150.

69. Benjamin, *Selected Writings, Vol. 2*, 507–30.

70. Benjamin, *Selected Writings, Vol. 3*, 101–33.

71. R. L. Rutsky, "Walter Benjamin and the Dispersion of Cinema," *Symploke* 15, no. 1—2 (2007): 17.

72. Laura U. Marks, *Touch: Sensuous Theory and Multisensory Media* (Minneapolis: University of Minnesota Press, 2002), 333.

73. Ibid., 333. This form of embodied perception is taken up by Marks in greater detail in *The Skin of the Film: Intercultural Cinema, Embodiment, and the Senses* (Durham, NC: Duke University Press, 2000). It also informs works such as Vivian Sobchack's *The Address of the Eye*. The phenomenological approach taken up in these texts can also be found in Ruiz's reflections on the "poetics of cinema."

74. Marks, *Touch*, 333.

75. T. J. Clark, "Malevich versus Cinema," *Threepenny Review* 93 (Spring 2003): 27.

76. Ruiz filmed a copy of *Medizin*, as the original was destroyed by fire in 1945.

77. Blackshaw, "Pathological Body," 399.

78. Siegfried Kracauer, *Theory of Film: The Redemption of Physical Reality* (1960; Princeton, NJ: Princeton University Press, 1997), 86.

79. See Oskar Strnad, "Projekt für ein Schauspielhaus," *Der Architekt* 23 (1920): 49–64, and Silke Koneffke, *Theater-Raum: Visionen und Projekte von Theaterleuten und Architekten zum anderen Aufführungsorten, 1900–1980* (Berlin: Reimer, 1999), 174.

80. Koneffke, *Theater-Raum*, 146–51.

81. "Alles dreht sich—alles bewegt sich" / "Everything turns—everything moves."

82. Ruiz, *Poetics of Cinema 1*, 86–87.

83. Giuliana Bruno, *Atlas of Emotion: Journeys in Art, Architecture, and Film* (New York: Verso, 2002), 250.

84. Ibid., 250.

85. Andrew Benjamin, "Surface Effects: Borromini, Semper, Loos," *Journal of Architecture* 11, no. 1 (2006): 7.

86. Benjamin, "Surface Effects," 31.

87. Ibid.

88. Ruiz, *Poetics of Cinema 1*, 107–8.

89. Andrea Lant, "Haptical Cinema," *October* 74 (Autumn 1995): 53.

90. Ruiz, *Poetics of Cinema 1*, 107.

91. Ibid., 109.

92. Ibid.

93. Ibid., 121.

94. Ibid., 108.

95. Galt, *Pretty*, 15–20.

Ghosts with Open Wounds

Benjamin's Photographic Unconscious and Raúl Ruiz's Spectral Turn

Sabine Doran

> We navigate on the surface: even, smooth, transparent, or opaque
> surfaces; but never level. Silence and death—explorable depth—
> cannot be expressed directly. They can only, O paradox, be trans-
> lated, exposed through the insidious bias of the opposite. Thus we
> are made to hear silence, to live death.
>
> —Edmond Jabès, Book of Margins, trans. Rosmarie Waldrop
> (Chicago: University of Chicago Press, 1993), 182

At the end of Raúl Ruiz's *Three Crowns of the Sailor/Les Trois couronnes du matelot* (FR, 1983), the student comments, "but the oozing worms, emerging from the wounds of the living dead, that was truly disgusting," thereby highlighting one of the most haunting images of the avant-garde film, that of the passage between life and death, which the sailor dramatizes in his stories about a journey on a ghostly vessel, the *Funchalense*. The horror of worms pointing at the viewer from the realm of the dead is emblematic of what one could call Ruiz's *spectral turn*, which he begins to explore in his so-called pirate films of the 1980s and which he discusses in a collection of lectures delivered at Duke University in the early 1990s (published as *Poetics of Cinema 1*),[1] in dialogue with Walter Benjamin's writings on film. Ruiz's exposition of the living dead, the undead, or "bare life,"[2] as Benjamin (and later Giorgio Agamben) called the liminal state between life and death, is part of his aim to produce "new forms of virtualities";[3] namely, a dialogue with the real in the form of "virtual countries (with real people), virtual poverty (with real paupers)."[4] Grounding the revolutionary potential of film in Benjamin's notion of the "optical unconscious," Ruiz endeavors to trace what he calls a "photographic unconscious," which ultimately engenders a "cinematographic unconscious,"[5] as we will see in our examination Ruiz's *Three Crowns of the Sailor*. In short, I seek to show how Ruiz appropriates Benjamin's reflections on technology and media in an effort to harness its political potential at a time when the vaunted "death of cinema" is proclaimed (most famously by Jean-Luc Godard)[6] in the wake of the digital revolution.

What Jacques Derrida refers to in *Specters of Marx* (1993) as "spectral effects"[7]—the intertwinement of political and media-technological developments related to "the collapse of Soviet communism and the 'revolution' in global telecommunications"[8]—is, from a cinematographic perspective, already at work in the spectral imagery of Ruiz's pirate films. These films show how the ghosts of collective histories (of imperialism, of political and social oppression)—the forgotten and repressed histories that form the collective unconscious of our mass-mediated society—reemerge, haunting our present. The revolutionary potential that Benjamin ascribed to the medium of film— stating in his famous essay "The Work of Art in the Age of Its Technological Reproducibility" (1936) that filmic techniques such as the close-up and montage tear the "prison-world" of our perception asunder "with the dynamite of the split second"[9]—is at the heart of Ruiz's reappraisal of Benjamin's "optical unconscious," a notion that implies a radical change in our perception of everyday life: "Walter Benjamin called such an overturning of basic givens 'photographic unconscious.' He believed there was a corpus of signs capable of conspiring against visual conventions, even of destroying them."[10] These conventions of mainstream cinema can be understood according to what Ruiz calls "central conflict theory": "someone wants something and someone else doesn't want them to have it." The resulting story is then "arranged around this central conflict."[11] Ruiz's resistance to this reductive conception of cinematic narrative is manifested in a cinematography of centrifugal movements, one that emphasizes the figure of the fugitive at the margins, hovering between states of being—most iconically in *Three Crowns of the Sailor*.

The first feature film in which Ruiz crosses back from his exile in France to his homeland, Chile (from which he fled in 1973), *Three Crowns of the Sailor* is a film composed of ghost stories and histories of repression, namely, those of the "vast mass of invisible men" that Ruiz discusses in reference to Giorgio Agamben's *The Coming Community* (*La comunità che viene*, 1990):[12]

> The vast mass of invisible men whom we never see, and never wish
> to see, those whom the philosopher Giorgio Agamben calls "the

community to come." These universal exiles move from one land to the next, crisscrossing the world, changing languages and centuries. Enveloping them in utopian imagery and losing them there would be the best way of imprisoning them.[13]

Ruiz's appropriation of Benjamin's "optical unconscious" (which Benjamin first mentions in his 1931 text "Little History of Photography"), is charged with the potential to return the gaze from within the margins. Ruiz's implicit dialogue with Benjamin in *Three Crowns of the Sailor* thus unfolds in inner and outer frameworks, in *scènes en abîme* endlessly folded into each other, emptying the world of its center,[14] while giving access to forms of haunting, which in Ruiz—as in Benjamin—are shaped by surrealist imagery. In what follows, I investigate how the surrealist techniques used in Ruiz's film represent a commentary on and a development of Benjaminian ideas on photography, film, and violence.

From the Optical Unconscious to the Photographic Unconscious

Indeed, the close dialogue that *Three Crowns of the Sailor* maintains with Benjamin seems to encompass a larger scope of Benjamin's work than Ruiz's reference to the "optical unconscious" first suggests, in particular its surrealist dimension (although Ruiz is as critical as Benjamin was of surrealist metaphysics).[15] For, what is encrypted in Benjamin's notion of photographically reproduced images is not an unconscious aspect heretofore unknown; rather, the visual space is interwoven with an unconscious space into a technologically permeated space, or what Benjamin calls "body-image-spaces,"[16] as he observes in his essay "Surrealism" (1929):

> Only when in technology body and image so interpenetrate that all revolutionary tension becomes bodily collective innervation, and all the bodily innervations of the collective become revolutionary discharge, has reality transcended itself to the extent demanded by the *Communist Manifesto*.[17]

As Sami Khatib emphasizes, these "innervations" are not primarily of psychoanalytical but rather of neurophysiological origin; they refer to a transfer of energy between the neurological system and the mind, or between "a collective body and an individual psyche."[18] It is through these "collective bodily innervations" in a "body-image-space" that Benjamin arrives at a notion of the "optical unconscious": the idea that photography and cinematography are, in Benjamin's view, able to record aspects of reality that cannot be seen with an "unarmed eye."[19] Benjamin writes: "It is through the camera that we first discover the optical unconscious, just as we discover the instinctual unconscious through psychoanalysis."[20] Benjamin saw the change in perception enabled though developments in technological media as a parallel to the discovery of an optical unconscious, which Benjamin approaches first of all (as Freud does with unconscious impulses) as *inscribed*.[21]

In Ruiz's hands, Benjamin's "optical unconscious" is exposed as a form of bodily inscription, which Ruiz will reflect on through the theological concept of incarnation:[22]

> But in all these incarnations of an abstraction—God, power, universal history—exactly who plays the role of consciousness, and who the unconscious? Is it not clear that Christ, the head of state, and the actor are three types of abstract photography, and that to the extent that their photographs bring the abstractions into view, they render the contours of the support structure visible in their proliferation—as though a swarm of tiny concretions (themselves the microfilms of micro-abstractions) had all begun colliding? These accidents, these extremes of photography, the corpuscular incarnations of abstraction, can be called "the photographic unconscious."[23]

Through the theological framework of an "incarnation of an abstraction," Ruiz defines the "photographic unconscious" as an alternate technique of vision, a form of carnal vision. Although the "condition of carnality," the carnality of the flesh, wounded and inscribed, "refuses formalization," as Rosalind Krauss argues in her book *The Optical Unconscious*,[24] it nevertheless proliferates in *Three Crowns of the Sailor* in forms of abstraction: in letters, color patterns, and the enigmatic three crowns. As "incarnations of an abstraction," these demand to be read within the photographic framework of the film—in its stillness as it collides with the fluidity of movement: moving images in a standstill.

The "photographic unconscious" is revealed in Ruiz's emphasis on the graphic aspect of the camerawork. Thus, Benjamin's "optical unconscious" is embedded within the larger armature of allegorical images. In *Three Crowns of the Sailor* this occurs through the framework of open wounds. Literally seeing through inscriptions of open wounds exposes a form of viewing exemplified by the allegorical figure of the blind man, the Tiresias figure (the blind seer), of the film. For only the sailor, who has already entered an intoxicated state through his encounter with the blind man, can see what the other men cannot.

Benjamin's commentary on surrealism's experiments with and reliance on forms of intoxication as a kind of "introductory lesson" to a collective "image-space"[25] of politics is echoed in the (quasi-stereotypical) surrealist setting that opens *Three Crowns of the Sailor*, in which, as we will see, Ruiz situates his notion of the photographic unconscious in scenes of writing. An oblique reference to the surrealist idea of "automatic writing" through intoxication, the opening shot of *Three Crowns of the Sailor* features a close-up of a glass of wine in saturated color. As the "writer" (who only appears in the opening scene) begins to tell a story about a storm in the East Indies (one of the most contested places of imperial and neocolonial politics), a close-up of the hand writing with black ink on white paper precipitates a shift to black-and-white cinematography. In black and white we see the legs of a dead body pulled (presumably by his murderer, whom we do not see in the shot) into the scene. The camera comes to a standstill, showing the dead body with its hand in extreme close-up. The dead body, as we subsequently discover, is that of a professor and collector who had been murdered by his student in Warsaw—"for no good reason," as the student will comment, other than for a collection of coins (including three Danish crowns) and a ring that were in the professor's possession. While attempting to flee the scene of the crime, the student meets a sailor in search of three Danish crowns he had borrowed from the captain of his ship, the ghostly *Funchalense*. In exchange for the crowns and for telling his life's story, the sailor offers the student a place on his ship.[26]

The storytelling evolves out of scenes of intoxication, figurative as well as literal—such as getting drunk in a dance hall, leading the intoxicated sailor to tell his stories to the students. Intoxication unleashes the flow of story lines, enabling them to inhabit different planes of existence simultaneously, demarcating boundaries between individual narratives. Awakening from his intoxicated state in a bar (to which the blind man had taken the sailor), the sailor finds the blind man mortally wounded—as if in a bad dream. Ruiz's scenes of intoxication, as they unfold narratively as well as cinematographically in circular tracking shots and pendulum camera movements, dramatize and symbolize the surrealist process of entering the dream realm of the unconscious (such as through experiments with drugs, which also play an important role in Benjamin's work, including what he called "profane illumination").[27] It is in a state of intoxication that the sailor will find his way to the *Funchalense*—where he will soon realize that he is the only *living* soul on board and where he will thus be confronted with the spectral dimension of his own and his country's (Chile's—also Ruiz's country of origin) history.

Once the sailor enters the ship, he points on a map to the unknown places the ship is scheduled to visit. The map, which can be read as an allegorical figure of the unconscious, is seen through the frame formed by a close-up of a foot, a ghostly white foot with open wounds.

The wounds of the living dead (the ghostly shipmates) in the foreground condition the way we look at the sailor and the map in the background. In a form of an "inverse theology,"[28] the corporeality of the wounded flesh is transformed into a cartography of codes and signs through the captain's scene of writing; his logbook takes the form of an embroidery, into which he stitches a code. While looking at the embroidery as the captain works on it, one of the shipmates comments: "On board of this ship, we are all one. It's a big brotherhood. It's necessary, each one has its place." Each letter stitched into the embroidery is in fact "incarnated" by one of the shipmates. The sailor's incarnation of the letter "A," through which we enter his (intoxicated) vision, is also emphasized when the sailor frames and is himself framed by figurations of the letter "A" on his shore visits to bordellos during the journey. Extreme close-ups of his legs, or the legs of a prostitute, in the shape of a letter "A," are used as framing devices. Most iconically, Ruiz frames the blind man's bleeding wound through the sailor's legs in close-up, thereby exposing the framing device most explicitly as a *form of inscription* that conditions a reading of images through wounds.

Through the shape of letters (most prominently the letter "A"), Ruiz frames open wounds, frames *through* open wounds and torn body parts, thereby recalling the surrealist practice of monumentalizing the ephemeral (a bodily gesture) and the corporeal (wounds)[29] in cinematographic inscriptions. In this manner, it makes legible what would otherwise remain unnoticed, thereby effecting a cinematic performance of Benjamin's "optical unconscious." As Benjamin writes: "It is another nature which speaks to the camera as compared to the eye. 'Other' above all in the sense that a space informed by human consciousness gives way to a space informed by the unconscious."[30] Benjamin's understanding of technologically reproduced images is based on their affinity to, as Miriam Hansen explains, "the unseen, the overly familiar, the repressed—with anything that eludes conscious, intentional perception."[31] Through Ruiz's framing device—framing with wounds, with monumentalized and sculpted body parts—the "look of the other" haunts *Three Crowns of the Sailor*, exposing the otherness of the camera through a proliferation and foregrounding of otherwise invisible structures. This is why Ruiz relates his notion of the "photographic unconscious" to what one can call an "inverse theology" (or in Benjaminian terms "profane illumination").[32]

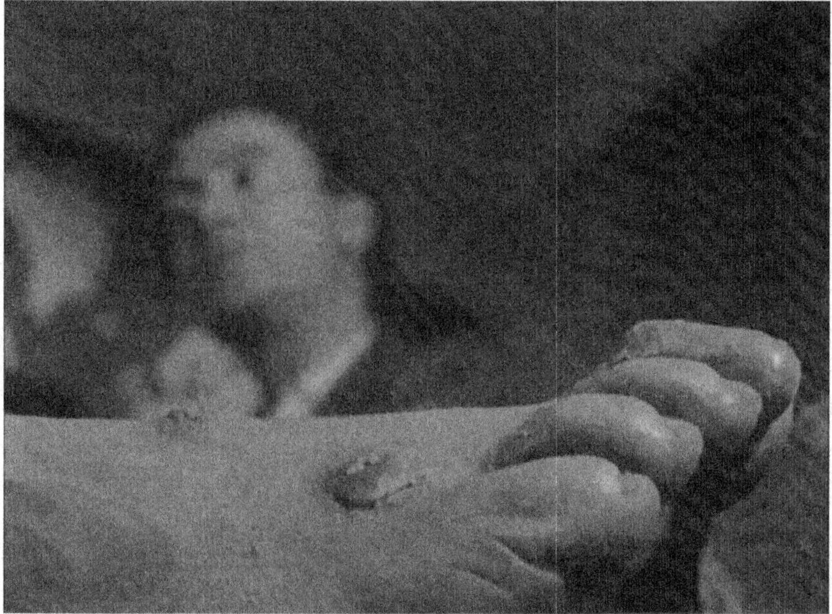

Cartographies of open wounds in *Three Crowns of the Sailor*.

The Cinematographic Unconscious

Between shot and counter-shot, image and anti-image, the return of the gaze is constructed as a return through open wounds, exposing a vulnerability at the limit of the senses that is looking back at us, haunting from within the liminality of open wounds. The moments when gazes are returned—as in the iconic image of the oozing worms, which in the shape of open eyes seem to be openings through which the dead reappear—perform a "cinematographic unconscious," the space felt between two shots, hovering between continuation and dispersion, stillness and movement:

> In *Othello* by Orson Welles, one character slaps and another: the beginning of the slap was filmed in Venice, the final part in Morocco a few months later. . . . Continuity and dispersion: two constant principles in cinematography. We see the images as if they were a continuum, knowing that each take is worlds apart. It is a feeling bordering on fear, accentuated by the passage of time. For those of us who attempt to remain conscious of the substance behind the cinematographic image this culminates in a sensation of abyss, of

multiple chasms that fissure the image at any given moment, lending the impression we are living realistic events which nonetheless
are hard to believe. This is a radical feeling, insofar as it makes us
suspect the cinematographic unconscious could be photography
itself: as though to look at it were to see all and nothing at once.[33]

As a "sensation of abyss," this state of suspension between shots becomes
manifest as an opposition of extremes. Ruiz's extreme close-ups combined
with deep-focus camerawork dramatize the very space between proximity
and distance within a single shot, thereby exposing the oscillation between
photography and cinematography. In constructs of images that are the mise-
en-scène of a montage, Ruiz combines, as it were, the two major schools
of filmmaking.[34] Aligning his own filmmaking with directors such as Dalí,
Buñuel, and Welles, filmmakers who considered what "happens between
two fragments to be worthy of attention," and who were also branded as
"pranksters," Ruiz observes: "And yet it is well known that every joke conceals a serious problem. The problem could be put in these terms: what
happens between two shots, between two frames, between two films zapped
on television?"[35]

Ruiz saw the advent of a cinematographic unconscious first and foremost in Welles's cinematography (indeed, the extreme close-ups of *Three
Crowns of the Sailor* in combination with low-angle shots are reminiscent
of *Citizen Kane*, and the search for cinematic truth echoes Welles's biopic
F for Fake):

> What would happen if the moving image were nothing but a con-
> tinuous circulation of images and anti-images, like couples in a
> permanent state of divorce and reconciliation? Couldn't the rever-
> beration provoked by this constant renovation of image/anti-image
> configurations be called "aura"? Why not conclude that aura and
> cinematographic unconscious are one and the same?[36]

In other words, the "cinematographic unconscious" is a marker of cinematic truth or *authenticity*. Ruiz's theorization of the cinematographic unconscious, which circles back to a form of photography and "could [even]
be photography itself," emerges from within collisions, puncturing them in
between opposites, in the "in-betweens of a new world-memory."[37] From
within the collision of "images and anti-images," of photographic images
(in a standstill) and cinematographic images (in movement), of analog images (inscribed into celluloid) and digital images (numerically constructed),

Benjamin's notion of the "optical unconscious" is folded into the graphic aspect of a photo-cinematographic writing.

In *Three Crowns of the Sailor*, we find an excellent example of the cinematic unconscious in the dramatization of the paradoxical figure of the prostitute called "Virgin Mary." In opposition to the other prostitutes (who appear, explicitly as allegories of meat, as when one of the prostitutes' legs are shown in a close-up that is juxtaposed with meat on a barbecue), the "Virgin Mary" is presented as an angelic figure, dressed in white. She first appears shadowlike behind a curtain, reading, and it is behind the curtain that we see the sailor embracing her. As shadowlike figures, they harken back to the first "cinematic spectacle" in Plato's cave allegory.[38]

The scene unfolds in the room of the "Virgin Mary," in which animated dolls hang from the ceiling, looking down, emphasizing her childlike innocence, while stories of oppression and dependencies are told. Haunted by her late father's debts, the figure of the "Virgin Mary" is also haunted by her own looming death, suggested by the coffin placed in her room; her father had bought the coffin for her when she was very sick as a child and was not expected to live. The sailor, who compares in a flow of associations the coffin to a ship, thus exposes an analogy between the ghostly vessel that he himself inhabits and the coffin, in which the "Virgin Mary" keeps her belongings and which marks her open wound. Still childlike, she was already almost dead, now undead, living a "bare life" haunted by the past, which prevents her from moving on. She is stuck in a state of permanent suspension as she tries to pay off her late father's debts by selling herself. Constantly hovering (like her dolls) over an abyss, she is the incarnation of the aforementioned "sensation of abyss" through which Ruiz defines the cinematographic unconscious, that is, she is the incarnation of a "dialectic at a standstill." However, most of all, as a prostitute, she is, in Benjamin's words, "the incarnation of a commodity";[39] a commodity in both image and body, she is an allegorical figure of capitalist modernity.[40] Ruiz thus performs through the allegorical figure of the "Virgin Mary" "the allegorist's gaze that allows things to become writing."[41]

The "Virgin Mary" also records her life's story through a form of inscription, decorating her coffin with the gum she chews while meeting her customers. A line of seventeen chewing gums decorates the coffin. The image of the lineup of chewing gums on top of her coffin—a testimony to her pain as well as to her loss of virginity—is recalled toward the end of the film in the lineup along a bar table of the "family members" the sailor has acquired during his journey, with the "Virgin Mary" placed first in line. Superimposed on the lineup of "family members" is the secret message the

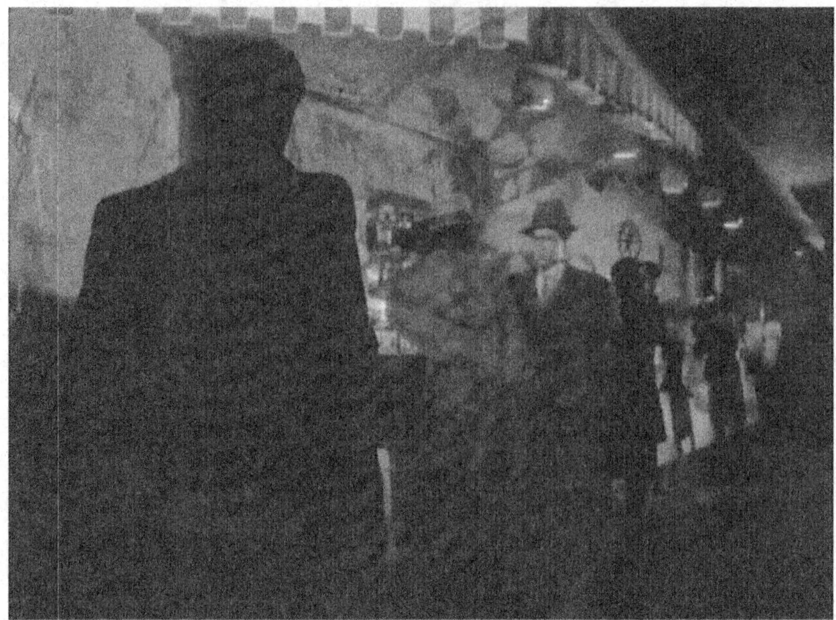

Superimposition of family bonds in *Three Crowns of the Sailor*.

captain of the ghost ship stitches into his embroidery, his logbook, in which he records his "family members" on board. The superimposition of images and texts interweaves the family bonds that the sailor has created on his journey (on his shore leaves with the living—such as a prostitute, a dancer, prisoners—and on the ship with his dead "brothers"). What is interwoven, literally held together with the captain's red thread, is the construct of a family, an invocation of Agamben's "community to come." Following Agamben, Ruiz attempts to think a community without unity, a community of "universal exiles" (from Tangier, Singapore, Dakar, Valparaíso), with "whatever singularities" that nonetheless co-belong without presupposing a form of identity.[42] In their diversity, the "family members" of Ruiz's "community to come" are dispersed in an endlessly continuous line, each member with his/her back to the other, a community without identity, and yet, interwoven with each other in their relationship to the sailor and their common status as "universal exiles."

The red thread woven through this allegorical image of an inscription marks not only the letters of a secret code—an encrypted code; its red color also marks the wounds and vulnerabilities on which the family bonds are based. As an allegorical image of an inscription of wounds, the cryptic text appears toward the end of the film again, this time written in blood on a wall in the apartment of the murdered professor, literally bleeding into the black-and-white cinematography. The return of the captain's haunting message, incarnated in blood, takes on an auratic quality as it returns the look from the realm of the dead, while it literally bleeds into the reality of the sailor, substantiating the bond between the living and the dead. Ruiz's suggestion that Benjamin's "aura and cinematographic unconscious are one and the same" appears to assert itself at this point, when the captain's secret message takes on a form of spectral agency:[43] the captain's inscription looks back from the realm of the dead, materializing itself in the space between life and death. In other words, the "cinematographic unconscious" is a marker of cinematic truth and existential *authenticity*.

In close dialogue with Benjamin's theory of the optical unconscious, Ruiz insists on reading images at the level of *inscription*. For it is in the pulverizing and decentering potential of the camera itself, its superimpositions and close-ups (compared, as mentioned above, to shattering our "prison-world" with the "dynamite of a split second")[44] that images are decomposed into constructs of images, allegorical images. As such, they insist, in Ruiz's as well as in Benjamin's allegorical world, on being read as what W. J. T Mitchell calls "imagetexts":[45] neither pure image nor pure text, writing is here seen in its graphic form as a kind of "suturing of the visual and the verbal, the 'imagetext' incarnate."[46] The dialectic between image and word in Ruiz's suturing of "imagetexts" thereby hovers between the living (the sailor's living family members) and the dead (the captain's logbook of the dead on board his ship), marking the *entredeux*[47] of open wounds, the wounds of the living-dead, as they demand to be read.

Notes

1. Raúl Ruiz, *Poetics of Cinema 1*, 2nd ed., trans. Brian Holmes (Paris: Dis Voir, 2005).

2. Walter Benjamin, "Critique of Violence," in *Selected Writings, Volume 1 (1913–1926)*, ed. Marcus Bullock and Michael W. Jennings (Cambridge, MA: Harvard University Press, 2004), 236–52.

3. Ruiz, *Poetics of Cinema 1*, 42.

4. Ibid.

5. Ibid., 69.

6. Ibid., 108. See Michael Witt, "The Death(s) of Cinema According to Godard," *Screen* 40, no. 3 (1999): 331.

7. In a lengthy footnote, Derrida discusses the notion of a "weak messianic power" in Benjamin's work and concludes that "we should quote and reread here all these pages—which are dense, enigmatic, burning-up to the final allusion to the 'chip' (shard, splinter: *Splitter*) that the messianic inscribes in the body of the at-present (*Jetztzeit*) and up to the 'strait gate' for the passage of the Messiah, namely every 'second'" (*Specters of Marx: The State of the Debt, the Work of Mourning, and the New International*, trans. Peggy Kamuf [London: Routledge, 1994], 181).

8. Allen Meek, "Guides to Electropolis: Toward a Spectral Critique of Media," http://pmc.iath.virginia.edu/text-only/issue.996/meek.996, accessed August 9, 2016.

9. "Then came film and exploded this prison-world with the dynamite of the split second, so that now we can set off calmly on journeys of adventure among its far-flung debris" (Walter Benjamin, "The Work of Art in the Age of Its Technological Reproducibility: Second Version," in *Selected Writings, Volume 3 (1935–1938)*, ed. Howard Eiland and Michael W. Jennings [Cambridge, MA: Harvard University Press, 2002], 117).

10. Ruiz, *Poetics of Cinema 1*, 32.

11. Ibid., 11.

12. Giorgio Agamben, *The Coming Community* (Minneapolis: University of Minnesota Press, 1993).

13. Ruiz, *Poetics of Cinema 1*, 41–42.

14. "Walter Benjamin made a decisive step forward in our understanding of the Baroque when he showed that allegory was not a failed symbol, or an abstract personification, but a power of figuration entirely different from that of the symbol: the latter combines the eternal and the momentary, nearly at the center of the world, but allegory uncovers nature and history according to the order of time. It produces a history from nature and transforms history into nature in a world that no longer has its center" (Gilles Deleuze, *The Fold* [Minneapolis: University of Minnesota Press, 1993], 125).

15. See Michael Calderbank, "Surreal Dreamscapes: Walter Benjamin and the Arcades" (2003), www.surrealismcentre.ac.uk/papersofsurrealism/journal1/acrobat_files/Calderbank.pdf, accessed August 8, 2016.

16. See Sigrid Weigel, *Body- and Image-Space: Re-Reading Walter Benjamin* (London: Routledge, 2003).

17. Walter Benjamin, "Surrealism," in *Selected Writings, Volume 2 (1927–1934)*, ed. Michael W. Jennings, Howard Eiland, and Gary Smith (Cambridge, MA: Harvard University Press, 1999), 217–18.

18. "As a result, innervation concerns the intersections, interplays, and interdependencies of (1) an individual corporeality [*Körper*] and a collective spirit—or, to use a Marxian term from the *Grundrisse*: 'general intellect'—and (2) a collective body [*Leib*] and an individual psyche" (Sami Khatib, "'To Win the Energies of Intoxication for the Revolution': Body Politics, Community, and Profane Illumination," *Anthropology and Materialism* 2 [2014]: 7).

19. This term is found in Benjamin's "The Work of Art in the Age of Its Technological Reproducibility."

20. Benjamin, "Work of Art," 117.

21. See Miriam Hansen's discussion of Benjamin's "optical unconscious" in the context of new technologies of inscription in "Benjamin and Cinema: Not a One-Way Street," in *Benjamin's Ghosts: Interventions in Contemporary and Cultural Theory*, ed. Gerhard Richter (Stanford, CA: Stanford University Press, 2002), 63 (originally published in *Critical Inquiry* 25, no. 2, *Angelus Novus*: Perspectives on Walter Benjamin [1999]: 306–43).

22. We should also note that the number "three" in the title of the film suggests, of course, the figure of the Trinity.

23. Ruiz, *Poetics of Cinema 1*, 68.

24. Rosalind Krauss, *The Optical Unconscious* (Cambridge, MA: MIT Press, 1994), 191.

25. Benjamin, "Surrealism," 217.

26. Michael Goddard points out that "singular stories play a vital role in the relations between human lives and money, so that currencies seem to take on the vital qualities of singularity, while life becomes infinitely multiple and exchangeable." In Ruiz's gift economy, the film becomes an "inexchangeable currency, in relation to normative models of cinematic production and narrative construction" (Goddard, *The Cinema of Raúl Ruiz: Impossible Cartographies* [New York: Columbia University Press, 2013], 74).

27. See Walter Benjamin, *On Hashish*, ed. Howard Eiland (Cambridge, MA: Harvard University Press, 2006). See also Margaret Cohen, *Profane Illumination: Walter Benjamin and the Paris of Surrealist Revolution* (Berkeley: University of California Press, 1993).

28. Norbert Bolz coins the expression "inverse theology" with respect to his view that Benjamin's notion of theology is cloaked in a "secular incognito" (Bolz, "Rethinking History," in Richter, *Benjamin's Ghosts*, 232).

29. See Caroline Levitt, "From the Walls of Factories to the Poetry of the Street: Inscriptions and Graffiti in the Work of Apollinaire and the Surrealists," *Papers of Surrealism* 9 (Summer 2011). www.surrealismcentre.ac.uk/papersofsurrealism/journal9/, accessed August 9, 2016.

30. Benjamin, "Work of Art," 117.

31. Hansen, "Benjamin and Cinema," in Richter, *Benjamin's Ghosts*, 66.

32. See note 29.

33. Ruiz, *Poetics of Cinema 1*, 69.

34. Ruiz calls them the "partisans of montage" and "the partisans of *mise-en-scène*," in ibid., 116.

35. Ibid., 117.

36. Ibid., 62.

37. Timothy Murray, *Digital Baroque: New Media Art and Cinematic Folds* (Minneapolis: University of Minnesota Press, 2008), 20.

38. See Plato, *Republic*, Book VII.

39. Benjamin writes in his "Central Park": "The commodity seeks to look itself in the face. It celebrates its incarnation in the whore" (quoted in Weigel, *Body- and Image-Space*, 96).

40. See Laleen Jayamanne's reading of *Three Crowns of the Sailor* in dialogue with Benjamin's notion of baroque allegory and its close ties to surrealist imaginary: "'Life Is a Dream'—Raúl Ruiz was a Surrealist in Sydney: A Capillary Memory of a Cultural Event," in *Kiss Me Deadly: Feminism and Cinema for the Moment*, ed. Laleen Jayamanne (Sydney: Power Publications Sydney, 1995), 221–51. Jayamanne's interpretation of *Three Crowns of the Sailor* in dialogue with Benjamin's notion of the baroque allegory focuses on the allegorizing ontology of the film with respect to figures of tormented flesh and the maternal as a form of emblematic memory. However, it is Ruiz's reference to the "photographic unconscious" that motivates my reading of the allegorical figure of the "Virgin Mary" as a figure that transforms "things into writing." (Weigel, *Body- and Image-Space*, 95).

41. Ibid.

42. Agamben, *Coming Community*, 5.

43. Esther Peeren develops the notion of "spectral agency" in her exploration of figures of the "living dead": "Being forced to align their looks with the marginalized characters or with a camera that is clearly looking with rather than at these characters makes it harder for audiences to approach these films in a voyeuristic mode" (*The Spectral Metaphor: Living Ghosts and the Agency of Invisibility* [London: Palgrave Macmillan, 2014], 44).

44. See note 10.

45. W. J. T. Mitchell, *Picture Theory: Essays on Verbal and Visual Representation* (Chicago: University of Chicago Press, 1994), 95.

46. Ibid.

47. Hélène Cixous discusses the *entredeux* as the site of vulnerability in Mireille Calle-Gruber and Hélène Cixous, *Hélène Cixous, Rootprints: Memory and Life Writing* (London: Routledge, 1997), 9.

Raúl Ruiz's "Lost" Chilean Film

Memory and Multiplicity in *Palomita blanca* (1973)

Ignacio López-Vicuña

Since Chile's return to democracy in 1990, a number of films have attempted to grapple with the difficult topic of memory in a postdictatorship, neoliberal society. During the 1990s, Chilean filmmakers attempted to break the silence and collective amnesia surrounding the events of Allende's Popular Unity government and of the Pinochet military regime. At the same time, films such as Patricio Guzmán's documentary trilogy *La Batalla de Chile/ The Battle of Chile* (VE/FR/CU/CL, 1974–79) originally filmed during the Allende government, were shown in Chile for the first time. Alongside this well-known film, however, one would have to place Raúl Ruiz's *Palomita blanca/Little White Dove* (CL, 1973). *Palomita blanca* was finished in 1973 but disappeared after Chile Films, the national film production center, was occupied by the military, when installations were destroyed and film stock burned.[1] The film was believed lost, but was rediscovered shortly after Chile's return to democracy, and shown for the first time in 1992.[2]

Palomita blanca, a film capturing everyday life under Allende, and in particular focusing on the young, was not intended as a memory film, but rather as a sort of mirror, a reflection upon Chileans' attitudes, hopes, and dreams, as well as a record of everyday speech, gestures, and humor, in the style of Ruiz's earlier film *Tres tristes tigres/Three Sad Tigers* (CL, 1968). However, since the film disappeared and was only shown twenty years later, after the end of the military dictatorship, it became, in spite of itself, a document of memory. *Palomita blanca* is thus profoundly marked by an air of

---

This chapter is a revised and updated version of the article "Raúl Ruiz's 'Lost' Chilean Film: Memory and Multiplicity in *Palomita blanca.*" *Studies in Hispanic Cinemas* 6, no. 2 (2009): 111–24. Reprinted with permission.

untimeliness, and its irruption into the contemporary Chilean cultural landscape remains awkward and uncanny.

For a number of reasons, including its experimental nature, rejection of linear narrative, and lack of a clear-cut political message, the film has failed to attain a place of importance in the Chilean discussion on memory and history. In this chapter, however, I argue that *Palomita blanca* is a document of vital importance for this debate, and that it deserves to become a significant point of reference for contemporary Chilean film. Furthermore, it is precisely because Ruiz's film rejects narrative closure and embraces an aesthetics of dissonance and fragmentation, I suggest, that it constitutes an essential point of departure for revisiting the Allende period as well as for reimagining the link between the past and the future.

During the transition to democracy, films such as *Amnesia* (Justiniano, CL, 1994); *Chile: La memoria obstinada/Chile: Obstinate Memory* (Guzmán, CA/FR, 1996); and *Fernando ha vuelto/Fernando Has Returned* (Caiozzi, CL, 1998) directly addressed the question of memory as resistance to the silence and "amnesia" imposed by the military regime and tacitly accepted by the later transitional governments. Although such films attempt to challenge what Tomás Moulian has called the "whitewashing" of recent Chilean history, it is only in the past decade that films such as *Machuca* (Wood, CL/ES/ UK/FR, 2004) and the biographical documentary *Salvador Allende* (Guzmán, BE/CL/FR/DE/ES/MX, 2004) have begun more actively to engage the legacy of Allende's Popular Unity government in order to understand potential futures the military regime closed up.[3]

Ruiz's films stand out among Chilean cinematic productions, especially when contrasted with Patricio Guzmán's narrative and emotionally charged documentaries, such as *The Battle of Chile* and *Chile: Obstinate Memory*.[4] Whereas such films offer coherent, linear, and epic narratives of the rise and fall of popular forces in Chile, *Palomita blanca* views the Popular Unity through an entirely different lens, focusing on dissonances, fragmentation, and heterogeneity, and thus opening up a different view of memory and narrative. In keeping with Ruiz's critique of "central conflict theory" in his *Poetics of Cinema*, the film is not organized around a central conflict between the popular and elite sectors, but rather multiplies microconflicts and digressions in an attempt to capture the rhizomatic complexity of everyday life.[5]

When it was shown in Chile during the transition to democracy, *Palomita blanca* could not help but offer an uncanny experience comparable to viewing a time capsule in the form of a motion picture. The film served as a window into the past, an image of a time long gone that remained strange and nearly impossible to assimilate within the new, postdictatorial and neo-liberal Chile. For many among the younger generation who came of age under Pinochet, Ruiz's film offered an image of a radical *otherness*, portraying a country whose existence they could barely imagine. Unlike many of the films dealing with memory and struggle, *Palomita blanca* portrayed a past that was richly heterogeneous, full of dark humor, and abounding in the absurd. It did not propose a coherent narrative of Chile's recent history, but rather challenged the idea that the nation's past (or future) could be mapped out in a straightforward, linear manner.

It is perhaps for this reason that *Palomita blanca* has failed to become a canonical Chilean film and remains commercially unavailable, in spite of the excitement generated by its release in 1992. At that time, film critic René Naranjo called the film "Chilean cinema's missing link" ("el eslabón perdido del cine chileno").[6] He writes that the film "puts the national spectator in the singular position of recovering the time gone by. . . . A Chile in black and white that now returns in full color and in a new copy."[7]

The phrase *eslabón perdido*, "missing" as well as "lost" link, suggests something that was lost and subsequently recovered. For Naranjo, the film helps Chileans to reconnect with their past, in particular with the cultural traits and ways of being that existed in Chilean society before Pinochet. Naranjo's remark that the film recovers a "black and white Chile" that now returns in a "new copy in full color" should be understood in the context of the ongoing struggle over memory. Attempts to challenge the triumphant narrative of modernity in post-Pinochet Chile were often sustained by reference to images of the past: black-and-white photographs of the *desaparecidos*, the "disappeared" victims of Pinochet's regime, or black-and-white film footage from the Popular Unity period. These images betray a distance from the present, a time dominated by the highly saturated color of advertisement and neoliberal consumer society. As cultural critic Nelly Richard points out, the portraits of the disappeared "do not go with anything" in this new, colorful, publicity-oriented cultural landscape.[8]

By contrast, *Palomita blanca* restores to the viewer not only the colors of 1970s Chile but also the sounds, the music, the slang, the diverse social registers and cultural tensions of that immensely vital time just before the military coup. Although *Palomita blanca* is not a film *of* the postdictator-ship period, I would argue that it intervenes *in* the ongoing postdictator-ship debate on memory. It is also a film that deconstructs understandings of memory and history, and thus does not lend itself to a narrative recon-struction of memory, but rather celebrates memory as always already open to chance and heterogeneity.

Palomita blanca: Reading the Romance

Palomita blanca was made during the last year of Allende's government, and finished shortly before the military coup (September 11, 1973) that ended Chile's socialist experiment. The story line of the film, however, is set during the time immediately preceding the election of Allende in 1970, and portrays a country segmented by class, gender, politics, and cultural divisions. Unlike other films of the period, *Palomita blanca* does not posit a unitary popular subject that will ultimately resolve these contradictions. Although Ruiz himself was in a sense an "organic intellectual," working within the Socialist Party and within Allende's political project, he rejected the dominant aesthetics of documentary realism, choosing instead to focus on the multiplicity of voices, fragments of narrative, and elements of popular and mass culture that create a dissonance, a splintering into many planes that coexist simultaneously and elude reconciliation.

Based on Enrique Lafourcade's best-selling novel of the same name (1972), *Palomita blanca* follows the doomed love affair between sixteen-year-old María, a romantic girl who lives with her godmother in a *conventillo* (a lower-class multifamily dwelling) in Recoleta, a poor neighborhood of Santiago, and Juan Carlos, a rich boy from a politically reactionary, upper-class family. Although Juan Carlos is ostensibly apolitical, his brother, a militant of a fascist group, manages to draw him into the plot to kidnap General René Schneider.[9] In the film, the failed kidnapping plot leads to Juan Carlos's sudden escape from Chile, which thwarts María's dreams of a long-lasting romance.

In an interview, Ruiz tells of how the novel *Palomita blanca*—by reactionary author Enrique Lafourcade—caught the attention of the Socialist Party during the Popular Unity government. Because the novel contained right-wing messages meant to satirize the revolutionaries' aspirations of eliminating class divisions, yet ironically proved extremely successful and "popular" (in both senses of the term), militants thought it would be fun to exploit the novel's popularity for their own purposes. They had the somewhat perverse idea, says Ruiz, of using it to make a commercially successful film in order to raise money for the revolution. Ruiz, as a militant of the Socialist Party, accepted the project, but his intention was to take the film in less conventional directions: "Obviously, what intrigued me was to offer a sort of critical reading of the novel, to deconstruct it in some sense."[10] The challenge was therefore to take a reactionary novel—whose main premise was the impossibility of love across class divisions—and, rather than merely reversing it (in order to show the triumph of the popular forces, for example), to take it apart and use its narrative elements and sentimental conventions as points of departure for new explorations.

The film is full of ironies. For example, in contrast to the highly politicized pro- and anti-Allende climate—expressed in the lyrics of the song that opens the film, "O dependencia colonial o independencia nacional" (Colonial dependency or national independence)—Juan Carlos is opposed to politics and searches for spiritual purity instead, following new-age spirituality, only to end up involved with a right-wing terrorist group. For her part, María, in spite of her class background, self-identifies as a supporter of right-wing candidate Jorge Alessandri, following the example of her godmother. María's mother and stepfather, staunch Allendistas, are portrayed as irresponsible alcoholics (which is why María lives with her godmother). The basic story line, however, serves merely as a framework. Ruiz is more interested in the "background"; that is, in the everyday lives of María, Juan Carlos, and those around them. Absurd situations, conversations that ramble on (as in the films of Godard), fragments of popular culture and political clichés, acquire a life of their own. Although there is a narrative framework, the film also incorporates fragmentary modes of storytelling and abounds in narrative subplots that lead nowhere.

In deconstructing the novel, Ruiz also deconstructs subjectivity and, obliquely, the Popular Unity's conception of a united popular front. To deconstruct, however, does not mean to undo or to dismiss, but rather to take apart or analyze, using playfulness and irony to undermine orthodoxy. Ruiz's perspective is profoundly ironic, and irony becomes integral not only to his cinematic project but to his political stance as well. In an interview given in exile, Ruiz affirms the importance of irony as a political and aesthetic strategy:

> It is not a question of pessimism, but for me irony is an important tool of political analysis. The present tragic situation is the result of a certain political process: it is important to be lucid rather than bemoan our fate; irony is necessary to refresh and clarify our perception of things.[11]

In the context of this assertion, it is possible to understand Ruiz's departure from realist modes of filmmaking as a political impulse to create new forms of consciousness, while remaining grounded in regional history and culture. His rejection of mainstream narrative (Hollywood) cinema therefore echoes both the concerns of avant-garde cinema and the call for cultural decolonization in Latin America. As Michael Richardson writes:

One feature we can discern which is consistent throughout his work is its political intent. Even though this may not be manifest in the content of the films as such, it is clear that Ruiz has never left behind the concerns of his earliest work in Chile, especially the critique of cultural imperialism and the impact of Hollywood production methods.[12]

In portraying everyday life in the Chile of that period, Ruiz has an excellent ear (and eye) for the sentimental and kitsch (what Chileans call *cursi*) in María's life. A large part of the narrative consists of María's voice-over narration (addressed to her diary) retelling her everyday life. María's interest in the (fictional) telenovela *María Isabel*, her prayers to the Virgin Mary, and her trite romantic turns of phrase all form a cultural matrix that underpins María's experience and the experiences of the popular sectors more generally.

Rather than presenting melodrama as the "truth" of popular experience, however, Ruiz uses María's monologues as a point of departure for a fragmented and nonlinear presentation of discourse and subjectivity. This becomes evident in the early scenes, particularly in María's account of meeting and falling in love with Juan Carlos.

The film opens with a rock festival at Piedra Roja (just outside of Santiago), a sort of Chilean Woodstock that serves as the setting for Juan Carlos and María's first meeting. Over the images of young hippies, the innovative rock music of Los Jaivas can be heard with the lyrics "O dependencia colonial o independencia nacional" (Colonial dependency or national independence).[13] After a series of images of the festival, we cut to María and Juan Carlos driving out to the beach. María's voice-over informs us (in reality addressing her diary) that Juan Carlos offered to drive her home after the concert, but they decided to drive out to the coast instead. When they arrive at the beach, Juan Carlos undresses and tells María to do the same so they can go for a swim. María's voice tells the story: "Llegamos a la playa, se bajó, me dijo que me desnudara. A mí me dio vergüenza, porque estaba con toda la ropa rota, qué sé yo, y él con su ropa tan linda" (We got to the beach, he got out, he told me to undress. I felt embarrassed, I had my clothes all torn, I don't know, and he with his really nice clothes). Her description of Juan Carlos as handsome and refined matches her idea of him as a Prince Charming, contrasting with her self-image as a poor and shabbily dressed Cinderella.

Halfway through this monologue, the track of María's voice unexpectedly doubles upon itself, giving rise to a superposition of the same (or possibly variations or different "takes" of the same) monologue. The monologue(s) run over each other asynchronously so that similar phrases clash

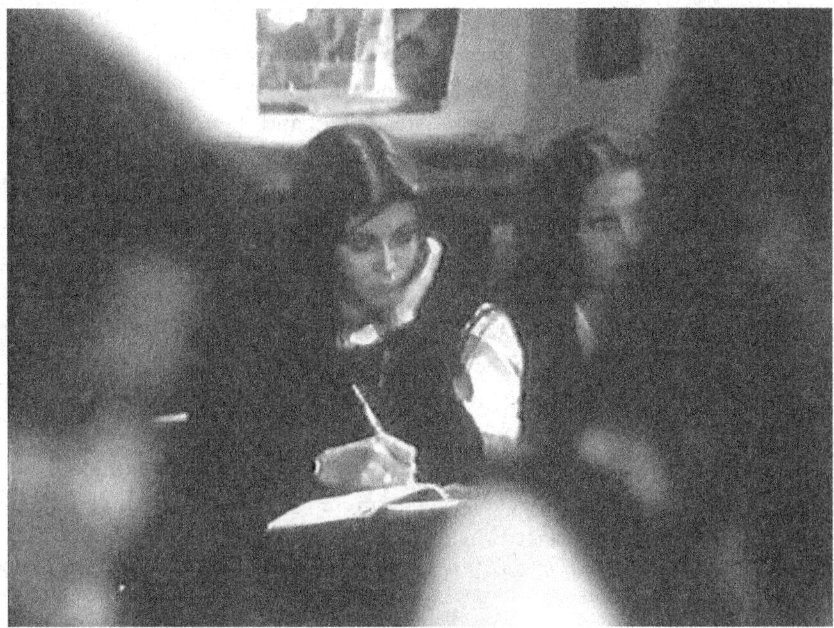

María at school in *Palomita blanca*.

with each other, making it difficult to make out everything that is spoken. This vocal layering suggests a splintering of María's subjective voice into multiple voices, multiple "versions" of the truth she seeks to communicate (to set down in her diary) regarding her meeting with Juan Carlos and her feelings about him.

A similar moment of subjective splintering occurs later in the film. While enjoying a weekend picnic at Parque Forestal with her family and a school friend, María reads some of her letters aloud to her friend. These include love letters and also a suicide note. After reading the letters, the girls burn them while they critique the style and mood expressed in each one. Regarding the suicide note, the friend comments: "está linda" (it's pretty) and "un poco larga" (a little long) before they burn it. The expression of María's self and feelings in the letter, to say nothing of the ritualistic reading and burning performance, complicate any sense of authenticity or truth.

A few feet away from the girls, María's mother and godmother become involved in a political discussion, each of them arguing her point by appealing to slogans and clichés. María's mother, for example, states that when Allende comes to power each and every one of them will live in a large house, and they will force the rich out of their mansions. The *madrina* (godmother) replies that if Allende wins the election, young children will be sent to Cuba for political indoctrination, something she will never stand for. While the women talk, María's stepfather and a friend sing, and their singing becomes more passionate and loud (presumably from drunkenness) until it drowns out the political discussion. This creates a moment in which neither the political discourse nor the popular song is clearly audible.

Ruiz presents here an eloquent picture of the dissonances created by everyday discourse during the Popular Unity period. Competing voices talk simultaneously, over each other, political discourse and popular culture vie for legitimacy, every discussion becomes immediately politicized, and public life is filled with constant political debate and conversation. Although projected onto the near past right before Allende's election, Ruiz's vision can be seen as a comment on the Popular Unity period itself. Furthermore, Chilean society's polarization reflects a deeper, more radical heterogeneity at the heart of any nation and society, suggesting that "the people" is not a unitary category, and that *el pueblo unido* (the people united) remains a rhetorical fiction.[14]

If *the people* is a rhetorical fiction, then any idea that social contradictions will be "resolved" through a revolutionary struggle becomes relativized and displaced. In another scene, the tenant who boards at María's house is shown pacing up and down in his room, thinking out loud in what appears to be a parody of Marxist dialectics. The dominant class, he says to himself, subjugates and assimilates the dominated class through the mass media, using it to disseminate its values. Hence, he reasons, if a girl from the dominated class falls in love with a boy from the dominant class, she will feel her ambitions realized, since she has internalized the values of the dominant system.[15] This class-based analysis constitutes a metanarrative commentary on the film itself, an exposure of the romance novel framework in order to create a distancing effect upon the viewer. As such, it also exposes the film as artifice and invites a critique of the media's role in perpetuating class stereotypes.

The tenant's musings, however, are cut short by the irruption of the unexpected. When he is just about to get to the synthesis of his dialectical argument he stops mid-sentence, stares out the window, and suddenly begins to shout at the people outside: "¡Qué estás haciendo ahí huevón! ¡Cuánto te pagan los yanquis, desclasado de mierda!" (What are you doing out there jerk! How much do the Americans pay you, you class-traitor shit!) The camera follows his gaze out the window, where we see young men painting slogans on the wall in support of Alessandri (that is, they are supporting a right-wing candidate in a heavily working-class neighborhood). The tenant continues shouting insults, calling the men *vendepatrias* (traitors to their homeland) and sellouts to the Yankee dollar.

Oblivious to the shouting, the *madrina* continues hanging up the laundry, barely paying attention, and as the camera pans we see boys on rooftops fighting (or play-fighting) with sticks. The panning movement of the camera displaces the tenant's altercation with the Alessandristas, staging one of Ruiz's cinematic principles: the background is as interesting as the foreground. We have already seen how Ruiz deals with the authenticity of subjective voice by multiplying and parodying speech/sound, and how he ends a political discussion (between María's mother and godmother) by drowning out the argument with singing. In this case, a dialectical analysis is not resolved, but rather interrupted, cut short by violent confrontation. It is ambiguous whether this moment indicates a call to action or simply a rejection and displacement of any attempt to "synthesize" contradictions.

In turn, the confrontation itself becomes an element in the background as other elements come to the fore and the camera keeps moving. These examples of "rational" political discourses being interrupted by "noise" (loud singing, fighting, shouting) recall—yet predate—the famous scenes in Buñuel's *Cet obscur objet du désir/That Obscure Object of Desire* (FR/ES, 1977) when the revolutionaries' explanations of their political motivations are drowned out by the sounds of airplanes or trains in the background, thus rendering political discourse unintelligible, equivalent to noise. This could be seen as an effort to deconstruct and blur the boundaries between rational arguments and ideology, between insight and alienation. It can also be seen as rejecting the idea of a single, central overarching conflict.

Ruiz's Poetics of Multiplicity

Ruiz has become well known for his critique of "central conflict theory" and for the baroque complexity of his films. However, critics have tended to associate such complexity and philosophical explorations with Ruiz's later "European" films (assuming a distinction between his "Chilean" and "European" films can be made). In this section, I would like to dwell on Ruiz's *Poetics of Cinema* in order to suggest how his thinking on cinema emerges out of early explorations in films such as *Palomita blanca*, films with a strong Latin American and Chilean flavor, and in dialogue with a very concrete political situation. My intention is to suggest that there is really no break between the "Chilean" and the "European" Ruiz.

Palomita blanca's procedure of displacing and multiplying conflicts is consistent with Ruiz's later films and with his writings on cinema. Laleen

Jayamanne suggests that Ruiz is often labeled a "surrealist" filmmaker merely for lack of a better term. A more accurate description would be "a late-twentieth-century baroque allegorical filmmaker."[16] Jayamanne writes that for Ruiz "the baroque is a multiplication of points of view, of an object, a space, a body."[17] Ruiz developed further this aesthetics of complexity and multiplication in his lectures on cinema, collected in *Poetics of Cinema 1* (1995), *Poetics of Cinema 2* (2007), and more recently in *Poéticas del cine* (2013). Although he covers many themes in these books, I will concentrate on his critique of "central conflict theory" and on his reflections on memory-images in cinema.

In *Poetics of Cinema 1*, Ruiz contends that reality is too complex to be viewed in terms of a single central conflict, and there is no reason why film should limit itself to central conflicts, excluding marginal elements and parallel story lines. Against the dominant aesthetic in Hollywood and mainstream cinema, which privileges a central conflict leading toward confrontation and resolution, Ruiz defends a cinema of subconflicts and story lines that proliferate and multiply, prompting an endless flow of "image-situations." Life, Ruiz argues, is full of interrupted situations, non sequiturs, conversations that ramble on, dreams and memories that invade the present moment and make it difficult to separate sleeping and waking life.[18] Against the lure of action cinema that "cuts to the chase," Ruiz defends the pleasures of "boredom." It is boredom, he argues, that allows us to view the cinematic image in a state of near sleep, creating a unique experience of dreaming while awake. The films of Michael Snow, Yasujiro Ozu, and Andrei Tarkovsky, he argues, possess this quality of boredom.[19]

In order to assume a central conflict as the organizing principle of film, Ruiz argues, we need to believe that a person has a single, unitary center of decision. In other words, we have to have a theory of consciousness as unitary. But what if we believe instead that within each person there are many wills competing against each other or even diverging completely? Ruiz illustrates this idea by reference to a well-known Chinese meditation manual, *The Secret of the Golden Flower*.[20] This manual guides the student through the different stages of deep meditation. In fact, Ruiz's reference is more precisely to an illustration of a monk meditating:

> An anonymous author illustrates the four steps in meditation with a drawing showing a monk meditating; by sheer force of concentration he divides into five small meditating monks, after which each of the five divides in turn into four new monks. These

semi-independent substructures are capable of taking power over the whole and of making major decisions.[21]

If we apply this image of consciousness to film, Ruiz argues, we can compose films in which characters have "many sides" (like dice), or many characters within, each guided by different motivations (such as strategy, attraction and repulsion, randomness, cheating). As a game played on many levels, the film becomes a space of multiple games and chance occurrences without a central conflict or resolution.

Ruiz's portrayal of Chilean society is novel and revolutionary in its own way: he presents society not merely in terms of the dominant, overarching conflict between Left and Right, but also by multiplying subconflicts and perspectives in a baroque manner. It is also consistent with Ruiz's project of developing an alternative "national" cinema that resists the dominant schemas of Hollywood cinema. Although he was also working within a revolutionary political context, Ruiz's aesthetics diverge radically from what Solanas and Getino describe as "third cinema." In their seminal manifesto "Towards a Third Cinema" (1969), the Argentine filmmakers argued for a politically engaged cinema of liberation that rejected both Hollywood models and European auteur cinema. Such auteur or "second" cinema, they argued, could only hope to capture a niche audience among the more "alternative" sectors of bourgeois society; it could not aspire to transform and displace bourgeois society.[22] Instead, a politically engaged *third cinema* would circulate among politicized sectors organizing to overthrow the bourgeoisie and bring about social revolution, as in Solanas and Getino's *La hora de los hornos/The Hour of the Furnaces* (AR, 1968).

Even though sharp distinctions between *second/auteur* cinema and *third/militant* film may be considered outdated in contemporary discussions of Latin American cinema, they should be kept in mind when trying to understand the context in which Ruiz was working. Once a student of Fernando Birri in Santa Fe, Argentina, Ruiz ultimately rejected what he saw as the dogma that documentary realism was the only way to film Latin American reality, and instead developed his own version of avant-garde cinema.

The point here is that *Palomita blanca* inhabits what could be seen as a middle space between "second" and "third" cinema, working as it does within Chilean cultural forms and idioms, and particularly as an engagement with a complex and contradictory political event such as the Popular Unity government in Chile. In other words, the "avant-garde" nature of this film emerges out of the political situation itself, out of the contradictions of the revolutionary and modernizing process Chile was undergoing. Furthermore, taking this history into account allows us to read even some of Ruiz's most avant-garde films as reflections on the Chilean experience and its implications for socialism more generally.[23]

Ruiz's cinematic poetics also involves an explicit concern with memory-images, most overtly in films such as *Mémoire des apparences/Life Is a Dream* (FR, 1986)[24] and *Le Temps retrouvé/Time Regained* (FR/IT/PT, 1999), but generally present in most of his cinema. In *Poetics of Cinema*, Ruiz posits that images must be allowed to express their secret underlying associations and connections so they can tell their own story. The narrative aspect of memory thus becomes, for Ruiz, subordinate to images' ability to enter into new (aleatory) combinations.[25]

Elements of Ruiz's conception of memory as open and fragmentary are already present in *Palomita blanca*. María's infatuation with Juan Carlos is strongly mediated by films, romance novels, and telenovelas. Thus her memories of Juan Carlos, ironically, precede the reality of Juan Carlos. On the surface, this might appear to be merely a critique of María's alienated self-understanding and, by extension, a critique of Latin America's experience of cultural imitation and "inauthenticity" vis-à-vis cultural imperialism. While there is some truth in this interpretation, it is consistent with Ruiz's project to see María's lack of "authenticity" as the expression of a process of multiplying levels of reality and experience. It is therefore possible to read María's memories of Juan Carlos as a comment on the fictive elaboration required by any coherent narrative of the self.

In a scene in which María pays a visit to Juan Carlos's sister, a snobbish young woman who manages a boutique in Providencia, the sister's inquisitiveness leads her to question María about her family, which María characterizes sarcastically as "gran conversación gran" (big conversation). The sister wants to know all about María: where she lives, how her family support themselves, what her plans are after high school. The scene reveals the underlying class tensions between the two young women (expressed in their attitudes, clothing, verbal styles, and accents), but is full of irony as well. As they talk, the camera moves slightly, leaving the sister out of frame, thus producing the absurd effect of María talking to a disembodied voice while she appears to be addressing a stuffed dog.

Juan Carlos's sister asks how María and her brother met, to which María answers that it was at a music festival. Then the following, slightly surrealistic, dialogue takes place: "Me trae muchos recuerdos ese festival" (That festival brings back many memories), says María. "¿Recuerdos de qué?" (Memories of what?), asks the sister. "De una película que vi que se llamaba Woodstock" (Of a film I saw that was called *Woodstock*). The sister asks if it was the one with Joan Baez and Jimi Hendrix:

(María) "Sí, me trae muchos recuerdos." (Yes, it brings back many memories.)

"Pero recuerdos de qué?" (But memories of what?)

"De Juan Carlos." (Of Juan Carlos.)

"¿Por qué?" (Why?)

"No sé, Juan Carlos me habla mucho de Jimi Hendrix también." (I don't know, Juan Carlos often talks to me about Jimi Hendrix as well.)

Juan Carlos's sister asks more about María's family, her plans, and her job prospects. The conversation concludes:

(Sister) "¿Te gusta Juan Carlos?" (Do you like Juan Carlos?)

"Sí, podría ser. Me trae muchos recuerdos." (Yes, could be. He brings back many memories.)

"¿De qué?" (Of what?)

"De muchas películas que he visto." (Of many movies I have seen.)

This circular interlacing of memory makes evident a temporal disjointedness, creating a sense of future memories that have not yet been actualized, that float without fully attaching themselves to their objects. María is thus able to answer the question "memories of what" (*¿recuerdos de qué?*) by referring to events that may have never happened in actuality. Thus María's perspective—and the outcome of her love story—encapsulates an unrealized, potential future.

Conclusion: Memories of the Future?

Palomita blanca's status as a document of memory in Chilean cultural history is fraught with complexities. It provides a "window into history," recapturing memories of that "other Chile" that existed before the military regime. But, one is tempted to ask, as Juan Carlos's sister asks María: "memories of what?" The Chile that the movie captures proves contradictory, heterogeneous, and multiple because its images enter into unforeseen combinations. At odds with the idea implicit in films such as *Amnesia* and *Chile: La memoria obstinada* that the release of suppressed memories will lead to a process of anamnesis—a total recollection of images from a previous life, thus making possible a restoration of memory as a coherent narrative,[26] *Palomita blanca* offers a baroque, resistant texture. The images it makes available to memory emerge as multiple and open, contaminated by multiple voices, by uncertainty, chance, and heterogeneity. Ruiz thus opens up memory to a different understanding: no longer representing the recovery of a coherent past, it suggests instead the opening up of the past to the aleatory and uncertain possibility of the future.

Palomita blanca thus turns the idea of memory as narrative continuity on its head. It suggests that efforts to impose narrative order upon the past end up suppressing that past's heterogeneity. The question that Ruiz's film poses—an aesthetic as well as a political one—is whether the nation's story can be told in terms that do not presuppose unity but rather embrace heterogeneity and fragmentation. This requires envisioning the nation otherwise: not as a unity, but as a multiplicity. The idea of national cinema as a form of liberation from cultural imperialism is crucial in *Palomita blanca* and accurately reflects the political climate in Chile during Allende's government.[27] It is all the more significant, then, that Ruiz refused to understand national liberation in terms of unity or univocity, affirming instead multiplicity and heterogeneity.

There is a sense in which Ruiz was working within the revolution in an effort to develop national cinema as part of the reform program of Allende's socialist government. This raises the question of the status of creative work *within* a revolutionary situation, a question that was essential to the debates about the place of the artist/intellectual in relation to social movements in the 1960s and '70s.[28] *Palomita blanca* asks whether it is possible to revolutionize aesthetics and modes of perception from within a revolutionary situation.[29]

Palomita blanca's "in-between" status as both national liberation and avant-garde cinema is unique. As a document of Chilean and Latin American cultural history, it provides an important point of reference as a hybrid space between national, anti-imperial struggles and deterritorialized, cosmopolitan critiques. Although critics sometimes emphasize Ruiz's cosmopolitanism at the expense of his local references, it would be a mistake to overlook the significance of the regional within his production. Jonathan Rosenbaum, for example, writes that what makes Ruiz's films interesting is "a lack of fixed identity or allegiances," which "is essentially the condition of the exile which Ruiz has shared since 1974." From this point of view, Ruiz's earlier Chilean films were "'pre-Ruizian' to the degree that they are Chilean or Latin American in subject, hence regional."[30] However, a film like *Palomita blanca* troubles this distinction, since it simultaneously engages the event of the Popular Unity while also embracing the "lack of fixed identity" that characterizes Ruiz's later "European" films.

On another level, it is possible to say that Ruiz's film conveys a crucial truth about the Popular Unity period: its unprecedented opening up and mixing of social classes and political factions. It remains a revolutionary film even if it does not situate the revolution within a narrative teleology; rather, it suspends temporality in order to capture the heterogeneity of the moment. Deleuze and Guattari's words can be applied to Ruiz's cinematic practice: "Becoming-revolutionary remains indifferent to questions of a future and a past of the revolution; it passes between the two."[31] In other words, it is not a question for Ruiz of where the revolution will lead or what its end (in both senses of the term) will be. *Palomita blanca*'s exploration of multiplicity and dissonance, its irreverent humor at the expense of both left and right, its rejection of narrative teleology and any mythology of national identity, its questioning of the unitary subject, these are all revolutionary in themselves.

If it is true that *Palomita blanca* constitutes the "missing link" in Chilean cinema, current cinematic production has not fully claimed this legacy. In the last few years, Chilean films such as *Machuca, Salvador Allende, Nostalgia de la luz/Nostalgia for the Light* (Guzmán, FR/DE/CL, 2010), and *No* (Larraín, CL/US/FR/MX, 2012) have attempted to open up a dialogue with the past, not only with the trauma of the military dictatorship but also with the revolutionary opening of the Popular Unity period. What is unique about Ruiz's film is its untimely irruption into a present that sees the revolutionary legacy of the Popular Unity as fully contained and closed, while also denying the continuity of the military dictatorship and its effects into the democratic neoliberal present. Ruiz's strange film will continue to shatter both the narrative of history and the immanence of the present. Perhaps its distant chorus of echoes and dissonances will persist as a challenge to the politics of consensus and univocity that have dominated Chilean culture since the return of democracy in 1990.

Notes

1. For an excellent overview of Ruiz's career, see John King, *Magical Reels* (London: Verso, 1990), 171–81.

2. According to Ruiz, the negatives had disappeared from Chile Films in 1973, after the military government banned the film. Nearly twenty years later, during a meeting at Chile Films in 1991, an assistant indicated that at the end of a hallway, in a corner under some stairs, there was something: "In reality it was *Palomita blanca*, and we understood it was she who had hidden it there" (Ruiz quoted in Bruno Cuneo,

ed., *Ruiz: Entrevistas escogidas—filmografía comentada* (Santiago: Ediciones Universidad Diego Portales, 2013), 296.

3. Tomás Moulian, *Chile: Anatomía de un mito* (Santiago: LOM, 1997), 31–37.

4. Patricio Guzmán's documentary *The Battle of Chile* played a crucial role in challenging the "official story" and opening up a debate about the Popular Unity period. This film had never been shown publicly in Chile until 1996, when Guzmán returned to the country and showed it to different audiences with diverse class and political backgrounds, capturing their reactions on film (the basis for *Chile: Obstinate Memory*).

5. See Raúl Ruiz, "Central Conflict Theory," in *Poetics of Cinema 1*, trans. Brian Holmes (Paris: Dis Voir, 1995), 9–23.

6. René Naranjo, "Palomita blanca: El eslabón perdido," *La Nación*, August 1992. In *Le cinéma de Raoul Ruiz*. Website. Accessed September 16, 2014.

7. "pone al espectador nacional en la singular posición de recuperar el tiempo ido. . . . Un Chile en blanco y negro que ahora vuelve a todo color y en copia nueva."

8. Nelly Richard, "Notas sobre 'La Memoria Obstinada' (1996) de Patricio Guzmán," *Revista de Crítica Cultural* 15 (1997): 52–55.

9. In a desperate attempt to prevent Allende's accession to power, extreme right-wing groups decided to kidnap the commander in chief of the army. Apparently they hoped to put the blame on left-wing insurgent groups (such as MIR) and thus sway Congress (which had to confirm Allende's election) or provoke military intervention. The plot backfired when General Schneider resisted and was mortally wounded in the crossfire, which discredited far-right opposition to the Popular Unity and ensured Allende's victory. See Brian Loveman, *Chile: The Legacy of Hispanic Capitalism*, 2nd ed. (New York: Oxford University Press, 1988), 295–96.

10. Raúl Ruiz and Benoît Peeters, "Palomita Blanca," *Rouge* 2 (2004). Website. Accessed September 18, 2014.

11. Ruiz quoted in King, *Magical Reels*, 177.

12. Michael Richardson, *Surrealism and Cinema* (New York: Berg, 2006), 177.

13. The soundtrack of the film, by the progressive rock band Los Jaivas, would merit a study of its own. The band mixes rock styles with traditional Latin American instruments such as Andean wood flutes, charangos, etc. The lyrics to the songs include political references as well as popular sayings (notably in "La cueca de los refranes") and indigenous musical styles from *cueca* to *huayno*.

14. Historians of the period often comment on the lack of internal cohesion among the Left in Chile. Loveman, for example, writes that "President Allende lacked a revolutionary army to carry out his will; he headed a precarious multiparty coalition lacking both internal cohesiveness and underlying agreement on the pace and character of change to be implemented in the Unidad Popular government" (Loveman, *Chile*, 296). Ruiz's critique, however, extends beyond the immediate conjuncture of the Popular Unity and presents an image of the constitutive heterogeneity of the nation.

15. "Ahora bien, que es lo que pasa si una niña de la clase dominada llega a andar con alguien de la clase dominante. Indudablemente por un tiempo siente cumplidos todo lo que son sus sueños, todo lo que son sus objetivos, porque está influenciada por los valores de la clase dominante, a través de los medios de comunicación."

16. Laleen Jayamanne, *Toward Cinema and Its Double* (Bloomington: Indiana University Press, 2001), 161.

17. Ibid.

18. In this regard, parallels with Buñuel's later French films are striking, in particular *Le charme discret de la bourgeoisie/The Discreet Charm of the Bourgeoisie* (FR, 1972); *Le fantôme de la liberté/The Phantom of Liberty* (IT/FR, 1974); and *That Obscure Object of Desire*, as mentioned above. In *The Discreet Charm of the Bourgeoisie*, for example, there is a scene in which a group of military officers is called away from the dinner table, but before they can go back into action, they are asked to wait and listen while one of the officers recounts a dream, which is subsequently discussed and interpreted.

19. Ruiz, *Poetics of Cinema 1*, 13.

20. *The Secret of the Golden Flower*, trans. R. Wilhelm and C. F. Baynes (New York: Harcourt, Brace, and World, 1962). It was translated into German by Richard Wilhelm in the 1920s and introduced to the European public by C. G. Jung.

21. Ruiz, *Poetics of Cinema 1*, 19.

22. Fernando Solanas and Osvaldo Getino, "Towards a Third Cinema," in *Film and Theory: An Anthology*, ed. Robert Stam and Toby Miller (Oxford: Blackwell, 2000), 265–86.

23. This is evident in films such as *Diálogos de exiliados/Dialogues of Exiles* (FR, 1975) and *Mémoire des apparences/Life Is a Dream* (FR, 1986). Even a film as seemingly intellectual as *La vocation suspendue/The Suspended Vocation* (FR, 1978)—ostensibly based on Pierre Klossowski's novel and portraying the controversies between Jesuits and Jansenists—can be read as a comment on the factionalism within the Socialist Party and within the Left more generally.

24. For an original reading of *Mémoire des apparences*, see Alejandro Bruzual, "Raúl Ruiz: *Mémoire des apparences/La vida es sueño*," *Osamayor* 16, no. 16 (2004): 97–113.

25. It is for this reason that both volumes of *Poetics of Cinema* invoke classical theories of "the art of memory" in order to illustrate the power of images to impose order upon memory. See in particular Ruiz, *Poetics of Cinema 1*, 95–96, and Ruiz, *Poetics of Cinema 2*, trans. Carlos Morreo (Paris: Dis Voir, 2007), 13–22. See also the classic study by Frances Yates, *The Art of Memory* (Chicago: University of Chicago Press, 1966).

26. Chilean cultural critic Hernán Vidal has proposed this idea. Vidal writes that Chilean society needs to overcome the effects of "posttraumatic stress" (amnesia and political paralysis): "The overcoming of posttraumatic stress comes about with an eventual capacity to integrate the catastrophic events into a narration that totalizes and consolidates them in a stable place of memory." Hernán Vidal, "Postmodernism, Postleftism, and Neo-Avant-Gardism: The Case of Chile's *Revista de Crítica Cultural*," in *The Postmodernism Debate in Latin America*, ed. John Beverley and José Oviedo, trans. Michael Aronna (Durham, NC: Duke University Press, 1995), 282–306.

27. It is important to recall here that this was the time when, under the auspices of the Allende government, Dorfman and Mattelart published their groundbreaking

work on the analysis of imperialist ideology in Disney comic books, *Para leer al Pato Donald* (1972), published in English as *How to Read Donald Duck*, trans. David Kunzle (New York: International General, 1975).

28. See for example the polemics between Julio Cortázar, Mario Vargas Llosa, and Óscar Collazos in Óscar Collazos, ed., *Literatura en la revolución y revolución en la literatura* (Literature in revolution and revolution in literature) (1971).

29. An illustrative comparison in this regard would be Tomás Gutiérrez Alea's film *Memorias del subdesarrollo/Memories of Underdevelopment* (CU, 1968), made within the framework of the Cuban revolution (although Ruiz is less focused on the drama of the artist and more interested in trans-subjective and collective resonances).

30. Jonathan Rosenbaum, *Placing Movies: The Practice of Film Criticism* (Berkeley: University of California Press, 1995), 227.

31. Gilles Deleuze and Félix Guattari, *A Thousand Plateaus: Capitalism and Schizophrenia*, trans. Brian Massumi (Minneapolis: University of Minnesota Press, 1987), 292.

Raúl Ruiz's Surrealist Documentary of Return

Le retour d'un amateur de bibliothèques (1983)
and *Cofralandes* (2002)

Andreea Marinescu

You can never go home again . . . but I guess you can shop there.

—*Grosse Pointe Blank*

The 1969 New Latin American Film Festival in Viña del Mar is remembered today for solidifying the ideals of militant cinema.[1] During the festival's Encuentro de Cineastas, Che Guevara was declared honorary president, while the screening of *The Hour of the Furnaces*[2] prompted public reactions of solidarity. However, the use of cinema as a vehicle for militant politics spawned dissent from some filmmakers, who expressed doubts about the inherent risks in homogenizing militant artistic practice to complement a formula of continental political change modeled on the Cuban revolution. Raúl Ruiz spoke publicly on behalf of a minority of filmmakers who were dissatisfied with the film festival's emphasis on militant politics with little consideration for cinema:

> The way in which things are being discussed—declamatory, vague, and parliamentary—is incompatible with the Chilean way of being.

This chapter is a translated and updated version of the chapter "El surrealismo documenta el regreso: *Le retour d'un amateur de bibliothèques* (1983) y *Cofralandes* (2002) de Raúl Ruiz," in *Efectos de imagen: ¿Qué fue y qué es el cine militante?*, ed. Óscar Ariel Cabezas and Elixabete Ansa-Goicoechea (Santiago: LOM Ediciones/ UMCE, 2014). Reprinted with permission.

> We talk about things differently. What we hear here are clichés
> about imperialism and culture that you can read about in any maga-
> zine; and then Fernando Solanas comes to recount *The Hour of the
> Furnaces,* which we've already seen last night. We're going to go to
> the other room to talk about film. Whoever wants to come, can
> come with us.[3]

In contrast to what he perceived as an Argentinian-driven instrumentaliza-
tion of cinema in the service of revolutionary ideals, Ruiz countered with
the need to explore cinema on its own terms, avoiding nationalistic and
proselytizing tendencies.

Even during the Popular Unity (UP) government of 1970–73, despite
being actively involved in the state-owned production company Chile Films,
Ruiz remained something of an outsider because his approach to cinema was
more experimental and avant-garde, especially in his use of surrealist gestures.
Several critics have pointed out the director's desire to problematize transparent representations of reality through a visual language that revels in the im-
probable.[4] Ruiz depicts contradictions, unlikely events, absurd situations, and
fantastic elements not as the opposite of reality but as an integral and valuable
part of it. For example, Waldo Rojas speaks of Ruiz's "chaste realism," an aesthetic in which reality is not exposed, but hidden. Reality is not a given, but a
system of concealments.[5] Edoardo Bruno emphasizes Ruiz's surrealist perspective, which becomes visible in his use of situations in which "the impossible
. . . happens as if it were normal."[6] Luis Mora del Solar notes that during the
UP government, as the visual language of militant cinema became the new
canon, Ruiz's films acquired a critical distance from that prevalent tendency. In
contrast to the realist aesthetic typical of Latin American militant films at the
time, Ruiz's early works welcomed avant-garde influences such as the Brazilian
Cinema Nôvo and the French New Wave.[7] Malcolm Coad also sees Ruiz as a
director keenly aware of militant cinema's risks of falling into political reduc-
tionism. For Coad, Ruiz's work points to the political aspects of seemingly
apolitical gestures, such as daily routines or antiheroic acts, which in turn can
stimulate innovative ways of thinking politically.[8]

In line with his avant-gardist perspective, Ruiz rejected what he saw as the
institutionalization of art during the UP government. In a 1971 interview with
the Peruvian film journal *Hablemos de Cine,* Ruiz spoke against Chile Films'
uncritical imitation and application of the Cuban cinematic model, which
held no regard for Chilean reality or the specificity of the political moment,
particularly in the production of *documentales* (documentary films) and *notic-
ieros* (newscasts). In the interview, his position on documentary work is deeply

entrenched within a militant stance that fuses politics and aesthetics. However, his interest in the camera's capacity not only to record but also to *interpret* reality diverges from the traditional militant perspective, where film is mainly a political tool that represents reality without questioning it:

> I think that we have the possibility to definitively annul this difference between documentary and fiction film, integrating them around the camera's capacity to investigate parts of reality and simultaneously registering and interpreting them, giving them ideological content. This would automatically imply the annulment of all genre differences and establish an activity in which the political and aesthetic field would be almost indistinguishable, because they are one and the same thing. (My translation.)[9]

We can see that Ruiz was clearly interested in cinema's political potential, arguing that there is a reciprocal correspondence between innovative aesthetics and innovative politics. In other words, for Ruiz, a politically committed filmmaker contributes to political innovation through aesthetic innovation.

While the aforementioned critics analyze Ruiz's films during his clearly political years before the 1973 coup d'état, I argue that Ruiz continued to explore the relationship between cinema and politics after the coup and during the postdictatorship. In fact, his early problematization of Latin American militant cinema was only the beginning of a process of political innovation through the filmic form. In this essay, I argue that in Ruiz's documentaries about his return from exile, the explicit problematization of the realist documentary form reveals an epistemological impasse. Theoretically, realist documentary is based on "epistephilia, or the desire to know."[10] This definition implies that the images in realist documentary have a very specific purpose: to present visual evidence that satisfies the desire for knowledge. Therefore, it follows that if the documentary does not show the sought-after knowledge, then it cannot motivate social and political action. I examine how Ruiz explores and challenges the direct causal link between image, knowledge, and social commitment, which is the foundation of realist documentary. By taking realist aesthetics to its absurd extreme, Ruiz shows the inability of realist documentary to account for gaps in knowledge such as those produced by absences, trauma, or exile. In the following film analysis, I argue that Ruiz's political commitment does not rest in showing us what we should know, but rather is embodied in the relentless search for new art forms to illuminate the difficulties of memory and the impossibility of constructing and capturing a coherent narrative of the nation.

Documentary and the New Latin American Cinema

New Latin American Cinema (NLAC) increasingly and intentionally blurred the traditional divisions between documentary and fictional modes of production, yet it retained a commitment to accurately portray social reality and its transformations.[11] Most documentaries, even if they employed fictional techniques, were characterized by a "raw realism" that originated from the desire to "show things as they are" without regard for the problematics of representation.[12] Consistent with the historical context and political agenda of the NLAC movement, the use of realist filmic forms intended to counter the dominance of Hollywood's "dream factory" by portraying the harsh realities and marginalization of large sectors of society. A counterhegemonic discourse was embedded in the images themselves, serving as a source of information and education with a clear message for the urgency of social transformation.

NLAC filmmakers insisted on a socially engaged discourse based on flexibility, research, experimentation, and adaptation to the shifting dynamics of social struggles.[13] Fernando Solanas and Octavio Getino's manifesto, "Towards a Third Cinema," encapsulates the drive to use documentary as a revolutionary tool, to produce images that show the truth of a situation and resist commodification.[14] Solanas and Getino echo the Brechtian impulse to change the function of art as an institution by producing "indigestible" images that cannot assimilate within a capitalist system.[15] However, Brecht's techniques are meant to disrupt the realism of the artistic production and to reveal that social reality is itself a construct. Albeit concerned with problematizing hegemonic forms of production, the majority of New Latin American documentary production was paradoxically infused with a strong dose of realism. Therefore, an important theoretical impasse arose for NLAC filmmakers: How to negotiate the paradox of making "revolutionary" films and at the same time employ a realist style to portray national and political realities?

Although the majority of NLAC filmmakers combined the urgency of militant political practice with innovative use of cinematographic devices, the dangers of dogmatism became apparent. In a 1971 interview, Miguel Littín, then head of Chile Films, stressed the importance of creating a didactic cinema inspired by the realities of everyday life, which would connect directly with the public.[16] For Littín—a representative of the majority of Chilean filmmakers at the time—the role of cinema was threefold: to clarify the meaning of the ongoing revolutionary process at work in Chile, to be a "witness to reality," and to project future transformations.[17] This vision— guided by a belief in the immediate possibility of representing reality—was minimally concerned with the formal elements of the medium beyond strictly utilitarian purposes. Formal innovation mattered only in its capacity to display the relevant images to make the public understand "how imperialism affects their daily lives."[18]

After the 1973 military coup and the brutal censorship enacted during the military dictatorship, the social relevance of documentary had to be negotiated rather than assumed. As most filmmakers active during the Allende years were forced into exile, they lost contact with the initial drive behind documentary filmmaking: the hope and the possibility of social change. Nonetheless, there are points of continuity between the interest in social change characteristics of precoup films and the interest in the relationship between the individual and the collective through an emphasis on collective memory, a defining trait of exilic production. Exilic films reference the filmmakers' past, therefore maintaining one of the NLAC principles: using the historical as the basic intertext.[19] The documentaries function as memory-work to counter the dominant tendencies of censorship and amnesia during and after the dictatorship.

Although some critics have suggested that the experience of exile has undermined "the nation" as a thematic and conceptual focus of filmic production,[20] I believe it is important to examine how the representation of "the nation" is transformed through the lens of memory and exile. Indeed, the exilic experience adds complexity to the "national question" and complicates the position that filmmakers and spectators take in regard to *lo nacional*. However, given that the majority of films produced in exile have an explicit or implicit national subject matter, the desire to examine the meaning of "the nation" through the cinematic medium persists.

The Return of the Exile: Modes of Historical Representation in Documentary Film

In contrast to fiction film, documentary holds the promise of a visual form that has a direct link to the historical world. The indexical quality of the image allows it to serve an *evidentiary* function—the images *testify* by virtue of this indexical relationship to the historical world, thus corroborating the rhetorical argument of the filmmaker.[21] Given that documentary film generally relies on the guarantee of the camera at the profilmic event,[22] one of the ways in which exiled filmmakers can (re)gain access to the profilmic space is by returning to their homeland.[23] The cinematic medium has the capacity to act as a visual substitute for the spatial backdrop upon which the past reconnects with the present.

Motivated by this realist impulse, Miguel Littín and Patricio Guzmán returned to Chile intending to film and expose the hidden reality of the dictatorship. In *Acta General de Chile/General Statement on Chile* (CU/CL, 1986), Littín clandestinely returns to Chile in order to unveil the hidden traces of resistance against the regime and to bring personal memories of Allende to the forefront. In *Chile, Memoria Obstinada/Chile, Obstinate Memory* (CA/FR, 1997) and *Salvador Allende* (BE/DE/CL/FR/SP/MX, 2004), Guzmán returns from exile with the purpose of recovering the lost history of the Allende period, to collect and paste together the "restos" that were hidden from view, but that are still present beneath the surface. Faced with the concept of a lost collective due to military repression, both filmmakers turn Allende into the symbol of a collective dream that was shattered before it could become reality. However, the realist style Littín and Guzmán use to construct an alternative historical narrative ends up idealizing the Allende period to a point at which it becomes impossible to think beyond the possibility of politics after Allende. In the realist stride to uncover and show that which the official discourse has forgotten, these filmmakers do not examine the contradictions that made the dictatorship possible and therefore are unable to avoid a polarizing political dogmatism.

Raúl Ruiz: Documenting the Fictional Character of the Return

Albeit problematic, the importance of Littín's and Guzmán's documentaries lies in their insistence on the recuperation of political memory, as well as in linking the individual to the collective. While Littín portrays national history as an invisible or clandestine struggle for representation and Guzmán uses documentary images as weapons of resistance against forgetting, Ruiz explores the impossibility of transparent historical representation. Ruiz is also interested in political and historical memory, but his aesthetic practice opens different avenues for portraying the political.

In 1983, Ruiz received official permission to return to Chile, and that event inspired the film *Le retour d'un amateur de bibliothèques/The Return of a Library Lover* (FR, 1983), a short documentary about his memory of the day before the coup. Twenty years later, he produced *Cofralandes, rapsodia chilena/Cofralandes, Chilean Rhapsody* (CL/FR, 2002), a four-part documentary about the travels of a camera-witness that records Chilean idiosyncrasies while appealing to a shared cultural legacy.[24] In these documentaries, Ruiz employs surrealist techniques in order to access a dimension of political thought that questions the effectiveness of representation in light of one's experience of exile.[25] In contrast to Littín and Guzmán, Ruiz uses the return trope to de-romanticize the possibility of a full, complete return. The place he had left many years ago appears unreal. That is why, in his documentaries, the real is surreal.

Although he uses a first-person voice-over narrative, Ruiz goes beyond self-reflexive documentary as he questions the means by which reality is constructed.[26] Moreover, he explores how the cinematic medium constructs its own reality. By using documentary conventions and, at the same time, challenging them, he critiques the fundamental principles upon which documentary practice is built: truth and knowledge. In other words, he analyzes how cinema in general and documentary in particular can give the illusion of reality. His efforts aim to deconstruct the illusion in order to challenge the nature of representation. Ruiz's documentary practice draws its inspiration from Walter Benjamin's theories on the photographic unconscious of surrealism, which Ruiz discusses in detail throughout *Poetics of Cinema*. He thus transmutes Benjamin's work on photography to the cinematic medium, aligning himself with the "documentary unconscious," also present in other films, most notably in Luis Buñuel's surrealist documentary, *Las Hurdes/ Land without Bread* (ES, 1933).[27]

Surrealist Film and Surrealist Documentary

As opposed to classical or narrative cinema, which conceals the fundamental illusion of the film image by inducing spectator identification with a character,[28] surrealism exposes and works against the inherent identification process of cinema. Surrealist cinema, in turn, reveals the fictive unity of the human subject by exposing the fundamentally illusory quality of the filmic image.[29] Surrealism provokes emotions not through identification but through the creation of new images through concrete juxtapositions. The connection between documentary and surrealism arises when it is important to document the social dimension while simultaneously showing the inability to use filmic images as evidence of reality. The three discursive levels—image, narrative, and sound—become contradictory and destabilize the viewer's epistemic fantasy.[30] For example, in *Las Hurdes*, Buñuel does not seek to understand the Hurdanos—"the strange [ones]"—in order to integrate them into a national narrative by denouncing their poverty and the negligence of the state. This would domesticate their story and fabricate their helplessness for the viewing pleasure of a national audience. Instead, he wishes to visually show the strangeness of the familiar category of "the nation."[31]

In Ruiz's documentaries one surrealist strategy is to combine a lack of narrative logic with a "realistic" visual representation. The effect is that the generally objective voice-over narrator not only lacks coherence and thus loses credibility, but also the image cannot function to reinforce the narrative, as it does in a traditional documentary. In other instances, profilmic special effects are used. The profilmic effects are effects achieved before shooting the scene; they differ from the cinematic effects, which are achieved by manipulating the camera or the filmstrip. With the use of profilmic effects, the viewer does not feel a distortion in the perception of the image but does experience a feeling of strangeness since profilmic effects are acceptable in fiction films but not in documentaries.[32] Employing them in a documentary breaks the contract of verisimilitude between the film and the spectators. Thus, Ruiz seeks to show that regardless of filmic form, the cinematic image has the power to create an alternate reality, not only to imitate reality. In these examples, the focus is not on the representation of reality but on the revelation of the film as artifice.

The visual style created through these strategies produces what could be described as an oneiric vision of reality. In Ruiz's documentaries, there is a clear connection between dreams and the process of memory. Repeatedly, the narrator informs us that he literally falls asleep while trying to remember, thus drawing a parallel between the process of memory and the logic of dreams. I understand Ruiz's use of dreams in his work as a way to challenge the binary between memory and forgetting in order to introduce a tension between re-membering and forgetting the traumatic past. To illustrate this tension, Ruiz comments on the beginning scene of *Cofralandes*, which features a multitude of Father Christmases in the courtyard of his childhood home:

> At Christmastime in Chile, there are thousands of Father Christmases. In the summer they walk about and, by sheer force of numbers, they become intimidating. That makes one think of the military. It's child-ish, but it's oppressive. It's above all the idea of translating, in the most indirect way possible, the trauma of sixteen years of dictatorship. That happens in an ambiguous manner. On the one side, we seek to forget, but on the other side, we seem to remember. Sometimes we only think of that; sometimes we forget. It's a little bit like someone who has cancer. He cannot think of his cancer all day, so from time to time he manages to forget. It is as if the whole country had some kind of terminal illness. Sometimes he jokes around, sometimes he forgets. Sometimes he surrenders to the evidence.

Ruiz recognizes the impossibility of directly representing the traumatic past and employs familiar images such as the Father Christmases to unsettle the sense of familiarity and comfort generally associated with them. Blurring the

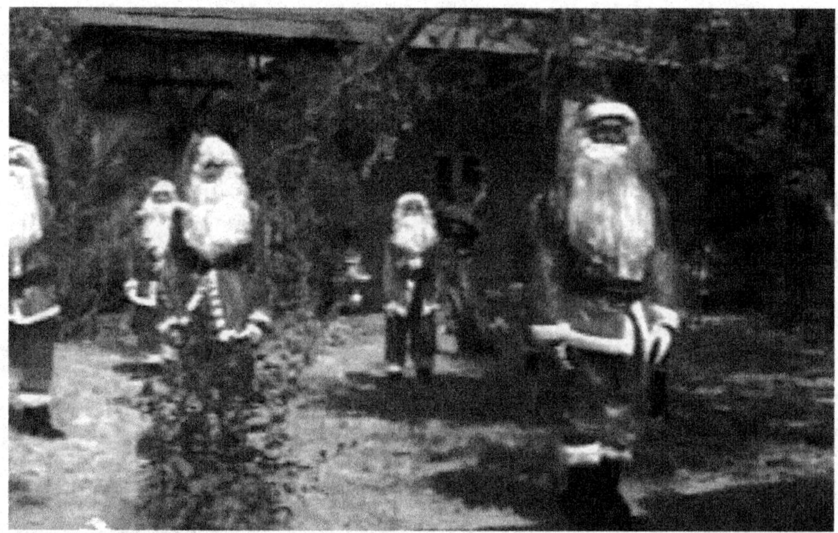

An army of Father Christmases in *Cofralandes*.

distinction between dream and waking life is analogous to making the familiar unfamiliar or to blurring the division between forgetting and memory.

This analogy further reveals memory as an ambiguous product of the collective unconscious. The use of these images emphasizes the social potential of surrealist cinema to reference the subject's inner conflicts. The oscillation between memory and forgetting destabilizes the unity of the subject, both individual and national. By using surrealist techniques, such as nonsynchronous sound and collage, the concept of the nation as a unified entity is challenged by the juxtaposition of disparate elements that have "Chile" as the common denominator. The documentary form is used for purposes other than legitimizing one's account through visual evidence. Ruiz's use of surrealist style, with its techniques of visually representing contradictions and ambiguity, is the concrete manifestation of a work that refuses to idealize the precoup past, while seeking new forms to represent the political: he uses ambiguity, rejects transparency in favor of elliptical forms of representation, and brushes reality against its own norms.

The Love of Books, the Search for Memory

Le retour prefigures the preoccupations that will be more fully explored in *Cofralandes*: the temporal and spatial return to his native country, the

185

relationship between dreams and memory, the refusal to romanticize the past, and the surreal aspect of reality. *Le retour* "documents" Ruiz's first trip back to Chile after his exile.[33] In the short film, the camera contemplates and records images of objects he reencounters upon his return, such as his old apartment and his personal library. Using a reflexive voice-over commentary, the director-narrator travels to various destinations in Chile in an effort to remember the night before the coup. Charles Tesson compares the narrator with a sailor who returns after having survived a shipwreck, only to find that he does not recognize his country or his childhood home anymore.[34] What was once familiar is now perceived as strange. The narrator knows that he is expected to remember, but he finds himself unable to recall important events from his past. This forgetting, however, is not the amnesia of the neo-liberal present. It is the uncomfortable oscillation between remembering and forgetting that Ruiz described when talking about the cancer patient in the last quote.

Le retour mimics the classic documentary form: the camera records the filmmaker's return by presenting images filmed from a car in motion passing by important landmarks in Santiago, as well as static images of private spaces, such as the filmmaker's childhood home. The images match our formal expectations of the documentary form, but they do not document the narrator's process of remembering. In the same way that traveling shots of the city alternate with static shots of the home, the voice-over narrator alternates between sleeping and waking. The narrator falls asleep when he encounters obstacles in his search, insinuating that he might obtain access to his forgotten memories by accessing his unconscious through dreams. The act of sleeping could also function as a defense mechanism. In any case, sleeping does not provide him with any useful information. In another example of the mimicking of traditional documentary form, two scenes employ the traditional interview format—static camera, interviewees speaking directly to the camera, medium close-up shots—but the interviewees' statements do not elucidate anything about the narrator's missing memory. The setup matches our formal expectations of documentary form, but challenges them through image and speech. Their interviews are testimony-like, but they do not give testimony directly.

The search for a lost book shows the deliberate lack of argumentative logic that characterizes this documentary. While he is at home trying to remember the day before the coup, the narrator notes that the house is different from how it was when he left. The logic is declared as follows: there is something missing from the house ∴ there is a color missing from the house ∴ a pink book is missing ∴ pink is the missing color in the homeland ∴

retrieving the book will restore the color of the country.[35] The thought process is presented as inductive logic, although it is, at best, associative logic. The confusion generated by this contradiction leads the viewer to a cognitive space outside of rationality, forcing him to break with rational thought. The activation of memory, then, has to go through a process that opens toward the unconscious. This action establishes a similarly nonlogical, yet fundamental, connection between individual memory (recall and find the book) and collective memory ("discolored" country).

Nevertheless, despite the lack of logic, the narrator begins searching for the book. Since all book lovers had burned their books and left for Australia (an indirect way of referencing exile), he tries the taverns. Again foiling the expectations set up by the voice-over commentary, the next scene is in a house. The mise-en-scène however, is characteristic of documentary-style interview, where a man is framed in a traditional medium close-up. Visually, the spectators are set up to expect to obtain information from him. However, these expectations are foiled because the only piece of information we obtain is that the last person who had the book was someone called Chico Leiva. The interviewee is an old friend whose political affiliation is subtly suggested: his right arm is shaking uncontrollably because of too much drinking, but his left arm is steady—"la izquierda, la que cuenta, es firme." Significantly, it does not bring us closer to the documentary's stated goal of remembering the day before the coup, but it is there as evidence of the repressive effects of the dictatorship.

While the search for the book continues, some scenes begin to repeat themselves, contradicting the expectations of "advancing" in the investigation through new images. As viewers, we are trained to follow a quest visually by going from place to place, finding new clues, and so advancing in our goal. In this case, the reverse happens: the repetition of the scenes frustrates our expectations of acquiring knowledge even as the camera travels throughout Santiago. The search for the book seems to have no end in sight, and the constant camera movement offers no clues that bring us closer to solving the mystery of the pink book. Likewise, the close-up static shots of books in the library do not allow the spectator to obtain any new knowledge about the pink book or the forgotten memories. Thus, the visual aspect of filmed reality refuses to support the narration's purported quest for memory.

After having abandoned the search for no clear reason, a strange incident makes the narrator recall the pink book two days before leaving. In a bar, he sees his best friend and wants to invite him to have a drink. At the same time, he knows that his friend has been dead for at least ten years. This contradiction intensifies when we see a close-up of the friend. The friend behaves very coldly and says he has nothing to do with Chico Leiva. While the camera remains fixed on the man, the narrator falls asleep and, during his sleep, he realizes that the man is speaking in many worlds at once, so he concludes that he must be his dead friend. The spectator does not have time to process this impossible conclusion because, immediately afterward, the narrator announces that he was sitting on a book that could have been none other than the pink one. Given the established interplay between dream and memory-work, it is no surprise that the book "materializes" following the act of dreaming. The book is *Cantos a lo divino y a lo humano en Aculeo*, an anthology of folkloric poems collected by Juan Uribe-Echevarría.

As a conclusion, the voice-over states: "And here I found the key to what happened on that night of Pinochet's coup." Our knowledge expectations are foiled, however, when we hear: "The key to it all was a poem from my childhood, which I had never managed to learn by heart. That night I realized that I would never manage to memorize it." The narrator's conclusion, the impossibility of memorizing a childhood poem, works against classic documentary's pretense to knowledge. If he is to remember something, it is that he remembers he has forgotten, which does not add anything new to what we already knew from the beginning. The documentary ends with a different voice-over reciting the aforementioned poem, "Julio" by the Uruguayan poet Julio Herrera y Reissig. Furthermore, the act of introducing new elements unrelated to the quest (such as the poem) frustrates any possible logical conclusion about *the meaning* of the impossibility of memory. Rather than filling the gaps in knowledge, the quest exposes the lack of knowledge.

Ruiz's surrealist documentary functions not as a tool for knowledge and rational understanding but as a means to explore Walter Benjamin's concept of "the optical unconscious." That is, by displacing our expectations of knowledge and by dampening our faith in the camera's ability to unveil the mystery of memory, we are challenged instead to access different spatiotemporal configurations.[36] In *Le retour*, surrealist documentary techniques work to destabilize the unity of individual and national subjects. This prefigures Ruiz's work in *Cofralandes*, where the director works to un-define the nation as subject. Through similar formal techniques, Ruiz shows how there is no possible sense of Chilean-ness. "Lo chileno"—and thus the sense of a unified national political project—is a fiction.

Cofralandes: Un-Representing the Nation

In *Cofralandes*, Ruiz returns to Chile again twenty years after making *Le retour*, this time while the transition to democracy is well underway. Sponsored by the Ministry of Education of the Concertación government, *Cofralandes* was intended as an educational piece on Chilean history, to be screened in schools and cultural centers. The film is a subjective representation that seeks to reach the public by evoking collective images and memories. The seven-hour, four-part series blends Chilean folklore, regional linguistic analysis, and observations of a neoliberal Chile that seems to have forgotten its past. Like *Le retour*, *Cofralandes* combines public spaces, such as streets and museums, but also private homes.

Here again, Ruiz undertakes the task of representing the nation, *lo chileno*, but he presents it not as an entity, but as a collage of differences. *Cofralandes* emerges as a critique of cultural nationalism by pointing precisely to the things that don't fit and that can't be accounted for within a national narrative. Images develop through a process that resembles dream-work: there are associations between scenes but the associations are not chronological and appear prompted by obscure mechanisms that intentionally disrupt narrative logic. Ruiz achieves these aims formally through a collage of disparate elements whose sole common denominator is their association with the idea of "Chile": popular culture through folklore (reenactments of folkloric tales, recorded performances of "cantos a lo divino"), references to the Popular Unity government, images of contemporary urban spaces, radio recordings of the bombing of the presidential palace, newspapers from Chile's national day, September 18, 1973, a week after the military coup. Furthermore, in order to destabilize the national aspect as the unifying factor, he introduces strangeness into the national landscape by inserting brief scenes from other countries, such as Japan, India, and Holland.

In this documentary film, Ruiz continues to destabilize the presumptions and drives of traditional documentary, showing the intrinsic impossibility of documenting for the purpose of acquiring *knowledge* of the object of study. For example, having just arrived from France, the exilic narrator observes how three foreign travelers examine the Chilean landscape. A French journalist writes travelogues about what he saw, "understanding without understanding," while the German traveler draws everything he sees and observes the others with curiosity. The German illustrator paints the landscape in order to try to decipher something about the psychology of the people inhabiting it.[37] He declares Chile a country of contradictions—"you can see it in the landscape"—while the camera contradicts him by contemplating a perfectly ordinary scenery made up of shrubs and greenery. Another foreigner, an English anthropologist, had initially come to Chile with the intent to study an area where there was a high incidence of suicides.[38] However, his object of study kept evading him: as he reached his research site, the suicides would stop, only to flare up in other regions, from Concepción to Antofagasta. After spending three years chasing after the object of study without ever reaching it, he gave up and settled in the village of Padre Hurtado. Disciplines such as journalism, botany, and sociology are tools for understanding, but despite their efforts, full comprehension keeps evading the practitioners of these professions. *Cofralandes* makes a fundamental critique of the impetus to document national reality through the "transparent" medium of ethnography. Ruiz's cinema refuses to become yet another inadequate ethnographic tool.

As we have seen in *Le retour*, for Ruiz, the political eye brushes reality against its own norms. Ruiz illustrates this idea by employing the documentary form while simultaneously questioning its capacity to access pure historical realities. Instead, all historical references are contaminated by other historical moments, giving way to an anachronistic collage of images and sounds, which point to the impossibility of a faithful reconstruction and recuperation of the past. For example, contemporary cityscapes are layered with the soundtrack of voices of soldiers during the Naval Battle of Iquique during the War of the Pacific against Peru and Bolivia (1879–84). The visual images of present-day Santiago continue even after a woman's voice interrupts the soldiers' cheers. However, the phrase she repeats, inviting her child to an afternoon snack—"La once está servida"—invokes uncanny memories of another more recent military intervention, the September 11 coup ("el once," as the coup is commonly called in Chile). To strengthen this idea, sounds of machine guns are added to the soundtrack. Through the layering of nonsynchronous sounds, the past asserts itself in the present, emphasizing competing ideological commitments over a unified historical trajectory.

Along with nonsynchronicity, anachronism emerges as an additional formal concept in Ruiz's work. The use of anachronistic techniques rejects the mimetic conventions of traditional historical representation and challenges the conception of progressive temporality. For example, the vignette titled "Dialogue between a Patriotic Priest and His Royalist Sister" continues the examination of the foundational values of the Chilean nation-state through a discussion about Chile's independence between two nineteenth-century characters: a proindependence priest and his sister, who supports the existing colonial order.[39] References to local cuisine and periods of profilmic, asynchronous sounds of motorized cars passing by punctuate the dialogue. These profilmic special effects interrupt the dialogue but are ignored by the two characters. However, the extranarrative undercuts the reception of the supposedly historical narrative, producing feelings of strangeness and distance toward the characters' heated debate around

Chile's future. Thus, the scene eludes a clear fixed meaning. Instead, it allows access to the "optic unconscious" via a multiplicity of relationships between images and signs, exceeding the simple notion of representation. The collective meaning of the unconscious dimension lies in the relentless interplay between the private (the conversation) and the public dimension of national history.

Other scenes connect Ruiz's own childhood memories with the country's historical memory. The "personal" childhood memories and the "historical" memories of the bombing of La Moneda palace are spatially and temporally brought together by the juxtaposition of private spaces and asynchronous sounds of radio transmissions during the day of the coup. For example, in one of the beginning scenes, while on screen we see a group of Father Christmases standing aligned in the filmmaker's childhood backyard, the soundtrack intersperses childhood memories with radio footage of Pinochet ordering the bombing of the palace and with the junta's radio communication and discourse of cleansing the country of communists. Later, sounds of gunshots and breaking glass are layered over images of the filmmaker's house, filled with motionless bodies covered by newspapers.

Even though the Father Christmases might seem innocuous, their uniform-like attire and their constant presence give them a threatening character because they remind one of the military, and thus, of military repression. The perceived threat does not only signal to the coup and the repression of the Pinochet dictatorship, but points to a deeper threat in the absolutism of advocating for one legitimate way of doing things or of seeing things—an oppressive ideological uniformity. Here the personal informs the historical, but Ruiz is very deliberate not to present the Pinochet dictatorship as a historical aberration. He takes a broader look at historical precedents to the military regime by looking at the functioning principles of the military, which might carry a desire for order and uniformity that transcends the historical Pinochet's regime, visually indicated by the perennial Father Christmases. Thus, we can surmise that the logical and visual disorder in Ruiz's documentaries functions as a formal rejection of ideological uniformity.

Ruiz goes on to show that this ideological uniformity is very much present in the current postdictatorial consumer society, where neoliberalism—an economic policy instituted during the dictatorship—is presented as the only viable option. For example, the camera records people standing in lines without knowing why they are standing in lines. While wandering the streets of Santiago, the camera focuses on a person having a heart attack, but the paramedics refuse to take him to a hospital before he writes them a blank check

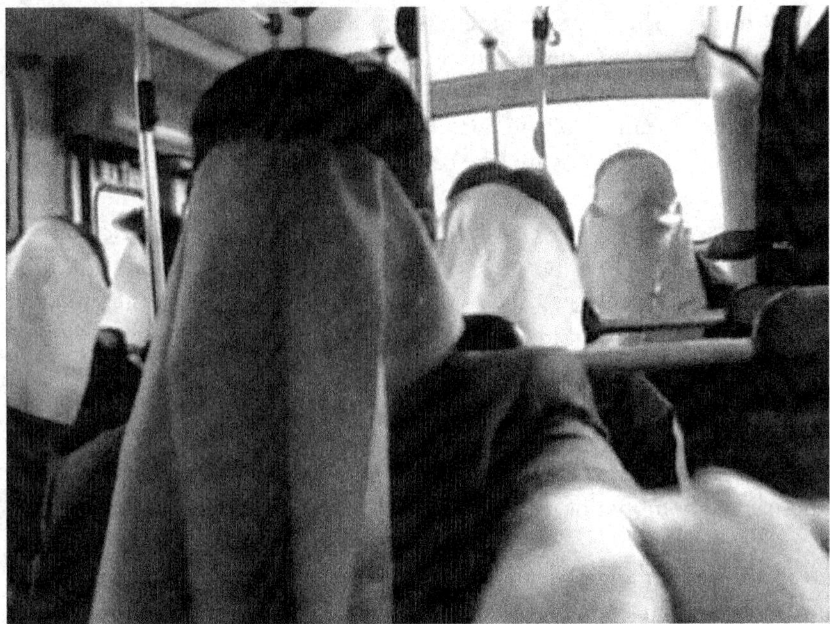

The alienation of life in a neoliberal society in *Cofralandes*.

to cover his future hospital expenses. We notice that the person's bank is Citibank, serving as a reminder of the ever-present flow of global capital. This scene compels the spectator to contemplate that an individual without the same financial means could not survive a similar incident. These and many other scenes portray absurd situations, seeking to show the disorientation of those filmed. The absurdity of the situation of daily neoliberal life prompts one to question the concept of reality itself. There is also a parallel between the alienation of the neoliberal subject and the exilic filmmaker behind the camera. While the dictatorship alienated its citizens through forced exile, today's consumer society alienates its citizens through economic exclusion. Members of both categories are rendered nonsubjects through their exclusion from political life.

As previously established in *Le retour*, Ruiz broadens the scope of his historical exploration and uses folklore and literary texts to access distinct aspects of collective memory. Here, for example, *Cofralandes* integrates a formal reinvention of Blest Gana's novel, *Martín Rivas*. Critics have indicated how this novel, "requisite reading in the education of Chileans as Chileans," plays a key part in the national imaginary.[40] After describing a visit to Rotterdam, making associations between a rainy day and a photograph immersed in water that sparks the memory of a tragedy in Valparaíso due to a fire sometime around 1950, the voice-over narrator remembers a novel by Blest Gana, but is unsure whether it was *Martín Rivas* or not. However, he does remember that it was required reading in schools. The narrator tries to summarize the story but keeps forgetting and invents characters' names and the relationships between them. On screen, we see an adaptation of the novel with static characters in period costumes.

Influenced by nineteenth-century Romanticism, *Martín Rivas* functions as a national allegory: fulfilled love as the allegory for conciliation between antagonistic regional and class interests.[41] However, the film's reworking of the *Martín Rivas* novel by reinventing names and relationships destabilizes the reading as of the novel as national allegory. While the details of the plot and the characters' descriptions receive little attention, the narrator places emphasis on the historical event that is portrayed in the book: the first Liberal attempt to challenge the autocratic and oligarchic tendencies of the Chilean political system guaranteed by the 1833 constitution.[42] This event, the first Chilean Liberal revolution of 1851, is experienced as a break—"y una mañana . . . revolución"—indicating a moment of interruption in the visual representation of the novel. While the images of the characters appear frozen in time, the narrative voice gives life to a new way of seeing the novel, where the interpretative weight is placed on the historical breakdown in the linear national discourse. The film's focus on historical crisis contrasts with the novel's overall optimistic representation of Chilean nationhood. Thus, while the novel has traditionally been interpreted to culturally reinforce nationalism, the documentary's focus on the rupture of the political fabric (the reformist Liberal rebellion) underscores a history of differences and divergent positions that traverse and interrupt the construction of national hegemonic discourse.

Ruiz's documentaries create a deliberately surreal version of reality, pushing the boundaries of representation through formal means. In the same way in which Ruiz had defied militant cinema because of its subservience to politics, his surrealist documentaries defy the fantasy of return to a lost "Chile" because it never existed in the first place. At the same time as he reveals the impossibility of return—not only to Chile but also to the past—he also disrupts the triumphant narrative of neoliberal democracy. By tirelessly exposing the disunity of the individual and national subject through formal means, Ruiz's cinema opens up a creative space for political engagement. Ruiz continues to be politically innovative through his innovative aesthetics.

Notes

1. Jeffrey Middents, *Writing National Cinema: Film Journals and Film Culture in Peru* (Lebanon, NH: University Press of New England, 2009), 11.

2. *La hora de los hornos/ The Hour of the Furnaces* (Fernando Solanas and Octavio Getino, AR, 1965–68).

3. Aldo Francia, *Nuevo cine latinoamericano en Viña del Mar* (Santiago: CESOC Ediciones ChileAmérica, 1990), 167–68. The original quote is: "La forma en que aquí se están discutiendo las cosas, en forma declamatoria, vaga y parlamentaria es reñida con la manera de ser chilena. Nosotros conversamos las cosas en otra forma. Aquí se están repitiendo lugares comunes sobre imperialismo y cultura que se pueden leer en cualquier revista; y luego viene Fernando Solanas a contarnos *La Hora de los Hornos*, que ya vimos anoche. Nosotros nos vamos a la sala del lado a hablar de cine. Los que quieran pueden venirse con nosotros. Ah, y tampoco nos gusta que nos tomen 'p'al fideo' al Che Guevara. Eso es igual a los españoles que, en las reuniones de cineastas, colocan una estatuilla de San Juan Bosco sobre la mesa."

4. In this section I refer mainly to essays from the collection *El cine de Raúl Ruiz: Fantasmas, simulacros y artificios*, ed. Valeria de los Ríos and Iván Pinto (Santiago: Uqbar Editores, 2010).

5. Waldo Rojas, "Raúl Ruiz: Imágenes del pasado," in De los Ríos and Pinto, *El cine de Raúl Ruiz: Fantasmas, simulacros y artificios*, 21.

6. Edoardo Bruno, "Ruiz Faber," in De los Ríos and Pinto, *El cine de Raúl Ruiz: Fantasmas, simulacros y artificios*, 43.

7. Luis Mora del Solar, "Ruiz ¿Díscolo o artista de vanguardia?," in De los Ríos and Pinto, *El cine de Raúl Ruiz: Fantasmas, simulacros y artificios*, 64.

8. Malcolm Coad, "Grandes acontecimientos y gente corriente," in De los Ríos and Pinto, *El cine de Raúl Ruiz: Fantasmas, simulacros y artificios*, 77.

9. Raúl Ruiz, interview by Federico de Cárdenas, Paris, *Hablemos de Cine*, July 1971, 11. The original quote is as follows: "Lo que creo es que se nos da la posibilidad de anular definitivamente esta diferencia entre lo documental y lo argumental o de ficción, integrándolas en torno a esa capacidad de la cámara de indagar en sectores de la realidad y simultáneamente registrarlos e interpretarlos, darles contenido ideológico. Esto implicaría automáticamente la anulación de toda diferencia de géneros y plantearse una actividad en la que difícilmente se distinguiría el campo político del campo estético, que son una sola cosa, y es realmente así."

10. Bill Nichols, *Introduction to Documentary* (Bloomington: Indiana University Press, 2001), 178.

11. Ana M. López, "At the Limits of Documentary: Hypertextual Transformation and the New Latin American Cinema," in *The Social Documentary in Latin America*, ed. Julianne Burton (Pittsburgh: University of Pittsburgh Press, 1990), 408. NLAC was aligned with Third Cinema, a wider trend of global cinematic innovation that arose from a widespread desire to counteract the hegemonic influence of Hollywood and its cultural domination over so-called Third World countries. As revolutionary cinema, Third Cinema's aim was to use the cinematic medium for the liberation of the socially and economically oppressed sectors of society.

12. Julianne Burton, "Toward a History of Social Documentary in Latin America," in Burton, *Social Documentary in Latin America*, 6.

13. Michael T. Martin, "Introductory Notes," in *New Latin American Cinema Volume 1: Theory, Practices and Transcontinental Articulations*, ed. Michael T. Martin (Detroit: Wayne State University Press, 1997), 16.

14. Fernando Solanas and Octavio Getino, "Towards a Third Cinema," in Martin, *New Latin American Cinema Volume 1*, 46.

15. Peter Bürger, *Theory of the Avant-Garde* (Minneapolis: University of Minnesota Press, 1984), 89.

16. Miguel Littín, interview by *Cineaste*, *The Cineaste Interviews: On the Art of Politics of the Cinema*, ed. Dan Georgakas and Lenny Rubenstein (Chicago: Lake View Press, 1983), 25.

17. Ibid., 30.

18. Ibid., 32.

19. López, "At the Limits of Documentary," 407.

20. Kathleen Newman, "National Cinema after Globalization: Fernando Solanas's *Sur* and the Exiled Nation," in *Mediating between Two Worlds: Cinematic Encounters in the Americas*, ed. John King, Ana M. López, and Manuel Alvarado (London: British Film Institute, 1993), 244–45.

21. Nichols, *Introduction to Documentary*, 106.

22. Philip Rosen, "Document and Documentary: On the Persistence of Historical Concepts," in *Theorizing Documentary*, ed. Michael Renov (Minneapolis: University of Minnesota Press, 2004), 72.

23. "Profilmic" refers to that which already exists in the world before the shoot. The camera films a reality that precedes the shot. Examples would be the actors' bodies or the location of the shoot.

24. Since documentary was crucial to the development of Chilean national cinema, it comes as no surprise that Ruiz was also a trained documentary filmmaker. He attended Fernando Birri's Escuela de Santa Fe in Argentina, the first film school in Latin America, but he abandoned the program shortly thereafter because of the strong emphasis on documentary filmmaking at the expense of formal experimentation. One of Ruiz's main points of contention was that documentary could very easily fall into political dogmatism because of its purported intention of faithfully representing reality.

25. Another Ruiz film that directly examines the theme of exile and memory is *Diálogos de exiliados/Dialogues of Exiles* (FR, 1974), but I will not include it in my analysis because it is not based on the physical return of the filmmaker. A future comparison between this film and the documentaries discussed here would be very fruitful in terms of the elements they have in common, such as the use of absurd situations, the interrogation of national categories, and the formal differences between documentary and fiction film.

26. Zuzana Pick, "Chilean Documentary," in *The Social Documentary in Latin America*, ed. Julianne Burton (Pittsburgh: University of Pittsburgh Press, 1990), 124.

27. See Catherine Russell, "Surrealist Ethnography," in *F Is for Phony: Fake Documentary and Truth's Undoing*, ed. Alexandra Juhasz and Jesse Lerner (Minneapolis: University of Minnesota Press, 2006), 99.

28. Christian Metz, *The Imaginary Signifier: Psychoanalysis and the Cinema* (Bloomington: Indiana University Press, 1986), xiii–xiv.

29. Linda Williams, *Figures of Desire: A Theory and Analysis of Surrealist Film* (Berkeley: University of California Press, 1992), 23.

30. Russell, "Surrealist Ethnography," 103.

31. Graham Roberts, "Surrealism and Documentary," in *The Unsilvered Screen: Surrealism on Film*, ed. Graeme Harper and Rob Stone (London: Wallflower, 2007), 93.

32. Williams, *Figures of Desire*, 49.

33. While some scenes were indeed shot in Chile, others were earlier unrelated shots *not* in Chile that Ruiz had filmed earlier and decided to add to this documentary (personal communication).

34. Charles Tesson, "Lettre d'un cinéaste ou Le Retour d'un amateur de bibliothèques," *Théatres au cinéma: Raoul Ruiz* 14 (2003): 132.

35. "∴" is the logical symbol for "therefore."

36. Walter Benjamin, "Little History of Photography," in *Selected Writings, Volume 2*, ed. Michael W. Jennings, Howard Eiland, and Gary Smith (Cambridge, MA: Harvard University Press, 1999), 510. The "optical unconscious" designates a new realm of experience that photography can open access to, similarly to how psychoanalysis aims to access the psychic unconscious. "It is another nature which speaks to the camera rather than to the eye."

37. This is most likely an allusion to Claude Gay, a French botanist and illustrator, who most famously drew the Chilean flora and fauna in the mid-nineteenth century.

38. This is most likely an allusion to French sociologist Émile Durkheim, who wrote a study on suicide in 1897. He examined the differing suicide rates among Catholics and Protestants.

39. This vignette illustrates the arguments for and against Chile's independence from the Spanish crown as advanced by the priest Camilo Henríquez (1769–1829), an intellectual promoter of the independence movement. This allegory illustrates the fundamentally religious underpinnings of the nation-state, despite the claims to Enlightenment ideals in the transition from the colonial system to national independence.

40. Jaime Concha, "Introduction," in *Martín Rivas*, by Alberto Blest Gana (New York: Oxford University Press, 2000), xiii.

41. Ibid., xxix.

42. Influenced by the values of the French Revolution of 1848, a new politically progressive movement, la Sociedad de la Igualdad, challenged what they considered an autocratic form of government and opposed Manuel Montt's presidency. The movement was swiftly repressed, and many leaders of the government went into exile. See Brian Loveman, *Chile: The Legacy of Hispanic Capitalism* (New York: Oxford University Press, 1979), 140–14. For the importance of this event in *Martín Rivas*, see the introduction by Jaime Concha.

Dialogue with Raúl Ruiz

Santiago, 1970

Cinema and Politics

Raúl Ruiz: I don't quite understand the expression "political cinema"; I remember a few classifications regarding the term: direct cinema, pamphlet cinema, ideological cinema—as in *The Hour of the Furnaces*—and a utopic cinema, which gives shape to a people's hopes based on real facts. What I do is political cinema in another sense. For me, filming a movie is a political act. I'm against the idea of film director as "the boss," or against [Jean-Luc] Godard's idea that everyone should make movies— and that they should do so in a general assembly. This parliamentarism has proved to be very sterile because, when it comes to filming, it's really Godard who does it, so the ten hours of previous discussion are useless. I believe in a collective cinema on another plane—a muscular plane— which attempts to develop a series of instincts, of behaviors that result in working together, like a sort of cinematic orchestra in which you simultaneously play a part and listen to it. But apart from that, I'm excited about the possibility of bringing this culture of resistance to light, especially in the case of Chile. My idea is that cultural methods of resistance make up a nonverbal language whose only way to become formalized and ascend to an ideological level—I employ this phrase with some reservations—is through film. These self-referential, decanted techniques form a group— not so much of syntagmas, but of stylemas:[1] arts in the middle of the road; arts of having a drink, of saying "cheers," of self-nullification, ul-

---

This is an extract from an important interview Ruiz gave in 1970, with poets Enrique Lihn and Federico Schopf. It was originally published in *Atenea: Revista de ciencia, arte y literatura de la Universidad de Concepción* 423 (July–September 1970) and reprinted in Raúl Ruiz, "Diálogo con Raúl Ruiz por Enrique Lihn," *Atenea: Revista de ciencia, arte y literatura de la Universidad de Concepción* 500 (2009): 265–79. All notes are supplementary notes provided by the editors.

timately. These stylemas can only be registered through film; they resist description because they are not verbal; it is a nonverbal language. This culture exists, we exist and the act of filming, which unites us with this culture, exists. It is in this sense that the act of filming, for me, is a political act. Filming is a bridge, a powerful way of establishing contact through gestures as timeworn as taking a photo in the park. To film is, in essence, to take a photo in the park.

Enrique Lihn: This, naturally, would influence the filming method, right?

RR: Of course. This implies an initial consequence: you must create a certain climate in which filming becomes possible, in which those stylemas emerge. Right away, this implies a distinct idea about mise-en-scène; it makes you change the dramatic structure of things.[2] The formula is quite simple. We work on the basis of a first model, of a group of opinions or things we have imagined; after choosing a general field and situation, we create what is called "a story." We take this previous model, constructed and enriched, to the field, where things begin to happen to us for the first time. We begin to investigate and then other types of situations surface, which confirm the previous model, modify it, or call into question its very structure. These three types of situations lead one to reject the model, to put it into practice, or to modify it. You try to avoid this temptation and, instead, to maintain all observations in terms of what they are—simple observations—until the moment they become embodied, when their quantity and magnitude tend to separate from the original model and conform to another by their own devices. And then comes the "cool" part: this new model that naturally arises from observation is set against the original model, but without discarding the original model. The two are utilized as opposite poles, and the events progress equidistantly to each model, creating a greater or lesser tension between the two. The models are not movie A and movie B, but rather outlines that exist outside the film; the film is that which exists in the midst of the events in tension between the two models. This is what concerns the dramatic structure. Then there is the issue of cinematography.[3] Working more like the photographer in the park than the paparazzi, establishing relationships between the cameraman and the actors, endeavoring a certain type of cinema in verse, so to speak. I'll give an example: in this room, there is a space naturally created by the everyday displacement of people. You compile these lines of displacement, and from that compilation, you extract a series of camera movements; but you don't make use of them in the area in which such movements occur, nor do you respect their magnitude. You make use of them from any part of the room, and you construct a situation that occurs in the entire room. Let's suppose that there are seven camera movements; with an arbitrary focus, you begin to move the camera according to the seven movements; when you arrive at the seventh, you start again, and so on and so forth, inserting events into the established mold (like in forced poetic verse),[4] which necessarily surpass that mold. This is what I understand as working with cinema in verse.

EL: The cinematographic language you are coining seems to attempt to eliminate the receptor, the signs directed towards the viewers' attention; it sort of reminds me of the surrealists' approach to language, who said it was misguided to consider language an instrument of communication. It would better serve to assess certain zones of reality that are difficult to access, or to use it in a negating manner, rejecting language within language. The technical procedures that you've detailed to register this culture of rejection seem to be as hermetic as the culture itself—and to duplicate this rejection at the formal level.

RR: That is to say, the method is consistent with the material it aims to extract. The fact that there is no pretense to reach [an audience] beyond the group in which it will be filmed makes it even more coherent. Ultimately, this has to do with Borges's prophecies. I remember this one: in the future, everyone will be his own Dante and his own Shakespeare; no one will pester the future with their brilliant ideas. I call this attitude "political" because it has to do with dislodging the intellectual from his privileged position and removing the disciplinary quality, scientific or mechanic, from artistic activity. Thus, once again, surrealism: everybody should be able to make art.

Cinema of Inquiry

RR: Currently, I see two very apparent attitudes. First, there is foundational cinema, which questions the meaning of filmmaking—concretely that of [Jean-Luc] Godard; the kind that *Cahiers du cinéma* presently endorses. On the other hand, there is the tendency to see film as a means to discover new and unique situations. The second attitude has one obvious limitation. Somewhere, [Paul] Valéry talks about the shock of realizing that the "terra incognita" disappeared from maps; there are no more territories to discover. Film, too, has already discovered all territories, has already seen the key places, including the most abject cases—like that of

[Gualtiero] Jacopetti—and six or seven years before that, with the emergence of the first Third World films. That's the other path.[5]

Now, to outline my own work's position, I'd use another framework specific to Latin America. Here, I see three clearly defined tendencies. On the one hand, a sort of civil cinema, which simply *shows* Latin America's concrete problems and presents the avenues by which they can be resolved—the case of *Hour of the Furnaces*. Didactic cinema. On the other hand, especially in Brazil, I see a metaphoric cinema that tends to *create* situations that synthesize the country's problems and unlock their solutions. Lastly, there is the type of cinema we try to create: a cinema of inquiry, in the sense of *searching* for national issues. By filming a situation, you complete it; you resolve it. This is the idea of the cinema of inquiry.[6]

Our work has precedents, but from the fields of sociology and anthropology: in the films of Jean Rouch, the Museum of Man, and Canadian cinema. This type of cinema never dared to include fantasy, to consider itself as art, as play. The idea of doing things very seriously ultimately ruined the possibilities of this cinema. I will talk about an experience connected with this type of film; I don't know who did it, nor exactly where. A group of filmmakers went to a fishing village, where they took one fisherman and had him talk for days. The movie went on for days. Later, without any editing, they projected all this material to the village of fishermen, who were constantly mentioned in it. The fishermen watched the film, and they changed—although I can't say what type of change it was. In any case, the film's intent was to influence reality, establishing a connection between filmic activity and real events, an influence that would not have been possible without film.

EL: When you begin to use cinema to influence the process of reality, doesn't that bring up an ethical problem for you? In what way—with what guidelines—would you influence what occurs in reality?

RR: I would contemplate that after having worked in cinema for a long time; for the time being, I'm not sure it really has any influence.

EL: But you would like this type of cinema to unfold into [class] consciousness-raising on the part of the actors-viewers . . .

RR: I am a little afraid of that expression; one generally alludes to something very specific when talking about "consciousness-raising."[7] Apart from that, it does not mean that people who do certain things say: "Wow! I do that." It is all about these gestures becoming a language, reflecting themselves in film, which can come to define them. I suspect that the culture of resistance conceals a great capacity for subversion, and that this resistance can only become subversion by completing itself through the medium of film.

EL: Subversion in what sense?

RR: In the most Bretonian sense of the word.

EL: If you had to put this subversion in political terms, against whom would you direct it?

RR: It's not about putting it in political terms.

EL: You worked with [Saul] Landau . . .[8]

RR: But this is something else. We're simply accounting for our militancy and our lack of militancy. It's a kind of ideological introspection for our entire crew: knowing where we are and trying to understand it by way of cinema. We believe that, through cinematographic work, we become in tune with each other, and that is what's valuable. . . . I do feel the need to be a part of the Marxist camp; I *feel* Marxist, but I would not venture to say that I *am* Marxist because I'm not familiar enough with Marxism [emphasis by editor]. But the wordplay in declarations of principles is something I dislike. I have no reason to reject everything that Marxist militancy gives me and that helps me to interpret the reality in which I move. What I do understand clearly is that cinematographic work has made me reconsider all kinds of political issues.

Federico Schopf: I don't think anyone can live, from the perspective of a permanent [class] consciousness, either as a Marxist or as an existentialist. For that to happen this perspective would have to become common sense in a society, and Marxism is very far from being that, at least in our Chilean society. Now, the encounter that Raúl is proposing, with everyday responses to the aggression of capitalist society, can of course coincide with Marxist thought, and in fact it should coincide to the extent that this thought conforms to reality. This is our hope. That is to say, he positions himself in a primitive point of view regarding the option of ideologies, but that does not necessarily mean that he does not agree with the notions of that particular thought—concretely, Marxist thought—in regards to our society. The crux, it seems, is that people do not build their lives on the basis of [class] consciousness. What is important is the premise of a perfectly coherent system that precedes the conscious construction of said system, and that, nevertheless, is present in every gesture and attitude, in the unconscious impulses of each of our country's inhabitants. One must look for the presence of such a system in public offices, for example, understanding that there is a whole system of mechanisms in place that allow a person to show up late to work every day. The system officially justifies that a public functionary can always arrive at work at ten o'clock instead of nine. If the system actually started to work correctly, a certain frustration would arise. For example, if an employee were to go cash a check, and the check were ready, or if someone were to tell him the bus would arrive at 9:30, and the bus actually came on time—this would all create chaos, at an unconscious level, for a middle-class Chilean.

RR: I was referring to the gradual nature of rejection; that is, more or less, what my divergence regarding Landau was about. He insists on considering these behavioral faults precisely as mere faults or accidents. There is the rational behavior, which consists of going to work, arriving on time, and doing a good job. Or, conversely, one directly rejects employment and fights against everything it stands for. The middle ground between these attitudes indicates underdevelopment. That is his point of view, and, in part, that of Wright Mills and the majority of Marxist sociologists who study the Third World. I suppose that this framework is valid and has the advantage of being extremely clear in that it allows for rapid cataloguing of all events as they arise. It has the disadvantage of creating—from the point of view of the results of our investigations—a sort of emotional paralysis. That is to say, it's impossible to sympathize with those who haven't made a decision, who are victims of underdevelopment—therefore, with all of us, to a greater or lesser degree. But let's look at somebody who participates wholeheartedly in political struggles, such as a MIR militant. You can easily detect in him—and Landau proved this in the movie *Fidel*—twenty or thirty characteristics indicative of an underdeveloped, Third World citizen, that is to say, a series of behavioral incoherencies. There is a general coherence but also twenty gestures that contradict it. For Landau—and for the majority of Marxist sociologists and European leftist intellectuals—this comes as a shock. This is demonstrated in Fanon's *The Wretched of the Earth*. We, as people of the Third World, to the extent that we participate in these incoherencies, we accept them as our own and put them into practice, and so we're condemned, that is, excluded.[9] We cannot be free, we have no possibility of escape from this world; we are condemned. The fact that they classify us this way brings us to a certain emotional tendency to reject these interpretations.

Translated by Tessa Allen de Oliveira

Notes

1. For a discussion of Ruiz's understanding of "stylema," see the introduction to this volume.

2. Dramatic structure here refers to both plot and staging, usually in theater.

3. The original phrasing is "puesta en imágenes."

4. A "forced poetic verse" (in Spanish, "pie forzado") is used in poetic competitions, as in the case of *payadores* (folk poets and performers). In Spanish Golden Age poetry, poets would also challenge each other with a verse, and the poet was "forced" to compose a poem in the meter and rhyme of that verse. Ruiz is most likely thinking of *payadores*, but the implication is to give a starting point, a direction for the artistic creation.

5. Gualtiero Jacopetti, Italian filmmaker, generally credited with the invention of the "shockumentary," especially in *Mondo cane* (IT, 1962).

6. Emphasis added to facilitate understanding.

7. The original phrasing is "toma de conciencia."

8. Saul Landau was an American leftist documentary filmmaker, who notably directed *Fidel* (US, 1969) about the Cuban revolution and *¡Qué Hacer!/ What Is to Be Done?* (CL/US, 1970) on the advent of Chile's UP government. Ruiz initially collaborated on *¡Qué Hacer!* but reneged on what he interpreted as dogmatic tendencies at work in the film. See 2008 interview in this volume.

9. The original phrasing is "fuera de valoración."

An Interrupted Dialogue

New York, December 9–10, 1989

This interview took place during the first retrospective exhibition of Raúl Ruiz's films in the United States, organized by Wendy Lydell (of Fox-Lorber Pictures) at the Public Theater. At the time, Ruiz was in the midst of collaborating with actors associated with the Wooster Group in preparation for shooting his movie *The Golden Boat* (1990) in New York. During the interview, Ruiz regaled his interlocutor with his remarkable erudition, his interest in colonialism and transculturation, experiences of exile, concepts and processes linked to the making of several of his films, and his commitment to cinema as a vehicle for constructing and transmitting Chilean national identity.

Catherine L. Benamou: Your work extends over many years, beginning at the start of the 1960s, right?

Raúl Ruiz: Yes, at the end of the 1950s.

CB: Could you describe the context in which you began to make movies?

RR: It's hard to say . . . our whole generation is the generation of cinema; it is a different generation now. Our generation lived surrounded by cinema, watching movies. I was accustomed to seeing five or six movies a week in huge movie theaters and triple features, and so the first gift I asked for was a camera. And they gave me a camera. So, I filmed with my friends—in other words, the starting point. . . . I'd say that, when I really started to apply myself, I wanted to do theater—that is, something different; and all of a sudden I took up film again as a way to be less serious. All this happened in Chile in the '50s, which was a very special moment: the end of the '50s and the beginning of the '60s. It was a moment of terrible culture shock, which provoked a kind of sudden interruption of national sentiment in Latin America in a very strong, overwhelming, in-

204

vasive way, rupturing all artistic activity and feelings of cultural identity. It was something maybe good or maybe bad, but it was a shock for all of us: leaving artistic activity behind as something secondary and focusing everything on political activity. Although no one did that; in their minds, it was a course of action no one wanted to take; no one thought about fully dedicating themselves to political activity. Somehow, they carried out any type of artistic work available to them, but they knew that it was an addendum to something much more important. Today, I—and the majority of my generation—we are people who've always felt like addenda. And making films in Chile directly leads to being an addendum because, in Chile, cinema is indeed an addendum to Chilean culture—one movie is produced every five years. And, fortunately, concurrently with that great cultural shock came another shock, which was the New Wave: people filming in the streets, making it possible to film the city. To film the city, to film the country, to play—for example, in *Three Sad Tigers* (1968) there is a joke intended only for Chileans. In Santiago people watched the movie in a theater called "La Bandera." The end of the movie takes place in the street, and the camera passes by that same theater. So, those who left the theater also left the movie onto the same street. It had a very small effect because it was produced only in that theater, but—for others and for me, above all—the idea is that, thanks to cinema, we were able to create elements of national identity, and everyone was involved in that important game.

CB: Yes, and there is the Cinema Nôvo movement in Brazil with Glauber Rocha . . .

RR: That was the second shock: Cinema Nôvo. After that, Cuban cinema. Of course, apart from Glauber Rocha, Brazilian cinema has another contribution that, for me, is much more important. There is a certain Hispanic prudishness that is very strong in Latin America, especially in Chile, which is the idea that every pretty image is in some way guilty, that images should be made without aesthetic content. Aesthetic content comes from pathos—we're all "Crocians," followers of Benedetto Croce: art is expression, not harmony. That's one thing. Then there was a certain dictatorship, a certain neorealist dogmatism that set in very quickly. And, quickly, the entire Left began to fight the New Wave, which had infused a considerable freshness, giving people the urge to make movies . . . they were completely irresponsible movies, and moreover, about love stories. . . . So, en masse, the entire Latin American Left immediately intervened—into culture, let's say—to try to impose the neorealist dogma, which ultimately meant working with things that had almost nothing to do with neorealism. In our case, that meant working with statistical data, investigating the social situation in the field—a job that was ultimately very boring (regardless of whether it was just or not). And it was in this context in which the Brazilians appeared, making highly political movies in which they freely created a collage of styles.[1] First, they were aware that cinematographic style is something separate from the reality effect of the camera. So, for example, they had their actors act like in Japanese movies; Glauber Rocha said he asks his actors to act like the actors in Japanese movies. . . . He said that unashamedly. He'd tell an actor playing a Brazilian peasant to act like Toshiro Mifune. The actor playing the peasant would make all the sounds and calls of Brazilian cinema and then, right away, he'd take up themes associated with Westerns. So, all those elements from Western films and all those Brazilian elements blended with folkloric music, and it all worked together. This was all very stimulating; it was a completely new means of expression. It was an explosion; it was a truly aesthetic influence whereas the other [Leftist tendencies in Latin America] were, more or less, moral instances.

CB: [Brazilian cinema] was an influence for you . . .

RR: I never did . . . when I did that, I created a sort of parody in *The Penal Colony* (1970); it was almost a jest at Brazilian cinema. But in any case, Brazilian cinema was unafraid of parodies—they self-parodied—a cinema where there was more happiness in filming.

CB: And later, Carnaval became a source of inspiration for them during the Tropicalist era . . .

RR: This, once again, forcefully became the new Tropicalist ideology, which the Left again criticized, calling it "Macondism" because of García Márquez's first novels. So, there was an immediate global criticism because [for the Left] everything that prompted pleasure was a sin.

CB: In that era, perhaps. You also mentioned Cuban cinema. *Three Sad Tigers* is based on the Cuban novel . . .

RR: No, it's not based on the novel. It's a Chilean play that came before the novel and shares the same name. . . . I couldn't change the title because it came before the novel. There is no connection other than the fact that they take place at night, and apart from including a lot of Bolero—not a lot, because there is very little music. It's for historical effect.

CB: That's interesting because I think one of the reports is mistaken since it mentions Cabrera Infante.

RR: Yes, they've talked about that a lot . . . no one has asked me. It's a work by Alejandro Sieveking, a playwright who continues to write a lot; it was the first time I did an adaptation of a play that was not mine.

CB: Yesterday we were talking about the idea that there were aesthetic positions that could correspond with political positions, which was an issue in Latin America in the '60s. There was a correlation in which one could adopt aesthetic issues to advance the political process . . .

RR: I've always been under the impression that every time one talked about aesthetics, it was really about ethics, and every time one talked about ethics, it was about aesthetics. For example, desiring a beautiful death is an aesthetic problem, not an ethical one. It seemed to be the ideal of an entire generation—dying in a beautiful way. And creating works of art that serve a purpose is an ethical problem and not an aesthetic one. Art was applied to solve ethical problems. It seems to me that there was an inversion of functions.

CB: And that era was characterized by ethical issues . . .

RR: With all that that implies. With such bad faith that later. . . . Somehow, in *The Suspended Vocation* (1978), I talk a lot about that part, more than I do about France. It's the situation Klossowski wrote about—very particular to the Catholic Church during the occupation—shown in a very indirect way. Klossowski's other vocation was to be a priest. And it shows the Church's behavior, this voluntary "Kafkaism." . . . That is, Kafka doesn't describe a metaphysical feeling of angst, but rather, that an institution deliberately utilizes that sentiment to rule. The Church applies a Kafkian method in order to preserve the illusion.

CB: What interested me about this movie was the insistence on the inscription of the profane in the sacred, which is very Catholic.

RR: It has often been said that a good Catholic doesn't believe in anything. The only Catholic religion is the Church, the structure of the institution. In the perfection of the institution, they find meaning in life. But belief isn't necessary.

CB: And that's the reason for the convergence of the church's two schools of thought at the end of the movie.

RR: Of course . . . in fact, there are three tendencies: the Marianists (those who follow the Virgin), the "black party" (who are, more or less, the Jesuits, but who—for Klossowski—were also vaguely agnostic Nazi collaborators). But they aren't in the movie. And then there are the Integrists. Ever since we began to discover that Paradise was not above, that Hell was not in the center of the earth, that the earth was not round . . . since the sacred texts were already in place, a compromise had to be found. So they created this distinction—fairly recently, first in the twelfth century and definitively in the seventeenth century during the Counter-Reformation—between the order of the world and the order of grace. In the order of the world, things are as they are. The order of grace is a purely allegorical one that imposes itself upon the order of the world to organize, to situate one spiritually within the chaos of the real world. This distinction was, and is to this day, abominable for the Integrists— the so-called Catholic Integrists, who believe there is no distinction and that, somehow, they must continue to believe that Hell is in the center of the earth, that the Virgin ascended in body and soul. . . . Just think: the dogma of the Virgin's ascent in body and soul is from 1950, it is recent. Aldous Huxley asked if she had entered into orbit. It's a dogma of faith. One must be a really good Catholic to believe that the Virgin ascended in body and soul . . . at a time when it was already known that there was no above or below. No, she went above, to a specific place. No, that's incredible . . . it's almost a coup d'état, and everyone is perfectly aware of that. But the Integrists believe that these things can't be separated. And the main character in *The Suspended Vocation* is an Integrist. Now, of course, the visual game is that two actors play the Integrist; he's no longer whole. And nothing is whole. The church is always two. There are two ways of looking at things within these three tendencies. And the Marianists are followers of a church that has no dogma, a populist church focused simply on the exaltation of the Virgin Mary—which is the exaltation of common life, of religious confusion, of popular festivities, of the church as it is in Latin America. The Latin American church is Marianist.

CB: In the movie I detected not only a slightly Borgesian narrative structure, but also a Chinese logic. Yesterday we were talking about a Hegelian, dialectical movement . . . through steps one must arrive at a transcendent, utopic stage. Only that, in these diversions, one sees that every thing produces its own opposite.

RR: I haven't thought so theoretically about something that, for me, is a practical problem—which is the problem of trying to make films that have something to do with the life I've been given. That is to say, in life there is a mediation between the things that are more or less determined by who you are and what you want, and a number of accidents. You occasionally anticipate them, and then you take them in and you reintegrate them into a sort of life plan. But, in general, one goes with the flow; these accidents take one in all directions . . . and the way in which these accidents occur is something that has always fascinated me. It has to be the main reason why I don't like the idea of "plot." Because, generally, accidents are considered errors in theater . . . there should be no accidents. If they do occur, they are always in the form of a "gag." On the other hand, in day-to-day life there is a play between chance and need, which cinema is particularly fit to capture, to show. It can intensely show "A" and "Z," something and its opposite. Moreover, the game of taking a sequence in one direction and all of a sudden abruptly changing it has more to do with this type of play.

Of course, one puts much more into a movie than intended. There are the two laws that José Ortega y Gasset called "complementary laws." One was called "the law of reduction" and the other was something like "the law of abundance." In every work of art, the artist always says less than he wants to; he doesn't fully say what he wanted to say. That is the law of deficiency. The artist means to say something from "A" to "M," but he or she only manages to say from "A" to "C." And, on the other hand, wanting to say everything, one somehow says more than that in what little one said. And that's the law of abundance. That is, there is an excess that you can't control. And Ortega y Gasset says that one can determine the quality of the work of art by comparing how these two poles operate. Too much efficiency generates too much excess, and the work becomes incoherent. There must be a maximum effect to what one wants to say, which will generate a minimum of overabundance but which will be a sort of halo around the work. It will give the work something . . . it will be something like the atmosphere around the earth. This generates life. It's an interesting idea . . .

CB: There is an analogy about the construction of language, of the language in *On Top of the Whale* (1982), in the sense that there is a real possibility of telepathy, of perfect communication. On the other hand, there is a complete misunderstanding—the impossibility of communication. The subtitles can change the entire work for you.

RR: You have the advantage of understanding almost every language. There's German, there's Dutch . . . and the voice-off is in French.

CB: Even if one does understand all those languages, there is a moment when—like this question of abundance—there are so many languages that they all blend into one. Or rather, you no longer know if you're hearing French or Spanish or English . . .

RR: Yes, because halfway through a sentence there is a switch to a different language.

CB: Yes, and we want to impose a mental logic to make everything intelligible . . . we will not recognize divisions between languages. On the other hand, there are moments, gaps, created by unintelligibility. And, at the same time, there is the question of polysemy in the indigenous people's language in *On Top of the Whale*. One word can mean many different things.

RR: It has to do with their description of the language—not the Yaghan people's but the others'—that every word is a metaphor. And that every word is a natural number. Thinking about it as a sexadecimal system, it would be a typical primitive language, in which arithmetical calculation is tied to vocabulary. The language in the film has only six words.

CB: In the Western world, we have separated arithmetic from linguistic development.

RR: At some point it branched off completely, of course. Further, numbers were invented or rather they became represented by signs and not by words. For example, in Hebrew, words—letters—and numerical symbols—numbers—are closely tied, and this allows for Kabbalah combinations. But imagine a sexadecimal system, sixty numbers that are the only sixty words in a language. There is a sexadecimal system— the Babylonian—it can work differently: instead of a decimal system, think of it as six and ten. It works. Also, in addition to being numbers, the words were also metaphors. So the combinatorial process grants you an enormous quantity, a true galaxy of words with which you can name one thing in a hundred thousand ways. I worked on this with a mathematician friend, an imaginary language. This isn't very important for the film, but it must be known that all language is a labyrinth. That's all you need to know. Also that indigenous language isn't necessarily a simple thing, but rather the opposite. . . . Not so with the Mapuche language; they were already using a *lingua franca* when the Spanish arrived. It was a more efficient, more "modern" language. But many indigenous people use a language closely tied to daily life and, therefore, capable of expressing complexities—capable of changing every day.

CB: That emerges as a theme in *The Penal Colony*, right? The character Napoleon Duarte says: "it is not a language because it changes every day." There are no rules, no grammar.

RR: But that—coming from a Latin American character—you don't know if he's lying or not. He could say that so that you'd leave him alone, to throw you off the trail.

CB: There's also the argument that violence is a cultural issue. . . . I thought that was an interesting subject for that era because it is an argument to defend difference.

RR: That was one of the reasons the movie made people angry—it mocked the fundamental Latin American dogma that cultural identity was inseparable from certain behaviors, like machismo, like this problem is ours and ours alone.

CB: And that the rest is colonization; and that democracy is a form of colonization.

RR: And that all foreigners are colonizers.

CB: Now, returning to *On Top of the Whale*, regarding the issue of colonization, stylistically there are two models of colonization within that movie. One is the model of the traditional Latin American oligarchical family that owns land. And on the land or on the fringes—or occupying the land without working—are the *indios*. So, it is a sort of colonization by negligence.

RR: The movie is full of allusions to that theme in other ways. It's the issue of the extermination of the natives of that region, the Alacalufe and the Yaghan. It is a very important issue in Patagonia; it was carried out by the Campos Menéndez family. It's a true fact, reported by a certain [José María] Borrero, a Spanish lawyer who wrote a book called *Tragic Patagonia*. The Menéndez family confiscated the book, bought every copy, and destroyed them. Borrero published another edition, they destroyed it again, and this continued throughout his lifetime. At some point the book began to sell, hand-copied, and people were able to learn about the details of the extermination of the native population and where it happened: how the Salesians tried to save them, how they systematically wiped them out by putting a bounty on their severed head; an ear was worth X amount, then the head. The movie supposedly takes place in Springhill, where they poisoned a whale with strychnine and invited the natives—whale is their favorite dish—to eat it and that is how they killed 1,500 indigenous people there.[2] That is to say, all the allusions in the movie are deliberately made so as to seem imaginary. But again, everything is real. The character's name is Narciso Campos, of the Campos Menéndez family, inasmuch as the name is real. The woman who plays the part of Sara Braun is Dutch in the film. Sara Braun was a German from Hamburg who came to work in a brothel in Punta Arenas. She was a prostitute, and she seduced one of the landowners, one of the members of the Menéndez Behety family. She married him, and she turned into someone like [Friedrich] Dürrenmatt's character, the old lady in *The Visit* (1956). She took revenge on all of society—the movie character is somewhat like that. But I can't say much on the matter because I will get myself sued by a very jealous family; they have three Argentine presidents, they own Patagonia on both sides of Argentina and Chile. A very powerful family. But any Chilean from the region will immediately understand all this, and they see a different movie; it's very different.

CB: The way the man who lost the wager treats Narciso is very interesting.

RR: All of Patagonia is the Latin American Far West, which is to say that everything was established through the strangest of wagers.

CB: There's also linguistic play here because it seems as if he doesn't understand the other language, and he manipulates that.

RR: There is a game of complicity, the complicity between the master and the valet. It is unclear where the power lies.

CB: And that these positions were arbitrarily determined at some point. Now, in the second part, once the woman becomes the mistress of the house, the natives begin to mimetize the colonizer . . . it's really mimesis. But what interested me—since the movie ends there, you can see it as a dystopic issue—is that we're always stuck in that game.

RR: The natives do mimetize but they continue to live elsewhere. They're there and they're not there; they can copy every gesture, they do it almost to be polite, but they're absent. They're always thinking about something else.

CB: And that aspect is very important in the film; the fact that it isn't complete. That is, on the one hand there is domination, but on the other hand the colonizer himself doesn't control the process.

RR: Patagonia, the "Tierra Austral," is a huge expanse of empty land, of empty territory. That's what the conquistadors found when they came to Chile, to the south, searching for gold. They were very hostile territories on one side and beyond that, there is emptiness, nothingness. The colonizers reached all the way to Puerto del Hambre,[3] to Tierra del Fuego.

CB: Well, returning to the issue, we'd talked about an ontological question in cinema; in other words, when one faces the camera, it's sort of like [Walter] Benjamin described it, but not completely. Something happens in front of the camera: something is lost but photogeny is gained. And, through that, one can extract a meaning that is not fixed. It's an ambiguous question that allows for the possibility of searching for another politics for cinema. Or rather, a politics through the ontology of cinema itself. This is in itself a political issue if one knows how to take advantage of it, or rather to refrain from trying to cover up these characteristics and instead to open them up.

RR: Film has a lot to learn from the other arts. It has a lot to learn from painting in that respect; using paint, at some point, came to mean using accident. Painting later got lost in that, disappearing into the air by putting itself into question, by playing with other mediums. One says, "of course this danger exists." But the power of film lies in its enormous capacity to produce a parallel discourse—if you take it into account, things appear in the movie, they are apparitions (this is another theoretical issue, the issue of apparitions). We can start with cinema's classical myths, with *Blow Up* (1966), Antonioni's film, which is the story of a friend of mine, Sergio Larraín, a Chilean photographer. That always happened to Larraín: he'd take a photo of a flower, but it would come out an airplane . . . but it was because he mixed up the rolls of film. There is a reality element. When you're filming something, there are obvious things that you don't see, that nobody sees.[4] There is a grotesque example: filming *Memories of Appearances: Life Is a Dream* (1986), we were filming the theatrical part, *Life Is a Dream* itself. And Rosaura was speaking, performing her monologue, "wild Hippogriff . . .,"[5] and she was there with her horse, and next to them was the servant,

Clarín, with a donkey. And the donkey got a terrible erection as the monologue was going on, and there were at least forty people watching the scene, and nobody saw the donkey. We saw it in the projection of that take; it was huge . . . and beyond that, noticeable! It's something of a constant function in film: the things that are true apparitions. Or rather, the combinations of lights or shadows produce unexpected valuations in certain parts of the image. This is slightly lost with the kind of photography, with the new kind of Kodak film,[6] with the new kind of illumination that tends to account for what the eye normally sees. But by working with lights and shadows, there are always apparitions. For me, it's very important to play with these apparitions, to manage these apparitions. It's almost a parallel world, a parallel movie.

CB: Yes, and you call attention to that in *The Suspended Vocation* by switching between color and black and white. Sometimes the same scene is in color and in black and white.

RR: Yes, there is a lot of play there, too. The idea is that there is a movie because the other one was censured. There is a movie that can't be seen. A whole movie, also made of two, that is outside.

CB: Now, regarding *The Suspended Vocation*, it also seems that there is a discussion about history itself in the sense that the visual style can show that this is in the past; that the occupation and that other movie are from the '60s. And, little by little, the characters disappear; they converge. This is also a formal game in the sense that there is the question of montage and "suture," of not showing the montage. But one becomes aware that a take of one situation is told in another take. So the consequences of a historical reading are interesting, and I wanted to know a bit more about your ideas concerning history and the historical process, its possibilities and its relationship to cinema.

RR: To respond at this time, when history is going through such a difficult moment. . . . It wouldn't be easy to live as a historian right now. These are situations that nobody foresaw, and we must engage in historical work to foresee what will happen. It's not new that people say that nothing is new. It's true that the majority of historical phenomena are systems of recurrence. I'm not a historian, I can't say; these are personal intuitions. It's sort of the central theme I'm working with now, with the expulsion of the Moors. These are movies about civilizations that were believed to be lost, but they are present; they're right next to you, they are present in behaviors that people possess without knowing where they come from, and they are behaviors that come from very far away. Presently, above all with the globalization of the world, this is becoming much more evident—a much more intense feeling: the non-territoriality of national sentiment, of new cultures that are emerging, the cultural mix, the fact that they begin in one country and end in another; they are cultural lands. Try to imagine the idea of the "cultural border"; it's a very strange idea. I had a public debate with Jacques Delors.[7] He was talking about defending France's cultural borders against American invasion. The characteristic of cultural borders is that they are always defined by a horizon, so they have the same problem as the horizon. When you arrive at the horizon, there is another horizon. And cultural borders fulfill this function. In other respects, it is a poorly thought out issue. It's called "the fallacy of the perfect location" (Whitehead): the belief that there is a privileged space for every object.

CB: That's sort of French, too. Order, Versailles as the architectural model . . .

RR: Yes, yes. The Spanish itinerant courts shocked the French, despite the fact that they were itinerant for a long time, too. One can reference Norbert Elias here.[8] In Spain, the king wasn't sacred like in France, but rather the first among his equals. He governed with a kind of voluntary protocol that ensured that there was no jealousy, which lent a certain coherency to the court. The king always systematically arrived late, excusing himself; and he entered through the side door. This infuriated the French. . . . And he ate with his friends when he was supposed to eat alone. There was no hierarchy . . . one day he was on that side . . . or he would sit on one side and begin to move around the table. Most politicians do it, constantly trying to show that they are men who make mistakes. If you look at the place where the king was in the Escorial Palace . . . in the center, where the king should be, is God (the cathedral). The king is "in the back to the left," in quarters no bigger than this room. And there is no throne. The king is in a vaguely central position; there is no symmetry. For the palace council meeting, a little farther above, there is a seat—but a very uncomfortable one. . . . This is all to say that the idea that there is a precise place and that one object is better than another does exist. There are cinematic theories that operate on this principle. Jean-Marie Straub,[9] for example, believes that if you come into a space, there is a privileged spot within that space to put the camera; it is there and nowhere else.

CB: The magic place . . .

RR: Yes, I made a movie just about him, or rather, making fun of that idea. For that to exist there would need to be such a thing as a pure place; and places are always superimpositions of distinct spaces.

CB: I think they do that in [North] American cinema by default, for pragmatic reasons, because in principle they deny the idea of an aesthetic or of a special angle, but in practice they do just that. And in television even more; there is "no aesthetic," it's purely technology . . . it is efficiency that determines the matter.

RR: Which is not true because the only objects that are 100% efficient—that are pure functionality—are satellites. They ended up creating an aesthetic through repetition because functionality *is* an aesthetic. That was the idea behind Bauhaus—all functionality is an aesthetic principle.

CB: But here, in the US, they seem to have misinterpreted that . . . functionalism grew, and they forgot about the other side of things.

RR: I've never had discussions with "industry" people; they refuse discussion.

[. . .]

CB: In the last thirty years in Latin America, it seems we've experienced a passage from an era in which there was hope to escape from a situation of dependence and foreign presence through political struggle, being able to reject these things by means of different methods. But there was always the idea that an authentic nationality existed beneath the surface of this situation and that it could be salvaged. Now, in 1989, I think that has changed a bit.

RR: For me, that's almost good news. I was shocked upon first reading Américo Castro.[10] I suddenly realized that our fight for Latin American identity and the expulsion of the foreigner (whoever they were), for the best reasons, could be read as a parallel to Spain's actions of expelling the Moors and the Jews. Oddly enough, it could be read that way. Because the same appeal to national identity that the Spanish made, who are a mix of everything, the Latin Americans made too, with even less reason, calling themselves *indios*. The murderers of the *indios* called themselves *indios*; it's the ultimate act of bad faith. Not content with killing the indigenous, they appropriated the term, transforming it into a sort of national flag. And behind this desire for purity there is something of the terrible aberration that is the Spanish "old Christian."[11] Somehow, all Latin Americans know that the *indios* are old Christians, the *indios* were declared "old Christians" anyways. "Old Christian" means only one thing: that they are not Jews; it doesn't mean anything else. I'm obsessed with these archaic structures that are submerged, that are in the "freezer" so to speak, and when the door is opened just slightly, they escape. And, wearing new disguises, taking other names, they reappear. Suddenly, Victorian morals, which everyone believed to be dead, are perfectly alive, and they reappear in the form of "sexual harassment," in certain aberrant forms of bodily control, like the systemization of modes of nourishment, suddenly reappearing in the form of "smoking/no smoking," prohibiting this and that. Anyhow, things that were believed to be dead reappear more strongly; suddenly we find ourselves facing the Four Horsemen of the Apocalypse. . . . Returning to the issue, there was that intense movement, which the whole world lived through. At some point, I got worried about this revelation itself, the simple parallel between the expulsion of the Moors and the expulsion of the North Americans. It's a dangerous and unpleasant idea; generally it is thought that the Moors were the victims and the North Americans are the oppressors. But, when you look at them in the same context, it's not that different. And, what remains the same are all the misunderstandings and aberrations that this general idea produces. All the Spanish ghosts reappear, the whole issue of *casticismo*, for example.[12]

CB: In cinema, what's happened is that, through this process of failures in the '70s . . . of that attempt, of various forms, as far as foreign debt, militaries financed by the North Americans, all that . . .

RR: Moreover, it has all failed, the Left, the Right, the Center, everything fails.

CB: Yes, the implosion of all these things that were outside, that had been expulsed.

RR: Once again, a repeated history, the repeated history of the seventeenth century . . . the history of the conquest, the history of Spain.

CB: Exactly. Anyway, in regards to all that, I believe there have been two processes in cinema: on the one hand, Cuba has recognized that the majority of the people of ICAIC[13] are white and that there are ethnic and sexual differences (women's and minorities' issues) within Cuban society and that this has created a certain pressure against the idea of national struggle, of national identity above all. And it has established a sort of crisis within artistic creation that has led to a search for *kitsch* and for a mix of Afro-Cuban elements with both Christian and Soviet revolutionary elements.

RR: I don't understand why it works so poorly in Cuba and so well in Brazil. But in Brazil, there is a real experience of syncretism. Lusitania has the best practice of schizophrenia. They've always known how to move between two nationalities.

CB: Now, on the other hand, other countries that are still capitalist or semi-capitalist have tried to create an international competition, to recognize that the only means by which film can survive is by doing North American or French coproductions.

RR: That is bad faith: handouts. . . . Coming up with general theories to justify a lack of money is a classified case of bad faith.

CB: Of course, but this has had aesthetic consequences, and also in terms of production values and all that.

RR: It could be interesting in the long-term . . . the fact that it forces an understanding of a multiplicity of cultures, which is my main interest. I was mostly interested in countries where they practice more than one culture simultaneously, where the people can move from one culture to another.

CB: Yes, for you it's been different, this process of coproduction.

RR: Oh no, I simply stay there. I've never done co-productions. I go to a country, and I disguise myself as someone who lives there to try to understand . . . and I've become accustomed to that, and it's become almost a lifestyle for me.

CB: The opposite, then; it's not an importation.

RR: I continue to be Chilean, but I allow myself to tell Chilean stories all of a sudden in Palermitan. Somehow, to quote Menéndez Pelayo, one of the great theorists of folklore, "there is nothing less national than national folklore." If there is a point at which nationality directly contradicts cultural facts, it is in folklore. Folklore is, by definition, international; it's a shocking idea. Say it to any Latin American, and he'll think you're crazy. In the moments of highest development for European folklore, in the nineteenth century, they are like weavings of distinct parts . . . you can see the same dances in different countries. Now the whole world believes that rock is a recent phenomenon, but that phenomenon has always existed. In Isabel I's[14] court, they danced popular Spanish dances; she was a great flamenco dancer. There are Arab dances in Spain; the Arabs arrived in Spain in the eighth century and they immediately disguised themselves as Christians. The phenomena of cultural encounters are very rich; the great nationalist taboo has destroyed them, and that has affected us.

CB: Latin American musical forms, such as rumba, tango, and cha-cha-cha, were invented for American consumption. Since the beginning, it was not pure . . .

RR: And thank goodness, because if not, these cultural forms would not exist. Yes, like flamenco. Had it not become a Spanish national stereotype, it would have disappeared. And now there is no risk of that. Now it's an industry.

[. . .]

CB: What fascinates me—and this is a difficulty I have with the representation of France here in the US—is that, for example *Dog's Dialogue* (1977) shows "the aberrant" element of France, which is a part of the French everyday. Or rather, you can't divorce the celebration of Notre Dame from the sources of the Seine, on that side too, which is petit bourgeois. It's the same when you talk about a working-class neighborhood; France is mostly petit bourgeois in its mentality. The merchant on the street corner is the real Frenchman.

RR: Strangely enough, fascism failed in France because it didn't have anything new to offer because people had always been like that. The fascist ideal is that one should revere his work, even if it's a small job. In France, barmen are absolutely proud just in completing their tasks, which is abhorrent in any other part of the world . . . and this type of pride in not being ambitious was sort of the new ethic that Italian fascism brought about. In Italy it is indeed the opposite. In France, it must have really shocked people to hear all these ideals because they had always been like that: they didn't need to be fascist, they didn't need a war or a movement to be what they always had been naturally—admirers of the state, respecters of the family in a very nonideological way . . . all the fascist values were already there. There's a book—not a very good one—from this new philosopher who wanted to prove that the French were not fascists, but rather the complete opposite. The French were the French just as they are, very petit bourgeois; they had created antibodies that prevented them from being fascists. The only aspect of fascism that really took off in France was xenophobia and fear of immigrants, the fear of being invaded. Apart from that, there wasn't any other aspect that altered them. They're just vaccinated.

CB: And there's also the question of language—that the whole world needs to speak French in France. Here in the US it's not that way; here being monolingual is more a question of negligence.

RR: Can you imagine [François] Mitterrand speaking to the Arabic community, saying three mangled words in Arabic (like Bush when he spoke to the Hispanic community in the US)? He would immediately lose the election. This aspect is truly distinct. Only in France. In Germany or Spain or Italy, xenophobia manifests itself in a different way; it's not the same sentiment. In France, it's almost metaphysical.

CB: That's caused problems for you, the issue of trying to be interpreted as a Frenchman. For example, the name "Raoul." I've seen it both ways: as "Raúl" and "Raoul."

RR: It's practical! If I call myself "Raúl" like in Spanish, I become "Paul." And it's a problem for computers, for "spell-checks." People always mess it up. I always write it in the Spanish way and for documents, in French. And in some movies, I've put in the French version. But I never create the credits. I have a phobia of credits, of movie titles. Someone else always does them, an assistant. That's another reason there are errors, lots of errors.

CB: I'm interested in this orthographic strategy mainly because it contradicts established theories of exile. One says that, once you leave your historical context, there's no way to . . . the only solution is through an autobiographical investigation towards the past, towards memory. Cinema is employed to express this effort. [Fernando] Solanas[15] sort of represents this position.

RR: Along with almost all writers.

CB: It's interesting because once this cycle starts, it gets repeated. Or rather, they continue alone, increasingly isolated from any situation. On the other hand, there are those who say that if an artist is an author, it doesn't matter what context [s]he is in, that [s]he transcends his/her context. And there are people who've made this argument about Orson Welles, for example . . . once he left the United States, it didn't matter that he shot his productions in Morocco, Italy, Spain, wherever. . . . So it seems to me that both positions are mistaken because they represent purist points of view.

RR: I have a theory that there are two types of artists: Chileans and Argentines. [Smile]. There is the artist who needs a center, who makes art to develop and amplify that center. That center is the artists themselves—tied to a territory, of course; if not, it doesn't work. They are the Argentines. I found out that the king of Tartessos[16] was called "The Argentine," which is very amusing because everything attributed to Tartessos applies to the Peronists. They were geezers; they were old. You know, Tartessos is the only civilization that destroyed itself, or rather, the only one that gladly accepted all those who beat them down. And they gave them everything. It's a metaphor for a certain way of making art: allowing all types of influence to invade you, with the condition of staying in one sole place, in a center from which you radiate, like the sun, so to speak. And then there are the others, the Chileans, as in "chile," which is a bird, a seagull; it's an interpretation of the word "Chile." They are artists who make works of art as a means to travel. It's not that there is no place, but rather that they go from one place to another. . . . For one, it's a problem of roots, and for another, it's a problem of wings, of fuel to travel far away. Some have problems with urbanism, others with aviation. The problem with aviation is that you must land. You must land; if not, it's no use.

CB: But it also seems that the two types exist in time; that is to say that there are historical moments that correspond more to one type . . .

RR: There are those who believe in roots and those who believe in wings. It has nothing to do with a loss of feeling . . . nothing is lost moving from one side to another. The fear is always the loss of national identity. You're an "exote"—Victor Segalen's term.[17] I really like that expression he invented: "exotes" are those who love the exotic at first, but they search other countries for difference and not for identity. They don't look for countries similar to the ones they're in, but rather ones that are different. And they manage to be true exotes when they come back to their own country and find that it is the strangest of all. They gain that possibility. They lose something, but they gain a lot. In some ways, I really feel like an exote.

CB: But it's a bit unique. . . . I haven't seen that attitude so much in the rest of Chilean cinema . . .

RR: Chilean cinema is very self-referential; Chilean movies are full of allusions to things that no one else understands. I have that tendency, too. I believe that "Chile" is an inside joke; all Chileans are members not of a country but of a club.

CB: This comes up in the movies from the 1960s, like *Three Sad Tigers* . . .

RR: In all of them . . . in my latest movie, too, but I know it's a joke. You can't make a movie exclusively for that kind of thing.

CB: There's a critical moment in *Three Sad Tigers* when they are in the bar, they've already fought with the other guy, and they go out to the street. They encounter a man in the street, and they decide to go drinking. And there is a political debate . . .

RR: An absolutely incoherent one . . .

CB: Yes, they change sides.

RR: Yes, because in the end you don't know who is who.

CB: There was a reference there perhaps to the political situation . . .

RR: No, no, no, they're just nonsensical games. There is an allusion to a type of debate in which there is total incoherence. Chileans are the inventors of "the tacit verb"; they speak with unspoken verbs. During the Allende period Chilean leaders left the German translators speechless—they were waiting for a verb that never came. They made extremely long speeches without any main verb. They talked sort of like . . . Łukasiewicz[18]—a logician who invented a system that puts functions before the subject. "Well, I'll explain that, when, even though, lest you think that, but rather that" and after seventy preambles like that, "I invite you to eat." It finally arrives, but you've forgotten everything. In Chile there is a certain prudishness in precision; it's a country where precision is obscene. When you arrive in France and everyone is willing to clarify what is being said—it's happened to me, and I was blushing all the time there. They would say to me: "And what exactly is it that you want?" I've never wanted anything exactly because it's impolite to want something exactly.

CB: Now I want to ask you a question about how you work with actors. I've noticed that there are some actors who reappear in various movies who aren't actors, strictly speaking, but people who are connected to the creative process in some way.

RR: Like my assistant, François, who appears all over the place, and Pascal Bonitzer. The French are always actors in some way or another. Explaining a role to a French actor is a waste of time because you won't get anything out of him. Godard said that. I've talked for hours, explaining how to move, what to do; they listen to you attentively, and then they do exactly what they do in every movie.

CB: So you haven't found it necessary to work with professional actors?

RR: Yes, yes, I always work with actors and stage actors, but for other reasons, because French theater actors have a lot of precision because they have a sort of presence, of impertinence. They're all presidents of the "Republic of Me," they speak very officially about themselves. Which allows for a whole rhetorical game; rhetoric becomes a daily occurrence. It's a prescribed language; everything has already been said. What you're going to say—when you start to say it—it's already said. And then there's a sort of respect to wait for the end of the sentence. What you've said is very precise, always formulated in the same way, more or less. Language has a pre-established rhythm. If you compare British English with North American English, above all, or Portuguese with Brazilian Portuguese. . . . There are always two languages: that which is emerging—what you're saying—and that which is underneath, which is fashioning the words, which erupts. It's full of the hesitations that are part of language, like "you know . . ." Sometimes there are many languages fighting below the surface that arise. This is very valuable for cinema. It's distinct every time, and the good actors know how to play with that. In French, you can't; it's another game. That's interesting, too. I'm not saying it's a limitation; it corresponds to the country. The biggest mistake in French movies is trying to have all the actors act like American actors do.

CB: What's your relationship with French filmmakers?

RR: The same as every French filmmaker: nonexistent. French filmmakers don't talk to each other.

CB: Each man for himself.

RR: They're like gang leaders, they never talk among themselves because they're potential enemies. I don't know a single one. By contrast, I know a lot of critics, many literary people, people from other fields. It's the opposite; they like to be together, to discuss and all that. Filmmakers are generally loners.

Translated by Tessa Allen de Oliveira

Notes

1. Editors' note: The implication is that Brazilian cinema worked against this general Hispanic prudishness and against the dogmatism of neorealism at the time. This is the important contribution that Ruiz attributes to Brazilian cinema.

2. On the extermination of native peoples in Patagonia, see for example, Pedro Mayorga Martinez, *Costumbres y extinción de los indios del Extremo Austral* (Santiago, 1972). A Salesian priest, Father Alberto de Agostini (1883–1960), who explored the region extensively, produced a Flaherty-like documentary, *Patagonia*, in 1928 that shows the last remaining members of the Tehuelches, Ona, Yaghan, and Alacalufe tribes in their native habitats. *Patagonia*, directed by Alberto de Agostini (Watertown, MA: Documentary Educational Resources [DER], 2007). Website. Accessed August 22, 2014.

3. Puerto del Hambre is a site south of Punta Arenas, near Tierra del Fuego and the Strait of Magellan.

4. Editors' note: Ruiz here is talking about how the camera operates on prefilmic reality. First, how the process of filming helps one see elements of the prefilmic reality that were not available to the naked eye. Second, how these elements of prefilmic reality captured by the camera can result in unexpected visual elements that he calls "apparitions" in the sense that these previously unseen elements appear or emerge in the filmic image.

5. The first line of Calderón de la Barca's play *Life Is a Dream*, on which Ruiz's film is loosely based.

6. According to Jean-Louis Seguin, an expert on the subject, "The late 80s saw the introduction of the EXR line, the first to use the new T-Grain structure." Jean-Louis Seguin to Catherine Benamou, e-mail correspondence via Association of Moving Image Archivists (AMIA) listserv, August 19, 2014.

7. French economist and politician (b. 1925), Jacques Delors was president of the European Commission from 1985 to 1994; he embodied the relaunch of the dynamics of integration that took place with the Single European Act (1987) and the Treaty of Maastricht (1992). See *Europe since 1914: Encyclopedia of the Age of War and Reconstruction*, ed. John Merriman and Jay Winter, vol. 2 (Detroit: Charles Scribner's Sons, 2006), 804–6.

8. In his book *Über den Prozess der Zivilisation* (*The Civilizing Process*) (1939), Norbert Elias argued that what westerners today perceive as Western civilization, with an emphasis on "civilized" personal manners, was a result of a long historical process, in which the movement from barbarity to civilization could be traced by examining books on manners. The internalization of this civility by the Western

individual, Elias argued, demonstrated his basic theory that the individual was not a static, self-contained unit, but a process, effected by society at large. See Mohammed Arkawi, "Elias, Norbert (1897–1990)," *Encyclopedia of European Social History*, ed. Peter N. Stearns, vol. 6 (Detroit: Charles Scribner's Sons, 2001), 89–90.

9. French film director, b. 1933.

10. Américo Castro y Quesada (1885–1972) was a Spanish literary critic and cultural historian. Most relevant to Ruiz's discussion are his *The Historical Reality of Spain* (1982), and, together with Raymond S. Willis, Julia Doerschuk, and Frederic Ernst, *Iberoamerica: Its History and Its Culture* (1967).

11. Editors' note: In Spain, it denoted a Christian with no Moorish or Jewish blood, a Christian from before the Reconquista conversions. By contrast, a "new Christian" was a converted Moor or Jew.

12. *Casticismo* from "castizo," which refers to that which is purely Spanish, and moreover "Castilian." In general it denotes the idea of purity, of pure blood.

13. The Cuban Institute of Cinematographic Art and Industry (ICAIC) was established by the Cuban government in March 1959, after the success of the Cuban revolution. See Michael Chanan, *The Cuban Image* (London: British Film Institute, 1985), 81–82, 89–110.

14. Queen Isabel of Castile, 1451–1504. Together with her husband Ferdinand II of Aragon, she presided over the final stages of the Reconquista, or expulsion of Jews and Muslims who did not convert to Catholicism, and also sponsored the voyage of explorer Christopher Columbus to the New World. For more information, see Peggy K. Liss, *Isabel the Queen: Life and Times* (New York: Oxford University Press, 1992).

15. Argentine filmmaker (b. 1936), exiled in Paris. See especially *Tangos: Los exilios de Gardel* (1985).

16. Tartessos was an ancient territory located near the Guadalquivir River in what is now Andalusia, Spain. They "practiced extensively agriculture, industry, and commerce by land and sea. They possessed a literature of their own, and annals, poems, and laws in verse." See Rafael Altamira [y Creveq], *A History of Spanish Civilization* (New York: Biblo and Tannen, 1968), 17. See also John B. Trend, *Spain from the South* (London: Methuen, 1928), 26–31.

17. Victor Segalen (1878–1919) was a French naval doctor, ethnographer, archaeologist, poet, explorer, art theorist, and chronicler, who traveled extensively in China and the South Pacific. In addition to his travelogues, archaeological studies, and poems, he was the author of an "Essay on Exoticism" and an experiment in synesthesia, of translating into written description paintings viewed in China. See Victor Segalen, *Peintures* (Paris: Gallimard, 1983). His medical thesis on the subject of "neurotics in contemporary literature" was published under the title "Les synesthésies et l'école symboliste" (Synesthesias and the Symbolist School). See Victor Segalen, *Essay on Exoticism: An Aesthetics of Diversity*, trans. and ed. Yael Rachel Schlick (Durham, NC: Duke University Press, 2002), 7. For Segalen exoticism generally denoted "the ability to *conceive otherwise*," although he also located the sensation in time and in space; ibid., 16. See also Charles Forsdick, *Victor Segalen and the Aesthetics of Diversity: Journeys between Cultures* (Oxford: Oxford University Press, 2000).

18.   Jan Łukasiewicz (1878–1956) was a Polish logician and philosopher who introduced mathematical logic into Poland, became the earliest founder of the Warsaw school of logic, and one of the principal architects and teachers of that school. His most famous achievement was to give the first rigorous formulation of many-valued logic. He introduced many improvements in propositional logic and became the first historian of logic to treat the subject's history from the standpoint of modern formal logic. See Peter Simons, "Jan Łukasiewicz," *The Stanford Encyclopedia of Philosophy*. Website. Accessed September 30, 2016.

Conversation with Raúl Ruiz

Aberdeen, Scotland, April 23, 2008

Andreea Marinescu: Knowing that you started your artistic career writing for the theater and later continued adapting plays into film, I want to ask you about the relationship between film and theater.

Raúl Ruiz: I incorporate more theater into film than is typically adopted in the cinematic world. I've been thinking about the relationship between film and theater for a long time, and one of the metaphors I've encountered is that of the Real Presence.[1] It's because of this metaphor that so many people have died, as in the war between Catholics and Protestants. The Catholic principle says that God is corporeally present in church. God is there. For the Protestants, God is never there. Therefore, churches are *ecclesia*, assemblies of people who believe that they can enter into contact with God through faith, and thus they can be saved. Catholicism must be the only religion in which faith is not so important. According to Catholicism, one can be saved and go to heaven if he/she fulfills certain bureaucratic procedures—like going to church every Sunday or confessing once a year—even if he/she is not a believer. For me, in the context of the theater, the importance of Real Presence lies in the mystery of theatrical representation.

AM: How does this concept translate to film?

RR: Film is Protestant. There is no Real Presence. In film, pieces of things come together . . . because you film one scene here, another there, you do one before lunch, the other after lunch; in one scene the actor hasn't eaten the spaghetti, in the other he has; and the scenes come, one after another—you can see this discontinuity in the actors' faces. Now I want to work seriously with the theoretical notions of the Real Presence, which is much more complex than what I've just described. It is important to understand that theologians are very intelligent people . . . at first, principles are foolish; someone conceives an idea and says "it is so," and later the intellectuals emerge to justify the idea. I was saying . . . faith is a problem. The three theological virtues are faith, hope and charity. For Catholics, faith is less important. Hope is essential, but charity—mutual help and acts—is paramount. For Catholics, faith is worthless without acts.

AM: Those could be contradictory . . . faith and charity . . .

RR: Up to this point, there is the Muslim theologian—the greatest of all: Al-'Arabi[2]—who, in his time, was called "the son of Plato," always playing with words, like Heidegger. Heidegger didn't know he was Arab . . . always playing with etymologies, with the roots of words. Al-'Arabi says that there are three possible monotheistic religions: Judaism, Catholicism, and Islam—by order of appearance. In Judaism, there is *hibrit*: "the right path" in Arabic; for Muslims, there is *mehme*: "submission to the will of God"; for the Christians, the Nazarenes, *nazare*: "mutual help." Thus, there are three priorities that create the perfect religion when combined.

AM: Is Real Presence something like transubstantiation?

RR: That is exactly what it's about . . . the officiator has the power to transform a piece of bread into God and eat it. Another approximation about the nature of theater comes from Rabaut Saint-Étienne,[3] one of the French Revolution's enthusiastic philosophers. Synthesizing what he says, theater is the point of contact between astronomy and agriculture, that is, astronomical ceremonies. Astronomical theater exists. I've seen it. It consists of putting people into a small territory, no bigger than a soccer field . . . putting people in places from which they can see the stars. Everyone assumes a character—which is one of the stars—and each one starts to sing his song. They move with the stars throughout the entire night. This happens in Brazil and in northern Africa. It happens here too, in northern Scotland, where the stars are indeed important. One mustn't forget that *Hamlet* was originally a cosmic myth. Hamlet is strolling around, looking at the sky, and suddenly the stars form into the shape of a face and Hamlet says, "I know this man," and the face says, "Of course, I'm your father." That's where it all starts . . . and vengeance must be wrought. I've used Hamlet in film. He is a recurring character for me. In *La recta provincia* (CL, 2007), someone encounters a bone on his patio;

it has holes and looks like a flute. He plays that bone like a flute, and a voice emerges that says, "I am your father. Avenge me."

AM: It's the father's bone . . .

RR: Yes, it's the father's bone, and he must carry out its justice. Borges repossesses this, along with other deeds of Saxo Grammaticus's Danish kings and heroes.[4] (Shakespeare didn't know that version; apparently, he knew the version in the Norman Chronicles.) In this version, there must be a madman in the court. What happens if this madman is to become king? They can't kill him; crazy people can't be killed because they speak with the voice of God. Madmen, fools, the poor . . . it's an ancient myth that the romantics reclaimed. So, there could be a version of *Hamlet* in which the villain, the usurper, who assassinates Hamlet's father, *Orvelde*[5] . . . this character would have to kill Hamlet, who is the legitimate successor to the throne. And to kill him, he would have to prove that Hamlet is rational, that he's sane. If he proves this, he can kill him. Hamlet, then, is simulating insanity as salvation. From this point of view, *Hamlet*'s nature changes completely. The origins of *Hamlet* also come from Rome . . . from Brutus. The foolish brother . . . the mother starts them running into the world, and the one who arrives first will be the ruler of the land, that is, the king; everyone runs and Brutus falls to the floor, he kisses the earth and says, "I have arrived." So, astronomical myths are tied to theater in many ways. And in agriculture, there are seasonal rituals, and thus it is *tragos* of tragedy that has to do with cannibalistic rituals. To inhibit cannibalism, the scapegoat is sacrificed. In order to sacrifice him, he must do something foolish, he has to commit a crime—like eating a straw chair—and making him find the knife with which they'll kill him; these are the possible origins of *tragoedia* or tragedy. . . . Rabaut Saint-Étienne was not mistaken in saying that there is a connection between cosmic myths and the changing of the seasons. The moment in which hunters become farmers produces this connection. Today, everything changes every three years. The hunters haven't stopped hunting, and agriculture hasn't been this way for a while . . .

AM: And what would be the connection with baroque theater?

RR: Doesn't this all seem very baroque? The baroque has to do with the pre-eminence of the spiral. That makes me think . . . I don't know if you're familiar with [Erwin] Panofsky's essay . . . he's a character who has created a lot of intrigue. Panofsky[6] belongs to a group of Jewish intellectuals called the Pomeranians. They dedicated themselves to reinterpreting the history of art and turning it "upside down." Walter Benjamin said that he made great efforts to enter into the group, but they always excluded him because he was too Marxist, while they identified more with the Right. One of them, Ernst Kantorowicz,[7] has the strange and terrible privilege of having written Hitler's bedside book (being Jewish himself, he never wanted to republish it) about Frederick II, who I see as one of the most mysterious and enigmatic characters of the First Reich, Frederick II . . . not Frederick II of Prussia. He was emperor of Sicily, self-proclaimed emperor of the world and enemy of the Pope. We're truly talking about the conflict between material power and spiritual power, the possibility that spiritual power also lies in the emperor's hands. We know that among Christians there are, as far as I know, two or three cases of emperors who proclaimed themselves rulers of three religions. One is Frederick II, the other case is Alfonso I the Battler,[8] and there was a Portuguese one as well. Genghis Khan was emperor of something like 500 religions. . . . That is to say that Frederick II placed himself above Christianity and is the prefiguration of Hitler—he had to have found inspiration in this character to do what he did.

Kantorowicz later plays with another Christian dogma: "How can God come to the world and remain alive?" He reasons that the secularized version of this dogma exists unconsciously in the nature and internal structure of European power. This indicates the permanence of power: "the King has died, long live the King." Thus the king has two bodies; in fact, Kantorowicz's second book is called *The King's Two Bodies*. The king has his body that represents the State, which is his eternal body; apart from that, he has his tantrums—what do I know . . . he has marital problems or stomach pains. This is the tangible king, who is subject to temporality, who is going to die. But he is more than a representation; he is a real body. The dogma of the hypostatic reunion—the reunion between the eternal God and Christ's transience—was developed by someone who has become very popular in the leftist circles (something I don't understand): Carl Schmitt. Carl Schmitt takes his Catholic concepts (he is Catholic, which makes him even less pardonable; Nazism implied the destruction of the Catholic religion) . . . Carl Schmitt was capitalism's biggest critic, that much is certain.

I also do not understand today's cult following of Pavel Florensky.[9] I love reading his work, but to continue beyond that, transforming him according to the leftist path. . . . I don't know where to go with that. Now he is a saint—Saint Pavel Florensky—shot by Stalin. He wrote a book that is very cinematically interesting, called *The Inverted Perspective*, a study of Andrei Rublev's icons. If you study them closely, what could pass for naïve images—the icons displayed in the iconostasis—may have a vanishing point that exists behind the viewer. That is to say, they are Picassos . . . more than Picassos, they are Cézannes. Cézanne was obsessed with perspectival games and distortions. Up to that point, I accept and happily adhere to these truths; but to transform him into the only possible exit point from the European Left, I don't see where that point lies.

AM: When talking about Carl Schmitt, I think you can emphasize the concept of friend and enemy, the delimitations that exist within the concept of politics . . .

RR: I'm concerned with something else: the question of sovereignty and exceptional occurrences. It suffices to say that "all facts are exceptional" to justify the dictatorship. Since when does being a member of the Left imply being an advocate of the dictatorship? I don't know . . . [Schmitt's] *Theory of the Partisan*, the text about Raoul Salan's defense, the processing of the general who attempted a coup against [Charles] de Gaulle . . . he witnesses the process and defends it; it's a psychopath's text. Anyway, if I continue, I will be attacking all of the current Left . . .

AM: One must always be somewhat critical . . .

RR: At the Manheim Film Festival—where all the PhDs go—in a secluded conversation in an alcove, we ended up screaming at one another: the others saying, "Long live Carl Schmitt!" and me yelling, "Long live Hans Kelsen!"[10] Kelsen also analyzes the notion of dogma, which comes from theology—theology is everywhere—that is to say, a dogma exists and one makes conclusions about it. The conclusions are more important than whether the dogma itself is true or false; what is important is that the consequences are coherent and consistent with the originally proposed dogma. The "pure" law: the standard of law has nothing to do with morality or the economy. The norm of "pure law" is the assumption that a rule applies without any initial basis, other than saying, "this law exists."

AM: We've talked about theology, rights, the origins of theater and film . . . let's return to film.

RR: There is an American tendency to see film more as *teatrum*, as *speculum* . . . it is not *laberintum*, it's *teatrum*.

AM: There is a certain aspect of "performance" in "American" film . . .

RR: There are three ways to say "book": *teatrum, speculum, laberintum,* which have distinct meanings. *Teatrum* is the harmony of the spheres; the *comedia mundi* is a critical piece. . . . And this is tied to language. *If cinema were a language, it would be composed entirely of verbs. In film, only the present exists.*

AM: Why not the past?

RR: The past is filmed in the present. In film, future and past time do not exist, even though flashback and flash-forward do exist. They are expressions that don't say anything; no matter what, you are seeing the present: a present that takes place in the future [flash-forward], or a present that took place in the past [flashback].

AM: It's interesting that you mention this, because I've noticed that there aren't any flashbacks in your films.

RR: Well, there is something called *racconto*: "I remember when . . ." And there is a voice that can distort this present that exists in the past. In fact, in China the past doesn't exist linguistically. All verbs are in the present tense, making it the only language that favors cinema.

AM: How does one indicate the past in China, then?

RR: In Spanish, you can say: "1952. I am eleven years old. I leave the house and find myself among . . ." Cubans use this frequently. Groups whose maternal language is Quechua often use the future to indicate the past: "1952. I will be eleven years old." In other words, it is a future that is also the past, and both are the present.

AM: How does this translate to your films? How do you talk about the past in the present?

RR: Well, you must explain that it is the past, but in a certain way it is also the present. In a certain way, it is the Real Presence. There are indirect ways to deal with the past. In *Time Regained* (1999)—which is a way to play with past and present—there are many games . . . it is a film in which sound plays a much more important role than in the majority of my work. For example, the narrator of *Time Regained* remembers the past in distinct ways: he remembers voluntarily: "I want to remember the past," and so he recalls certain aspects of the past that are important to him. He performs both voluntary and involuntary memory, that is to say that the past appears by means of an interruption of exceptional events. He recalls that one of the characters died in an accident in World War I, the last time he saw him, he was singing a German song by Schumann enthusiastically as he was dying. There is also a more interesting form of memory, which is the "time machine." Memories grab you by the hair and pull you back—memory that is neither voluntary nor involuntary— they are something else; they are called *les felicités,* "the felicities." You find yourself in the past by accident. You remember that you've done this before; it's the body that remembers, the whole body. So I played with that idea in many ways. For example, there is a character who attends Robert Saint-Loup's funeral, and he begins to remember seeing him singing a German song. But the whole time that he is in the past, there is also a present, a double present: the past within the present but also the actual present, the soldier's speech as he eulogizes the dead man's bravery and patriotism. The present appears in every level of time. Saint-Loup appears on horseback, continuing along the beach, where he passes his own funeral procession. Those interested in folklore will immediately recognize the idea of [André] Breton's folkloric double vision (as well as visions of other worldwide folklores). This happens when you see a person and, behind him, you see his coffin; that is, you see him as already being dead. Myth and all, but I've seen it happen. A friend of mine had double vision; he knew it and he said it. I shook hands with someone in front of me at a cocktail party. He left, and my friend said: "this man is dead." And, after leaving the cocktail party, he died of a heart attack. So, I'm telling a folk tale, but it is a reality. The idea of double vision corresponds to a certain reality. I played with this concept in *Time Regained.*

AM: Memory is never the same.

RR: There are many memories. One must follow Daniel Schacter[11] regarding implicit and explicit memory; we remember everything. In some part of the body we have memory of everything that has ever happened to us, but this mixes with imagination. Imagination is another form of memory; it is a confabulation. Schacter's theory gave rise to a court case that led to a television series: one day he received a visit from an attorney who came to see if one can eliminate his memory of the things he has lived or if one can simply forget, which is the central theme of one of my films, *Life Is a Dream* (1986). What Schacter calls "implicit memories" are various ways of remembering. Schacter wanted to know why amnesic people can recall so many details and are always focused on specific things if they are supposedly so amnesic. He conducted a series of experiments in the '70s and almost proved that the brain stores all information. Now this is commonplace, but at the time it was very new. The consequences of this are that, if you are paid a salary to discover something in science of technology and you go to another company, you will use this technology—this knowledge—even if you don't want to; this is the legal point. MIT used this idea to argue that someone who left for another company was obligated to pay a quantity of money or to return to MIT. To be paid a salary for research involves a kind of slavery, so to speak. It was proven that one cannot forget, that one cannot avoid using knowledge, even if he doesn't want to use it. Since then, the concept of implicit memory has continued to develop. I believe it is an emotional element that occurs in film. So, you can integrate elements that are not going to go straight into the vicissitudes of the movie, the *peripeteia* of the movie, but that will emerge from somewhere else. They emerge when the film is finished and will continue, of course, later. Because it happens that people ask themselves why they cannot forget a film even if it seemed silly and boring. It is because something else happens that is emotionally touching. Implicit memory does not develop consciously. The entirety of the body generates the poetics of cinema. It is recalled in a more subdued manner. It's like when you have the flu, but the illness can't manifest itself because you've taken too much vitamin C.

AM: There's a documentary of yours—which is more of a "mockumentary"—about your character's return to Chile in 1982, called *The Return of a Library Lover*, in which he attempts to recall his memory of the night before the coup.

RR: Speaking of memory, I don't recall much about that film, but I believe the connection is that the character lost his book the night before the coup. The narrator—who is not me (like in Proust, where the narrator is not Proust)—goes looking for the book he had lost and is unable to remember why it is so important. . . . It's odd because, if you don't remember, that means that fiction has burst . . .

AM: I saw it in the British Film Institute, which probably indicates that it was a British production.

RR: It was a Channel 4 production. I made it in France, and I filmed it in France. And the voice—which is the voice of the actor in *Three Crowns of the Sailor* (1983)—is Jean-Bernard Guillard.

AM: Speaking of the narrator . . . in *Three Crowns of the Sailor*, there is a voice-off, like in *Life Is a Dream*.

RR: He (Jean-Bernard Guillard) is one of the characters; he is the dead brother.

AM: What role does choosing this method of storytelling play for you—the use of voice-off?

RR: In the majority of cases it is parodic, but the parody isn't meant to make people laugh when they know its model; the purpose is the opposite: to create a kind of distance. The voice moves away or comes closer; it is the vehicle that allows one to move into the film. It is not the voice that envelops, that allows you to tell a story, but you could say that it unfolds the story.

AM: Like a newscast?

RR: The news informs; it is a commentary about images. Here, the voice misinforms; what they are seeing is not what they are seeing. This pipe is not a pipe. The voice creates the illusion of information, but you realize that, in reality, it is misinformation. I've dealt with voice-off in many ways. For example, one voice says something and another superimposed voice says something else. In the documentary *Great Events and Ordinary People* (1979), Chileans made comments in French with a Chilean accent. There was another voice-off that merely corrected errors in pronunciation and syntax. This second voice-off was Jean Baudrillard (but he is not in the credits). We were good friends, and I asked him to make this joke for me.

AM: Speaking of the narrator and his function in distancing the viewer and drawing him closer, I wonder who your potential viewer is. . . . To whom do you direct the narrator?

RR: I don't work with the viewer. I've repeated this many times. I work with zero viewers. They are individuals, each of whom understands a movie distinctly, and there is space in the movie for this interpretation. Sometimes this is true; many of my films are simply narratives, it is not a principle I follow morally. I don't follow a moral principle, but rather an aesthetic one that is playful in some sense . . . contemplatively playful.

AM: I like the concept of "zero viewers" because it has an ideological position without worrying about monetary ends.

RR: I've been fighting constantly since I started making films. When I was in the US—I made three movies in the US—they repeated this idea almost obsessively: "we are working for a black laborer from Detroit whose mother is a drug addict, whose father is in prison and who wants to come home at night to watch a movie that engages him." If I were this black worker, I would have dedicated myself to reading novels by Dostoevsky; I wouldn't watch movies, at least not on television. Yes, the idea of having an audience implies profitability. It's true that in certain cases an audience—and in certain cases, an audience alongside a film—is something positive. It's true that comedy is better because everyone laughs together, and there is a kind of community. But this is not the theater's community; it is the spirit of the group. In theater, the actors are mediums: they know when "the room" is good and when it is bad; so with gestures, they successfully unite the audience and bring them to wherever it is they want to bring them. In film there is a kind of loss in doing this, I think . . . the gain is the opposite, in leaving the viewer free.

AM: It's not trying to convince . . . it's not moralist in this sense.

RR: Under no circumstances. There is no moral reason behind this. It's to give more, to enrich the expressivity of cinema.

AM: However, you made a movie during the Popular Unity's government called *¡Qué Hacer!/What Is to Be Done?* (1970) that had a strong ideological position.

RR: Yes, but I had very little to do with that movie. The absurdity of the situation has transformed into something almost interesting. I watched it a little while ago; I didn't think it was good. There are too many hands, you see the whole debate in the filming, and clearly, knowing what happened in the world after the film's release, you see the sinking of the socialist world. . . . Radical North Americans made it. They wanted to have enough Chileans in the making of the movie to say that it wasn't an American movie about Chile, that Chileans participated too. They never understood the ambiguity of the Chileans' behavior, for example, nor the ambiguity of political emotions. Political emotions, like all emotions, are double. True passion, true generosity, and the simple lust for power mix together. And they manifest in many ways. Americans think that one simply wins or loses (an allusion to the theory of central conflict in film). Now, *¡Qué Hacer!* was made before the Popular Unity government, and it ended with Allende's election.

AM: I mentioned this movie in order to contrast it with the others that you've directed. It is much more interesting to lose the viewer.

RR: Yes, it is the *laberintum*.

AM: It also gives agency to the movie's potential. To a certain extent, it gives the viewer freedom.

RR: Yes, awakening the capacity for invention. Making a film of the film. A movie is worth more based on the extent to which it watches you more than you watch it. That is to say, the film is a live being that is watching you. It watches what is happening inside you. This, more than just a metaphor, is a reality. Today, we know about the changes produced in the brain when you watch a movie (this is one of the reasons I'm in Aberdeen): you project your own movie. But this sort of movie must have an airport because, if not, there is no landing point. That is how you produce a kind of body that comes back to you.

AM: And the airport is the movie?

RR: No, the movie must have airports, open spaces; this implies a certain slowness, many ambiguous images, a lot of double vision. If what the neurologist Allan Hobson says is true, the changes that a movie produces in the brain transform the movie . . . to simplify this idea, we'll say that we see the film as much as we dream it. But to make this possible, the movie has to lend itself to it; it must have a dreamlike dimension. Hobson said that Fellini was the best example of this. Now, Fellini slightly overstated that point: his movies are *explicitly* oneiric from *La dolce vita* on, especially in *8 1/2*, where dreams and reality intermix.

AM: Perhaps these airports are spaces that permit memory.

RR: Precisely. If you watch a movie in photograms, you can see that every movie has at least a half-hour of black screen. This black screen is there, it accumulates and it condenses. There are many forms of black, but this type is accentuated in relation to the extent to which you are interested in the film, to the extent to which you are fascinated. The more fascination, the blacker the screen. There is an entire world to discover about the perception of cinema.

AM: How does this fact depend on each individual viewer?

RR: In a film, there is a certain quantity of blackness; everyone sees the same quantity. Now, what one does with his own black, with his own darkness. . . . I believe personal imagination comes into play. [There are so many things to discover. Simpletons always pose a possible risk . . . doctors might start saying that watching movies is dangerous, like smoking.]

AM: You were recently filming a television series in Chile. How does returning to Chile to film affect you?

RR: In Chile, I was filming a very long film, very ambitious, about six hours in three parts. They are stories; there's a version for television and a version for cinema. The financing comes from television. Chile is a country where they still give me a lot of freedom. In the US, the television officials impose a system, and if you err three times (meaning that the movie is not a box office hit), they don't allow you any freedom. In Chile, you can go wrong forty times a year, and it's no problem. In the US, they make very drastic decisions, and one has to pay the consequences. If they make a mistake, it is because they predict that the movie will be successful and it ends up failing. If they believe that it will be a success *because* it's bad, nothing happens, there is no punishment. Today, however, the distribution system is such that if the movie doesn't bring in money immediately, it will within ten years. All inexpensive American films recover in less than ten years due to international revenue and the distribution system that all theaters are obligated to accept, like it or not. They donate these movies to sell others, and that's how they recover. In the golden age system during the '40s and '50s, many movies were donated in order to spread the "commercial film," which was profitable.

AM: For many, Hollywood is their only reference in film; it marks a certain nationality, a certain patriotism.

RR: I think it's simply the fact that many people can't imagine a movie that is not in English.

AM: Many internationally famous actors, like John Malkovich, Catherine Deneuve, and Marcello Mastroianni, have performed in your films. How do you finance these films?

RR: John Malkovich isn't expensive; he charges 10 percent of the cost of the film, regardless of how much it costs to make it.

AM: How did you come to work with him?

RR: Some friends introduced us, and he wanted to work in Europe.

AM: In these conditions, working with prestigious actors must come from the initiative of the actors themselves.

RR: In regard to the well-known actors with whom I've worked, it's because they accepted working with me beforehand—Catherine Deneuve without even seeing the script. They want to do something unique, to move away from what they normally do. Catherine Deneuve is tired of playing the sexy mother-in-law. They don't work with me to make money. I told Marcello Mastroianni that my movies never make money. "Great!" he told me.

AM: Why you and not another director?

RR: Because I'm famous for being crazy, and this always attracts actors . . . in France. Beyond that, they do it for the aspect of "no pain, no gain" and nothing more.

AM: It's an inversion of the established practice in which the director (or producer) chooses his actors.

RR: This is the current situation; it's very new. I started working in France more than thirty years ago, and the movie director's position was the auteur position. There were auteurs who invented new forms; they were very prestigious . . . and this collapsed . . . more quickly in France than in other countries. And, as it collapsed in France, it began to rise in the US, England, and Germany. It has never subsided in the ex-socialist countries. The director is the demiurge, the one who creates things.

AM: The "master."

RR: Master, all around. Now there are fewer masters because people want to make money, not because they are less capable. Now they want to win an Oscar. They practically treated me like a living Buddha in Moscow. The Czech Republic is an exception. The Czechs, themselves depressed, bury everything. In the Moscow Festival, I couldn't believe the point to which sanctification can make you foolish. At one point, I started to believe everything. I looked into the mirror, "is it so?" . . . The first and second questions were: "What does it feel like to be famous?" I asked them, "How do you understand fame?" They told me, "It's simple. You must have more than a million hits on the Internet." It's funny that they tell you this when, two months prior in the Czech Republic, someone had asked me, "How does it feel to have worked so hard and remain unrenowned?" One of the great things about cinema is that sometimes movies are involuntarily good, regardless of those who make them. In Allende's era, we were given movies from all over the world, except from Poland, which was already capitalist. I saw very entertaining Romanian films, but I preferred the Bulgarian ones because they were very free. Since everything happened during the Middle Ages, there weren't any ideological problems. They had found a way to say what they wanted to say without censorship.

I remember that the Romanian filmmaker Lucian Pintilie made a film, *Reconstituirea/Reconstruction* (RO, 1968), about a group of filmmakers making a movie to prove that alcoholism is bad. And what they started to see was that everything is bad, that alcoholism is just one of the problems; in addition to the other detail that they were all drunk while making the movie. Ceausescu said that they didn't show the movie very much, that they only showed it to well-educated people in Romania. In 1969, it won an award in Locarno.

AM: Today in Romania, they have what Americans call the "New Romanian Cinema," which is characterized by young directors. Today, the Romanians win at Cannes.

RR: Yes, they are horrifying comedies or, more directly, tragedies—for example, *Moartea Domnului Lazarescu/The Death of Mister Lazarescu* (RO, 2005). Regarding socialist Romania, I have visions of the Chileans who went there before, in a group from a socialist party propaganda company. We sent a film crew to accompany the minister of exterior relations, Clodomiro Almeyda, on his last journey there. It was a trip to ask for help for Chile, part of a campaign where the paradoxical situation happened that the Soviet Union offered 40 million dollars—which was very little— while the fascist Brazilian government gave 100 million. They did a tour of all the socialist countries, and I remember that every time they would deplane, they would sing the song from the series *Mission Impossible*. There was an accident in Romania. A car crashed . . . the minister's car collided with a truck. The truck's driver saw that he had crashed into a government vehicle, and he died of a heart attack immediately. The Chilean journalists, with Western training, began to film the accident . . . the minister had only cut his finger; there were only a few drops of blood, but the cameras were there and the newspaper headlines said, "Mare catastrofa!" ("Great catastrophe!") They also had to send images to be televised in Chile every day of the trip, because they were propaganda. One of the transmissions was a clip in which the Chilean minister shook hands with Ceausescu. Ceausescu made a speech, but you couldn't hear it because it was mute. The minister answered, and you couldn't hear him either, but it had to reach the news for the next day. It was all so Ionesco-esque.[12]

AM: In a previous project about exiled Chileans living in Romania, I talked to the ex-Interior Minister during that period, and he told me that the

Romanian Socialist Party thought that Chile—near the end of the Popular Unity's government—was moving too far Left. He said that, in their opinion, Clodomiro Almeyda had become too radical.

RR: What they don't tell you is that the people were the ones who wanted to move towards the Left. The government, oppositely, was trying to control this movement. What they also don't tell you is that the parliamentary elections of March 1973 favored the Leftists, and that's when the coup became inevitable.

AM: I remember something Patricio Guzmán said in an interview when they started filming *Batalla de Chile/The Battle of Chile* in 1972. He said that they began filming because they knew *something* was going to happen . . . they didn't know exactly what, but they knew it would be a civil war or a coup. According to him, they anticipated a disaster . . .

RR: I would say that there was a desire to produce this disaster. This is the hardest part to understand. Suddenly countries begin running towards suicide. It couldn't have been any other way . . . you don't have to be very intelligent to know that, you didn't have to be a prophet to see that the people neither walked nor ran, but drove towards disaster . . . we drove.

AM: How?

RR: This is inexplicable. If you are not Elias Canetti, it is inexplicable. Elias Canetti explained it: *Crowds and Power*.

Translated by Tessa Allen de Oliveira

Notes

1. In Eucharistic theology the term "real presence" has been employed to refer to the concrete and material presence of Christ in the Sacrament (not figurative or symbolical), mediated by the bread and wine, prior to the faith of the congregation. See Monika K. Hellwig. "Eucharist," in *Encyclopedia of Religion*, ed. Lindsay Jones, 2nd ed., vol. 5 (Detroit: Macmillan Reference USA, 2005), 2876–78.

2. Muhyiddin Ibn al-'Arabi (1165–1240) can be considered the greatest of all Muslim philosophers; his works cover the whole gamut of Islamic sciences, not least Koran commentary, Hadith (sayings of Muhammad), jurisprudence, principles of jurisprudence, theology, philosophy, and mysticism. He has been called "the son of Plato" by Muslim thinkers, described as Neoplatonist by modern scholars, and he is the *Ash-Shaykh Al-Akbar* (the Doctor *Maximus*) to the Sufis. See William Chittick,

"Ibn Arabi," *The Stanford Encyclopedia of Philosophy* (Spring 2014 edition), ed. Edward N. Zalta. Website. Accessed July 21, 2015.

3. Jean-Paul Rabaut Saint-Étienne (1743–1793), French Protestant pastor and political figure. Inspired by Jean-Jacques Rousseau and by Enlightenment ideals, he played an important role in drafting the Declaration of the Rights of Man, but he was also critical of the abuses of power committed by the republican regime, which led to his execution in 1793. See Myriam Yardeni, "Rabaut Saint-Étienne, Jean Paul," in *Encyclopedia of the Enlightenment*, ed. Alan Charles Kors, vol. 3 (New York: Oxford University Press, 2003), 383.

4. Saxo Grammaticus (ca. 1150–after 1216) was a Danish historian whose writings (*Gesta Danorum*) constitute one of the few important early sources on Germanic mythology and religion. John Weinstock, "Saxo Grammaticus," *Encyclopedia of Religion*, ed. Lindsay Jones, 2nd ed., vol. 12 (Detroit: Macmillan Reference USA, 2005), 8141–42. Website. Accessed July 27, 2015.

5. In *Gesta Danorum*, Orvelde is Horvandillus, the name of the father of Amleth (Hamlet).

6. Erwin Panofsky (1892, Hannover, Germany–1968, Princeton, New Jersey) was a German American art historian who gained particular prominence for his studies in iconography. Panofsky was a professor of art history at the University of Hamburg, New York University, and Princeton University. He studied many iconographic, stylistic, and theoretical aspects of medieval and Renaissance art. His most notable publications are *Studies in Iconology* (1939); *Albrecht Dürer* (1943); *Early Netherlandish Painting* (1953), with Dora Panofsky; *Pandora's Box: The Changing Aspects of a Mythical Symbol* (1956); and *Meaning in the Visual Arts* (1957). See *Encyclopædia Britannica Online*, s.v. "Erwin Panofsky," Website. Accessed October 1, 2014.

7. Ernst Hartwig Kantorowicz (1895–1963) was a German Jewish historian of medieval political and intellectual history, known for his 1927 book *Kaiser Friedrich der Zweite* on Holy Roman Emperor Frederick II, and work of political theology *The King's Two Bodies* (1957). See Helene Wieruszowski, "Kantorowicz, Ernst Hartwig," *Encyclopaedia Judaica*, ed. Michael Berenbaum and Fred Skolnik, 2nd ed., vol. 11 (Detroit: Macmillan Reference USA, 2007), 772. Website.

8. Alfonso I of Aragon (1073–1134), byname Alfonso The Battler (in Spanish Alfonso El Batallador) was king of Aragon and of Navarre from 1104 to 1134. See José M. Lacarra, *Vida de Alfonso el Batallador*, 2nd ed. (Zaragoza: Caja de Ahorros, 1971).

9. Pavel Alexandrovich Florensky, born 1882, Russian Empire–died 1943, Siberia, was a Russian Orthodox theologian, philosopher, and mathematician. Florensky's chief contribution to Russian Orthodox theology is his 1914 essay on theodicy titled "The Pillar and the Ground of Truth," in which he argued that only through nonrational, intuitive experience could a person become consubstantial with all of creation and thus encounter God's reality and understand God's truth. See *Encyclopædia Britannica Online*, s.v. "Pavel Alexandrovich Florensky," accessed October 2, 2014.

10. Hans Kelsen (1881–1973) was an Austrian American legal philosopher, teacher, jurist, and writer on international law, who formulated the "pure theory" of law. Kelsen is most famous for his studies on law and especially for his idea known as "the pure theory of law." By "pure" he meant that a theory of law should be logically

self-supporting and should not depend on extralegal values. Among Kelsen's later books are *General Theory of Law and State* (1945) and *The Law of the United Nations* (1950–51). See "Kelsen, Hans," in *West's Encyclopedia of American Law*, ed. Shirelle Phelps and Jeffrey Lehman, 2nd ed., vol. 6 (Detroit: Gale, 2005), 115–16.

11. Daniel L. Schacter is professor of psychology at Harvard University. His research explores the relation between conscious and unconscious forms of memory and the nature of distortions and errors in remembering. Among his most important publications are *Searching for Memory: The Brain, the Mind, and the Past* (New York: Basic Books, 1996) and *The Seven Sins of Memory: How the Mind Forgets and Remembers* (Boston: Houghton Mifflin, 2001).

12. Romanian-born Eugène Ionesco is the inventor of the Theater of the Absurd.

Contributors

Catherine L. Benamou (Associate Professor of Film and Media Studies and Visual Studies, University of California–Irvine). She specializes in Hispanophone and Lusophone film and television. She is the author of *It's All True: Orson Welles's Pan-American Odyssey* (2007) as well as of numerous articles on Welles, documentary, gender and cinema, and Latinx diasporic film and media. She is also pro bono consultant to the UCLA Film and Television Archive and to the University of Michigan Special Collections regarding the preservation of Orson Welles's creative legacy.

Sabine Doran (Associate Professor of German, Pennsylvania State University). Her work traces the relation between literature and the visual arts (film, painting, video, plastic art), in terms of the genetic and figural connections between aesthetics, politics, and history. She specializes in twentieth- and twenty-first-century German literature and culture, film and film theory, media studies, art history, and Jewish studies. She is the author of *The Culture of Yellow; or, The Visual Politics of Late Modernity* (Bloomsbury, 2013).

Michael Goddard (Senior Lecturer in Film, TV, and the Moving Image, University of Westminster, UK). He has published widely on Polish and international cinema and media culture as well as cultural and media theory. He is the author of *The Cinema of Raúl Ruiz: Impossible Cartographies* (Wallflower Press, 2013). His current research centers on sonic cultures, including popular music as well as free and guerrilla radio stations, culminating in two edited books on noise, *Reverberations* and *Resonances*. His forthcoming *Guerrilla Networks* examines radical media ecologies in film, TV, radio, and radical politics in the 1970s from a media archaeological perspective.

Ignacio López-Vicuña (Associate Professor of Spanish, University of Vermont). His areas of expertise include contemporary Latin American literature and cultural studies, representations of urban space, queer theory, and Latin American film. López-Vicuña has published articles on Southern Cone writers and filmmakers, including Roberto Bolaño and Raúl Ruiz.

Andreea Marinescu (Associate Professor of Spanish, Colorado College). Her primary areas of specialization are contemporary Latin American film, literature, and cultural studies, with particular interests in twentieth- and twenty-first-century Southern Cone literature and film through the lens of literary and critical theory. She has published several articles on the relationship between politics and art in the works of Roberto Bolaño and Raúl Ruiz.

Valeria de los Ríos (Associate Professor, Aesthetics/Visual Studies, Pontificia Universidad Católica de Chile). She has published several articles on Chilean writers and filmmakers. She coedited *El cine de Raúl Ruiz: Fantasmas, simulacros y artificios* (Santiago: Uqbar Editores, 2010) and coauthored *El cine de Ignacio Agüero: El documental como la lectura de un espacio* (Santiago: Cuarto Propio, 2015). She is the author of *Fantasmas artificiales: El cine y la fotografía en la obra de Enrique Lihn* (Santiago: Hueders, 2015) and of *Espectros de Luz: Tecnologías visuales en la literatura latinoamericana* (Santiago: Cuarto Propio, 2011).

Alejandra Rodríguez-Remedi (University of Aberdeen, UK). Cultural researcher, educationalist, and digital filmmaker. Relevant publications include "The Arts as Means of Cultural Integration: A Chilean Case Study." Diss. UK/University of Concepción, Chile (2007), and "*Cofralandes*: A Formative Space for Chilean Identity," in *Visual Synergies in Fiction and Documentary Film from Latin America* (2009).

Janet Stewart (Professor of Visual Culture/German, Durham University, UK). She has published widely on Austrian and German literature and visual culture, cultural sociology, and urban history, including two monographs, *Fashioning Vienna: Adolf Loos's Cultural Criticism* (2000) and *Public Speaking in the City* (2009).

Select Filmography

A complete, annotated filmography of Ruiz is available in French at *Le Cinéma de Raoul Ruiz* (www.lecinemaderaoulruiz.com/) and an annotated filmography in English (up to 2005) at *Rouge 2: An Annotated Filmography of Raúl Ruiz* (http://rouge.com.au/2/index.html). See also the select filmography included in Michael Goddard, *The Cinema of Raúl Ruiz* (2013). For filmographies in Spanish, see Valeria de los Ríos and Iván Pinto, eds., *El cine de Raúl Ruiz: Fantasmas, simulacros y artificios* (Santiago: Editores Uqbar, 2010), and Bruno Cuneo, ed., *Ruiz: Entrevistas escogidas—filmografía comentada* (Santiago: Ediciones Universidad Diego Portales, 2013). Note: A short list of films commercially available on DVD may be found at the end of this filmography.

La maleta/ The Suitcase (CL, 1962)
El tango del viudo/ The Widower's Tango (CL, 1967)
Tres tristes tigres/ Three Sad Tigers (CL, 1968)
La colonia penal/ The Penal Colony (CL, 1970)
¡Qué Hacer!/ What Is to Be Done? (CL/US, 1970)
Nadie dijo nada/ No One Said Anything (CL, 1971)
La expropiación/ The Expropriation (CL, 1972)
El realismo socialista/ Socialist Realism (CL, 1973)
Palomita blanca/ Little White Dove (CL, 1973)
Diálogos de exiliados/ Dialogues of Exiles (FR, 1974)
Colloque de chiens/ Dogs' Dialogue (FR, 1977)
La vocation suspendue/ The Suspended Vocation (FR, 1978)
L'hypothèse du tableau volé/ The Hypothesis of the Stolen Painting (FR, 1979)
Des grands événements et des gens ordinaires: Les élections/ Great Events and Ordinary People (FR, 1979)
Petit manuel d'historie de France/ A Short Guide to French History (FR, 1979)
Het dak van de Walvis/ On Top of the Whale (NL/FR, 1982)
Les trois couronnes du matelot/ Three Crowns of the Sailor (FR, 1983)

La ville des pirates/City of Pirates (FR/PT, 1983)

Le retour d'un amateur de bibliothèques/The Return of a Library Lover (FR, 1983)

Manoel dans l'île des merveilles/Manuel on the Island of Wonders (FR/PT, 1984)

Mémoire des apparences: La vie est un songe/Memory of Appearances: Life Is a Dream (FR, 1986)

La chouette aveugle/The Blind Owl (FR/CH, 1987)

L'île au trésor/Treasure Island (UK/FR/US, 1987/1991)

A TV Dante (UK, 1989)

The Golden Boat (BE/US, 1990)

Trois vies et une seule mort/Three Lives and Only One Death (FR/PT, 1996)

Généalogies d'un crime/Genealogies of a Crime (FR, 1997)

Le film à venir/The Film to Come (FR/CH, 1997)

Shattered Image (US/CA/UK, 1998)

Le temps retrouvé/Time Regained (FR/IT/PT, 1999)

Comédie de l'innocence/Comedy of Innocence (FR, 2000)

Combat d'amour en songe/Love Torn in Dream (FR/PT/CL, 2000)

Les âmes fortes/Savage Souls (FR/BE/CH, 2001)

Cofralandes, rapsodia chilena/Cofralandes, Chilean Rhapsody (CL/FR, 2002)

Ce jour-là/That Day (FR/CH, 2003)

Días de campo/Days in the Country (CL/FR, 2004)

Le domaine perdu/The Lost Domain (FR/RO/ES/IT, 2005)

Klimt (AT/FR/DE/UK, 2006)

La recta provincia (CL, 2007)

Litoral: Cuentos del mar/Litoral: Tales of the Sea (CL, 2008)

La maison Nucingen/Nucingen House (RO/FR/CL, 2008)

Mistérios de Lisboa/Mysteries of Lisbon (PT/FR, 2010)

Ballet aquatique (FR, 2011)

La noche de enfrente/Night across the Street (CL/FR, 2012)

FILMS COMMERCIALLY AVAILABLE ON DVD (CHRONOLOGICAL BY ORIGINAL FILM RELEASE)

Dialogues of the Exiled. 1975. Chicago: Facets Video, 2010. DVD.

The Hypothesis of the Stolen Painting. 1978. Chicago: Facets Video, 2006. Includes *The Suspended Vocation* (1977). DVD.

Three Crowns of the Sailor. 1983. Chicago: Facets Video, 2006. DVD.

Three Lives and Only One Death. 1996. Paris: Blaq Out, 2016. [PAL] Blu-ray/DVD.

Genealogies of a Crime. 1997. Culver City, CA: Strand Releasing, 2005. DVD/Paris: Blaq Out, 2016. [PAL] Blu-ray/DVD.

Shattered Image. 1998. Santa Monica, CA: Lions Gate Films, 2003. DVD.

Time Regained. 1999. New York: Kino Video, 2001. DVD.

Comedy of Innocence. 2000. London: Artificial Eye, 2002. [PAL] DVD.

Savage Souls (*Les âmes fortes*). 2001. Paris: France Télévision Distribution, 2002. [PAL] DVD.

That Day. 2003. New York: Kino Video, 2006. DVD.

Klimt. 2006. New York: Koch Lorber Films, 2007. DVD.

Nucingen House. 2008. Paris: Blaq Out, 2011. [PAL] DVD.

Mysteries of Lisbon. 2010. Chicago: Music Box Films, 2012. Blu-ray/DVD.

Night across the Street. 2012. New York: Cinema Guild, 2012. Includes *Ballet aquatique* (2011). DVD.

BOX SETS

The Films of Raúl Ruiz (*Three Crowns of the Sailor/The Hypothesis of the Stolen Painting/The Suspended Vocation*). 1978–1983. Chicago: Facets Video, 2010. DVD.

Raúl Ruiz Collection (*That Day/Three Lives and Only One Death/Genealogies of a Crime/Klimt/Time Regained*). 1996–2006. Lisbon: Atalanta Filmes, n.d. [PAL] DVD.

Raúl Ruiz Collection (*Rarities*) (*Love Torn in Dream/City of Pirates/The Territory*). 1981–2000. Lisbon: Clap Filmes, n.d. [PAL] DVD.

Raúl Ruiz: 8 Rare Films (*Dialogues of the Exiled/Of Great Events and Ordinary People/The Suspended Vocation/The Hypothesis of the Stolen Painting/Three Crowns of the Sailor/The Divisions of Nature/Bérénice/La recta provincia*). 1974–2007. Paris: INA/Cinemathèque Française, 2016. [PAL] DVD.

Select Bibliography

Note: This bibliography is focused on academic publications written directly on Raúl Ruiz's work (such as books, peer-reviewed articles, and book chapters) as well as a selection of other texts that have had considerable impact on the current scholarship on Ruiz studies (such as essential interviews and film journal dossiers dedicated to his work). It is the editors' hope that the different language sections will illustrate the extensive range of scholarship on Ruiz and help guide and stimulate prospective researchers.

English

Adair, Gilbert. "The Rubicon and the Rubik Cube: Exile, Paradox, and Raúl Ruiz." *Sight and Sound* 51, no. 1 (1981): 40–44.

Bandis, Helen, Adrian Martin, and Grant McDonald, eds. *Raúl Ruiz: Images of Passage.* Melbourne, Australia: Rouge Press, 2004.

Beugnet, Martine. "Ruiz on Proust, or the Pathology of Vision." In *Le Temps retrouvé: 80 ans après; Essais critiques/Eighty Years After: Critical Essays*, 293–308. Oxford: Peter Lang, 2009.

Cisneros, James. "The Figure of Memory in Chilean Cinema: Patricio Guzmán and Raúl Ruiz." *Journal of Latin American Cultural Studies* 15, no. 1 (2006): 59–75.

Corrigan, Timothy. "The Commerce of Auteurism: Coppola, Kluge, Ruiz." In *A Cinema without Walls: Movies and Culture after Vietnam*, 101–36. New Brunswick, NJ: Rutgers University Press, 1991.

Doran, Sabine. "The Aesthetics of Postcolonial Cinema in Raúl Ruiz's *Three Crowns of the Sailor*." In *Postcolonial Cinema Studies*, edited by Sandra Ponzanesi and Marguerite Waller, 143–56. New York: Routledge, 2012.

Dowd, Garin. "Apprenticeship, Philosophy, and the 'Secret Pressures of the Work of Art' in Deleuze, Beckett, Proust, and Ruiz, or Remaking the *Recherche*." In *Beckett's Proust/Deleuze's Proust*, edited by Mary Bryden and Margaret Topping, 89–103. Basingstoke, UK: Palgrave Macmillan, 2009.

Elsaesser, Thomas. "Raoul Ruiz's *Hypothèse du Tableau Volé.*" In *European Cinema: Face to Face with Hollywood.* Amsterdam: Amsterdam University Press: 2005.

Goddard, Michael. *The Cinema of Raúl Ruiz: Impossible Cartographies.* London: Wallflower; New York: Columbia University Press, 2013.

———. "Hypothesis of the Stolen Aesthetics." *Contretemps* 3 (2002): 75–84.

———. "Towards a Perverse, Neo-Baroque, Cinematic Aesthetic: Raúl Ruiz's Poetics of Cinema." *Senses of Cinema* 30 (January–March 2004). Website.

Jayamanne, Laleen. "'Life Is a Dream'—Raúl Ruiz Was a Surrealist in Sydney: A Capillary Memory of a Cultural Event." In *Kiss Me Deadly: Feminism and Cinema for the Moment,* edited by Laleen Jayamanne, 221–43. Sydney: Power Publications, 1995.

Marinescu, Andreea. "The Dream of Memory in Raúl Ruiz's *Memories of Appearances: Life Is a Dream.*" *Framework* 55, no. 1 (2014): 7–31.

Martin, Adrian. "Hanging Here and Groping There: On Raúl Ruiz's 'The Six Functions of the Shot.'" *Screening the Past* 35 (2012). www.screeningthepast.com/2012/12/hanging-here-and-groping-there-on-raul-ruiz's-"the-six-functions-of-the-shot"/.

Martin, Adrian, ed. *Rouge 2.* Web journal. *Raúl Ruiz: An Annotated Filmography.* http://rouge.com.au/2/index.html.

Peña, Richard. "Images of Exile: Two Films by Raoul Ruiz." In *Reviewing Histories: Selections from New Latin American Cinema,* edited by Coco Fusco, 236–45. Buffalo, NY: Hallwalls Contemporary Arts Center, 1987.

Pick, Zuzana M. "The Dialectical Wanderings of Exile." *Screen* 30 (1989): 48–64.

Richardson, Michael. "The Baroque Heresy of Raúl Ruiz." In *Surrealism and Cinema,* 149–64. Oxford: Berg, 2006.

Rodríguez-Remedi, Alejandra. "*Cofralandes*: A Formative Space for Chilean Identity." In *Visual Synergies in Fiction and Documentary Film from Latin America,* edited by Miriam Haddu and Joanna Page, 87–104. New York: Palgrave Macmillan, 2009.

Rosenbaum, Jonathan. "Mapping the Territory of Raúl Ruiz." In *Placing Movies: The Practice of Film Criticism,* 222–37. Berkeley: University of California Press, 1995.

Ruiz, Raúl. *The Book of Disappearances/The Book of Tractations.* 2nd ed. Translated by Warren Niesluchowski. Paris: Dis Voir, 2005.

———. *In Pursuit of Treasure Island*. Translated by Paul Buck and Catherine Petit. Paris: Dis Voir, 2008.

———. "Object Relations in the Cinema." Translated by Jill Forbes. *Afterimage* 10 (Fall 1981): 87–94.

———. *Poetics of Cinema 1*. 2nd ed. Translated by Brian Holmes. Paris: Dis Voir, 2005.

———. *Poetics of Cinema 2*. Translated by Carlos Morreo. Paris: Dis Voir, 2007.

———. *The Wit of the Staircase*. Translated by Paul Buck and Catherine Petit. Paris: Dis Voir, 2012.

Thies, Sebastian. 2011. "Nomadic Narration and Deterritorialized Nationscape in Cofralandes: Rapsodia chilena (2004) by Raúl Ruiz." In *Screening the Americas: Narration of Nation in Documentary Film/ Proyectando las Américas: Narración de la nación en el cine documental*, edited by Josef Raab, Sebastian Thies, and Daniela Noll-Opitz, 273–96. Trier, Germany: Wissenschaftlicher Verlag Trier, 2011.

Topping, Margaret. "Photographic Vision(s) in Marcel Proust's and Raoul Ruiz's *Le Temps Retrouvé*." In *Le Temps retrouvé: 80 ans après; Essais critiques/Eighty Years After: Critical Essays*, edited by Adam Watt, 309–21. Oxford: Peter Lang, 2009.

Spanish

Bruzual, Alejandro. "Raúl Ruiz: *Mémoire des apparences/La vida es sueño*." *Osamayor* 16 (2004): 97–113.

Cortínez, Verónica, and Manfred Engelbert. *La tristeza de los tigres y los misterios de Raúl Ruiz*. Santiago: Cuarto Propio, 2011.

Cuneo, Bruno, ed. *Ruiz: Entrevistas escogidas—filmografía comentada*. Santiago: Ediciones Universidad Diego Portales, 2013.

De los Ríos, Valeria. "La pregunta sobre el barroco en el cine de Raúl Ruiz." *Revista Chilena de Literatura* 89 (2015): 113–31.

———. "Raúl Ruiz a través del espejo: De la representación a la alegoría." *Aisthesis: Revista chilena de investigaciones estéticas* 47 (2010): 115–27.

De los Ríos, Valeria, and Iván Pinto, eds. *El cine de Raúl Ruiz: Fantasmas, simulacros y artificios*. Santiago: Editores Uqbar, 2010.

Laddaga, Reinaldo. "Elogio de las imágenes partidas: Sobre la *Poética del cine* de Raúl Ruiz." *Revista de Crítica Cultural* 17 (1998): 18–27.

Marías, Miguel, Adrian Martin, Jonathan Rosenbaum, François Margolin, Jorge Arriagada, and Andrés Claro, eds. *Raúl Ruiz*. Madrid: Cátedra/ Filmoteca Española, 2012.

Martin, Adrian, and Raúl Ruiz. *Raúl Ruiz: Sublimes obsesiones*. Buenos Aires: Editorial Altamira, 2004.

Mouesca, Jacqueline. "Raúl Ruiz: Un cine sin fronteras." In *Plano secuencia de la memoria de Chile: Veinticinco años de cine chileno (1960–1985)*. Santiago: Ediciones del Litoral, 1988.

Ospina, Luis, and Emmanuelle Hamon. "Cenas y escenas con Raúl Ruiz." *Cinémas D'Amérique Latine* 20 (2012): 24–31.

Ruiz, Raúl. "Conferencia en el Instituto de Arte, Pontificia Universidad Católica de Valparaíso, 23 de septiembre de 2003." *Pensar y poetizar* 10 (2012): 93–101.

—————. "Diálogo con Raúl Ruiz por Enrique Lihn." *Atenea: Revista de ciencia, arte y literatura de la Universidad de Concepción* 500 (2009): 265–79.

—————. "Entrevista a Raúl Ruiz por Federico de Cárdenas." *Hablemos de Cine* (July 1971): 9–11.

—————. "Entrevista a Raúl Ruiz: Prefiero registrar antes que mistificar el proceso chileno." *Primer Plano* 1, no. 4 (1972): 3–21.

—————. *Poética del cine*. Translated by Waldo Rojas. Santiago: Editorial Sudamericana Chilena, 2000.

—————. *Poéticas del cine*. Translated by Alan Pauls. Santiago: Ediciones Universidad Diego Portales, 2013.

Raúl Ruiz. Madrid: Filmoteca Española, 1978.

Raúl Ruiz. Selections by José García Vázquez and Fernando Calvo. Alcalá de Henares: Filmoteca Española/Festival de Cine, 1983.

Sabrovsky, Eduardo J., ed. *Conversaciones con Raúl Ruiz*. Santiago: Ediciones Universidad Diego Portales, 2003.

Sánchez, Cristián. *Aventura del cuerpo: El pensamiento cinematográfico de Raúl Ruiz*. Santiago: Ocholibros, 2011.

French

Bax, Dominique. *Théâtres au Cinéma: Raoul Ruiz*. Vol. 14. Bobigny: Magic Cinéma, 2003.

Bégin, Richard. *Baroque cinématographique: Essai sur le cinéma de Raoul Ruiz*. Saint-Denis: Presses Universitaires de Vincennes, 2009.

Bovier, François. "*Tres Tristes Tigres*, fourchelangues et contes à rebours." *Décadrages* 15 (2009): 57–68.

Buci-Glucksmann, Christine, and Fabrice Revault d'Allonnes. *Raoul Ruiz*. Paris: Dis Voir, 1987.

Bullot, Erik. "La théorie et les rendez-vous: Sur quelques films documentaires de Raúl Ruiz." *French Forum* 35, no. 2–3 (2010): 233–48.

Ciment, Michel, and Hubert Niogret. "Raoul Ruiz ou Le Réalisme Magique (Special Section)." *Positif: Revue Mensuelle de Cinéma* 611 (2012): 90–112.

Le Cinéma de Raoul Ruiz. Website. www.lecinemaderaoulruiz.com.

Klekovkina, Vera A. "Proust's souvenir visuel and Ruiz's clin d'œil in *Le Temps retrouvé.*" *Esprit Créateur* 46, no. 4 (2006): 151–63.

Lagueira, Jacinto, ed. *Raoul Ruiz: Entretiens.* Paris: Éditions Hoëbeke, 1999.

Martin, Marie. "La Projection du peintre: Klimt de Raoul Ruiz." In *Biographies de peintres à l'écran,* 255–70. Rennes, France: Presses Universitaires de Rennes, 2011.

"Raoul Ruiz." *Cahiers du cinéma,* special issue, 345 (1983): 1–82.

Ruiz, Raúl. *À la poursuite de l'île au trésor.* Paris: Dis Voir, 1989.

———. *Entretiens.* Paris: Éditions Hoëbeke, 1999.

———. *L'esprit de l'escalier.* Paris: Fayard, 2012.

———. *Le livre des disparitions.* Paris: Dis Voir, 1990.

———. *Poétique du cinéma.* Paris: Dis Voir, 1995.

Ruiz, Raúl, and Benoît Peeters. *Le Transpatagonien: Roman.* Paris: Casterman, 1989.

Vera, Adolfo. "Les spectres de Raúl Ruiz: *La maison Nucingen* (2009)." *Appareil* 6 (2010). DOI: 10.4000/appareil.934.

Italian

Bruno, Edoardo, Lorenzo Esposito, Bruno Roberti, Daniela Turco, and Raúl Ruiz. *Ruiz Faber.* Roma: Minimum fax, 2007.

Index